Ownership, Control,
and the Future of
Housing Policy

Recent Titles in
Contributions in Political Science

Ownership, Control, and the Future of Housing Policy

EDITED BY

R. Allen Hays

Prepared under the auspices of the Policy Studies Organization
Stuart S. Nagel, *Publications Coordinator*

CONTRIBUTIONS IN POLITICAL SCIENCE,
NUMBER 316

GREENWOOD PRESS
Westport, Connecticut • London

363.58
097

Library of Congress Cataloging-in-Publication Data

Ownership, control, and the future of housing policy / edited by R.
  Allen Hays.
        p.   cm. — (Contributions in political science, ISSN 0147–1066
  ; no. 316)
      "Prepared under the auspices of the Policy Studies Organization,
  Stuart S. Nagel, publications coordinator."
      Includes bibliographical references and index.
      ISBN 0–313–28846–1 (alk. paper)
      1. Home ownership—Government policy.   2. Housing policy.
  I. Hays, R. Allen.   II. Policy Studies Organization.
  III. Series.
  HD7287.8.096   1993   92–35553
  363.5'8—dc20

British Library Cataloguing in Publication Data is available.

Library of Congress Catalog Card Number: 92–35553
ISBN: 0–313–28846–1
ISSN: 0147–1066

First published in 1993

Greenwood Press, 88 Post Road West, Westport, CT 06881
An imprint of Greenwood Publishing Group, Inc.

Printed in the United States of America

The paper used in this book complies with the
Permanent Paper Standard issued by the National
Information Standards Organization (Z39.48–1984).

10 9 8 7 6 5 4 3 2 1

Contents

Acknowledgments

I would like to thank Professor Stuart Nagel of the Policy Studies Organization, under whose auspices this work is being published. I would also like to thank the Graduate College of the University of Northern Iowa for its support for manuscript preparation. Finally, I would like to thank the contributors to this volume for their patience and cooperation during the lengthy process of putting it together.

Introduction: Ownership and Autonomy in Capitalist Societies

R. ALLEN HAYS

The chapters in this book are organized around the central theme of the role of ownership and control in the provision of housing. This book was undertaken because of a perceived need to address homeownership as a public policy issue in a comparative perspective. In several countries, government promotion of homeownership has been a major issue, and it deserves careful scholarly scrutiny.

Homeownership as a policy issue can be understood only in the context of the basic value questions it raises. These involve claims that homeownership contributes to both material and psychological autonomy for individuals and that it improves their relationship with society. In order to see how these value questions affect policy, one must examine closely the promise and the results of programs promoting homeownership. One must also look at other public policies that have attempted to confer greater autonomy on individuals with regard to housing. These include participation in collective management and ownership of housing by those living in the housing and by the neighborhoods surrounding it. These measures are defended in terms similar to those used to defend homeownership, and they provide alternative paths to similar goals.

In this introductory essay, basic philosophical issues raised by ownership and control of housing will be discussed and will be linked to the structure of the book and to the essays presented.

AUTONOMY AND HOUSING IN CONTEMPORARY SOCIETIES

The Dilemma of Autonomy

A fundamental social and political dilemma of modern societies has been the struggle of individual human beings for autonomy, that is, for control over their own destiny. Two major ideologies of modern society—democracy and capitalism—have, from their beginnings, promised the individual unprecedented freedom from the strictures of the state and the confines of a rigid social order. In the same year that Adam Smith was promising individual freedom through an unfettered market (1776), Thomas Jefferson was asserting an inalienable individual right to "life, liberty, and the pursuit of happiness." These themes have often been repeated in the ensuing two hundred plus years.

Yet despite these promises, individuals have found themselves increasingly isolated and imprisoned by the large institutions into which contemporary societies are organized—primarily corporations and government bureaucracies. Karl Marx and his followers responded to these frustrations by asserting that bourgeois promises of economic and political freedom were illusions designed to conceal the oppression and alienation of the great mass of workers through concentration of private wealth in the hands of the few. Only by seizing *collective* control of the means of production, they argued, would workers attain true autonomy. Nevertheless, institutions based on socialism have, in turn, been subject to challenge and overthrow in part because of *their* failure to deliver individual autonomy and dignity.

Both capitalism and socialism have viewed *material* well-being as the key to human dignity, freedom, and fulfillment. The ideology of the capitalist market promises fulfillment through freedom to appropriate whatever share of the national wealth the individual's talents and initiative will permit and through the ability to keep whatever is appropriated with minimum government interference. Socialists have promised fulfillment through contributing to and sharing from the collective wealth of society. They see the gross inequalities generated by the market system as obstacles to freedom, not as opportunities to exercise it.

These materialistic views have been supplemented in recent years by more psychologically based views of individual autonomy, in which it is not so much formal patterns of ownership embodied in large institutions that shape one's fate but the satisfactions derived from immediate relationships to those institutions. (See, for example, the works of Abraham Maslow, Chris Argyris, and other organization theorists.) The individual must experience a reasonable degree of personal control within the daily processes of the workplace and the community; otherwise, the abstraction of "ownership of the means of production" is meaningless. Moreover, the fact that large institutions may satisfy basic material needs is not enough. Material well-being is a necessary but not sufficient condition for individual fulfillment.

Attention has also shifted, as Marc Choko points out in chapter 1, from conditions in the workplace as the key to individual autonomy to the total conditions of life, including consumption patterns. The ability to consume the amount and type of material resources one needs and desires can be just as critical to freedom and control as the ability to influence decisions concerning one's work. The consumption decisions that are available are shaped by and shape basic life values.

Homeownership and Autonomy

Shelter is but one of many human needs, and yet it is frequently regarded as central to material and psychological well-being. Key contributions of decent shelter to material well-being include physical safety, health, comfort, adequate space, and housing costs that are not burdensome relative to income. Its contributions to psychological well-being include privacy, self-expression through the ability to alter one's dwelling to reflect personal needs and tastes, and security in the terms and conditions of tenure.

In capitalist societies, the enjoyment of these benefits has frequently been linked to private ownership of one's dwelling, although the intensity of this linkage has varied over time and between cultures. Some mature industrial societies, such as Sweden, Germany, and Switzerland, have low homeownership rates, while in others, such as the United States and the United Kingdom, substantial majorities of the population are homeowners. Critics of homeownership, such as Kemeny (1981), see this variation as evidence that ownership is not a prerequisite to the good life and go on to argue that alternative tenure patterns are more beneficial to the average citizen. Nevertheless, homeownership has become a powerful economic and cultural symbol in many societies, with a profound influence on policy outcomes. Therefore, it is necessary to understand the components of this symbol, even if one remains skeptical of its empirical justification.

Looking first at material rewards, the status of homeowner is viewed as beneficial because the owner accumulates equity in a real asset rather than paying thousands to others for housing as a service over a lifetime. Under capitalism, ownership of both real property and stock is highly concentrated at the very top of the income scale. Therefore, for most families, their home is by far the largest, and in many cases the only, real asset they will ever possess. They can purchase this asset because they do it simultaneously with the purchase of shelter, which is already a necessary expenditure. As Slitor (1976) points out, it is a form of enforced savings, and if the property's value appreciates, it may also be a profitable investment. Moreover, possession of this asset can contribute to financial security, particularly in old age when cash income declines for most households.

Of course, in these very advantages lie the inherent risks of homeownership. The family becomes responsible for maintaining the value of its asset through physical maintenance of the structure and through helping to maintain neighborhood quality. They incur long-term debt, and if the home's value declines or they are unable to repay, they may lose their investment. Both of these outcomes can result from forces beyond their control. These risks are seldom mentioned in the paeans to the virtues of homeownership delivered by policymakers in various countries, yet as the chapters in this book will show, they quickly become apparent as programs to promote it are undertaken.

It has also been argued that the capital gains associated with homeownership are illusory, because the household must reinvest them in housing in order to maintain a similar or higher-quality dwelling. Only by trading down or by opting out of ownership can these gains be realized. Also, the steady increase in prices that enables older families to reap these gains concentrates the impact of high costs on young families who must buy into the market at a time when their resources are limited (Kemeny, 1981). However, if one looks at homeownership from the perspective of households operating in the context of markets in which it is already the dominant choice, rather than the alternative (cost-rental) housing market that Kemeny posits as an ideal, equity accumulation still affords important advantages over renting.

In addition to its material benefits, homeownership has been strongly linked to psychological well-being, through the sense of pride and autonomy it is said to confer. The element of pride derives from the social status attached to the physical dwelling place and the surrounding neighborhood. In capitalist societies, social mobility and geographical mobility are closely related. With some notable exceptions, owner occupancy is the prevailing tenure for higher-income persons, so that families "naturally" move into ownership as their incomes and social status improve. In debates surrounding government promotion of homeownership in the United States, repeated references are made to its being part of the "American dream," a dream that includes a secure and respected status in the community. As the chapters by Choko and by Alan Murie (chapter 4) reveal, similar rhetoric can be found in other Western societies.

Homeownership contributes to autonomy, it is frequently argued, because the family's privately owned home, is theirs in a sense that a rented dwelling can never be, no matter how much freedom and security is granted by the landlord. Regardless of the indebtedness that accompanies homeownership, the fact that a family is in legal possession of the property gives the members permission to shape the physical space and decoration to suit their needs and tastes, within the limits dictated by their financial resources. This control extends not only to the structure but to whatever plot of land may surround it. In the U.S. context, Daniel Elazar (1969) suggests that by occupying and tending private plots of land in suburbia, Americans continue to participate in the Jeffersonian myth of the independent "yeoman farmer," even while they are living in urban areas for economic reasons.

In addition to conferring freedom from outside control, homeownership is linked to the nurturing of the individual's most intimate family ties. The link between ownership and family life was articulated with great rhetorical flourish by President Herbert Hoover in his 1931 address to the Conference on Home Building and Home Ownership:

> There is a wide distinction between homes and mere housing. Those immortal ballads, "Home Sweet Home," "My Old Kentucky Home," and "The Little Gray Home in the West" were not written about tenements or apartments. . . . They were written about an individual abode, alive with the tender associations of childhood, the family life at the fireside, the free out-of-doors, the independence, the security, and the pride in possession of the family's home—the very seat of its being. (U.S. President's Conference, 1931:3)

In spite of recent increases in home purchases by single adults, the formation of the nuclear family is still the point in the life cycle when most people turn their aspirations to homeownership, as will be elaborated in chapter 2 by Hazel Morrow-Jones. The private home becomes the haven and symbol of family life during child rearing and the point of return through which adult children maintain their ties to their family of origin. For this reason, too, the sale of the family home is often bitterly resisted by the elderly owner, since it symbolizes a retreat from independence and activity.

Homeownership and Social Stability

Individual autonomy is not the only socially desirable goal sought through promotion of homeownership. It has also been widely defended as a source of social and political stability. In what appears at first glance to be a paradox, proponents have argued that while owning one's home provides independence and choice, it also creates close ties to the local community. Homeowners are seen as people who care about and participate constructively in their community; renters' ties are more temporary and fragile, and thus they are not so concerned about the community's well-being.

The resolution of this paradox comes through the *financial* stake in the community that homeownership creates. Since the value of property is dependent on the quality of its surroundings, the owner has an incentive to keep the community peaceful and orderly. Beyond this, it is argued, owners feel a greater sense of participation in the collective wealth of the society, which will dissuade them from taking actions that radically disrupt it, even though, as in the case of working-class homeowners, they may have grievances that might otherwise make radical alternatives appealing. Dean (1945) quotes a U.S. senator named Calder who declaimed on the floor of the Senate in 1923, "Where there is a community of homeowners, no Bolsheviks or anarchists will be found" (p. 41). Of course, for many socialist critics of homeownership, from Engels to the present, this is precisely the problem (Saunders and Harris, 1988)!

Alternative Routes to Shelter Autonomy

Despite the special status that homeownership has acquired, many alternative ways for the individual to acquire more control and autonomy over her or his housing have been proposed and implemented. Just as participation in collective control over the means of production has been seen as an alternative route to personal freedom to the capitalist idea of individual ownership, collective control over housing has been seen as a way to enhance autonomy. Through participation in cooperative or collective ownership or management of housing, one becomes one's own landlord, thereby establishing control over the essential conditions of housing.

These shared methods of control have been seen as superior to private ownership in more than one respect. At a minimum, they offer a more economically feasible route to autonomy for those unlikely to accumulate the resources to purchase a home. More than this, collective ownership keeps the housing in question as explicitly a possession of the whole society, one that is used as a resource to meet its shared need for shelter, rather than isolating it as a commodity at the disposal of one household. Moreover, as Kemeny (1981) argues, collective ownership enables costs to be more equitably distributed among families, since the costs of older and newer units are averaged in determining rents.

During most of the twentieth century, the main vehicle for collective ownership of housing has been state ownership. For doctrinaire free market conservatives, any form of state ownership compromises the individual's freedom, no matter if the state itself is subject to popular control. Yet even for those who support public ownership in principle, it is troublesome that state ownership has created large bureaucracies that dominate the lives of individual tenants and discourage them from pride or concern in their dwelling units. (Gregory Andrusz's discussion in chapter 3 of the operation of "decommodified" housing in the former Soviet Union should add fuel to these concerns.) For tenants of public housing, the abstraction of democratic control of the state means little in contrast to the immediate, daily power struggles with the state as landlord.

One way out of this dilemma is for the state to retain a minimum of collective control but to provide for decentralization of decision making through democratic participation in the management of the housing. In this way, individuals are given control over their immediate housing circumstances, thereby benefiting both materially and psychologically. However, the housing remains a collective good, available for allocation to future generations. Chapters 7 and 8, by William Peterman and Daniel J. Monti, respectively, find both strengths and weaknesses in this particular resolution of the problem.

Another way is for the state to surrender control to collective entities or to encourage and subsidize the creation of such entities. This may be done through the creation of housing cooperatives, as Francine Dansereau describes in chapter 10 on the Canadian experience and in William Rohe and Michael A. Stegman's discussion in chapter 6 of the transfer of U.S. public housing to cooperatives. This may also be done through the decentralization of housing management to neighborhood-based groups rather than groups based on a single project, as is described in chapter 9 by Keith Rasey. They have a somewhat broader perspective than a group of tenants of one project, yet their closeness and commitment to the concerns of those living in a particular area give them an advantage over private landlords or public managers.

In most capitalist countries, the ideology of private ownership is so strong that the scale of these efforts and the public resources devoted to them are dwarfed by the preponderance of homeownership and the large government subsidies given to it through the tax system and other means. Nevertheless, they represent a third path that may become more attractive if ownership costs continue to rise relative to average incomes. Their very existence shows that the "yeoman" on his plot of private land and the "anomic" tenant in the public housing block are not the only choices.

Ownership, Control, and Poverty

The issues of ownership and control have been of particular importance when linked to the issues surrounding poverty in contemporary societies. The classical free market ideology includes little sympathy or concern for those who lose the competitive struggle or never get the chance to compete. However, public policy in virtually all capitalist societies reflects the acknowledgment by political and economic leaders of the need to deal with the problems of the poor—whether from compassionate motives or from the desire to stabilize the system and to legitimize it in the eyes of the masses. The "welfare state" addresses, often inadequately, what are considered the basic needs of those whose shares of market-generated wealth are too small to enable them to provide these needs on their own. Housing has universally been an important element in these welfare state arrangements.

The early efforts of various welfare systems to deal with housing focused on the need to provide physically adequate structures. Massive blocks of public housing were built after World War II, making the state a major, if not the major, provider of rental housing. As with other social welfare programs, the United States's effort was much smaller than in most European countries or in Canada, yet public housing still had a large and visible impact.

As public sector units became part of the physical and social fabric of the community, the quality of social life within units occupied by the poor became the object of controversy and debate. They were seen as failing to improve the lives of their residents, not because the units were physically inadequate (although this was sometimes the case) but because the communal life within them seemed to perpetuate and sometimes intensify the social problems faced by low-income people (e.g., crime, family instability, drug abuse). Simultaneously, large, bureaucratic management structures were seen as failing to provide residents with a sense of control over their housing, an attitude that spilled over into other aspects of their lives.

Both of these perceptions raised the issue of whether something more than adequate physical shelter should be provided to lower-income families, something that contributed to their dignity and autonomy, as well as providing a roof over their heads. Would not improvements in this psychological element of housing lead to improvements not only in the individual's quality of life but in the life of the entire community? For those with a free market ideology, only termination of state ownership by transfer to individuals would end these problems. For others, the proper vehicle was to act within the framework of public assistance to increase the degree of control and autonomy that the residents of public housing felt over their environment.

Thus, the stage was set in many countries for a variety of new approaches to the delivery of housing assistance. The construction of massive housing blocks were supplemented or supplanted by cash vouchers that allowed families greater choice in where they would live. Various experiments in tenant management or community-based management were begun. And, increasingly, homeownership was advocated as the best path to dignity and autonomy for the poor.

An early effort to encourage homeownership for the poor occurred in the United States in the late 1960s, with the enactment of the Section 235 program, which provided mortgages to eligible low-income households at a deeply subsidized interest rate. The rhetoric surrounding the creation of this program cited many of the virtues of homeownership already noted. Some proponents were primarily concerned with social stability, in the face of the widespread racial disturbances then occurring in American cities. Senator Charles Percy (R, Illinois), a major advocate of homeownership for the poor, stated bluntly, "People aren't throwing bricks through their own property" (U.S. Congress, 1967). Yet there also appeared in this debate a *transformative* rhetoric that would enter into subsequent debates about homeownership for the poor.

The thrust of this transformative rhetoric was that homeownership programs are uniquely capable of dealing with the problems of poverty, because the positive cultural values associated with homeownership can counteract the negative cultural values that the poor are perceived as possessing. The purchase of a home is seen as an incentive to work hard, practice thrift, plan for the future, and care about the physical condition of one's own dwelling and neighborhood. According to the widely held view in the United States that the poor possess a distinct and destructive "culture of poverty," it is precisely these middle-class values that the poor lack. (See Waxman, 1983, for a full discussion of the culture of poverty debate.) Thus, ownership transforms not only the housing or financial circumstances of the poor but, potentially, their entire value system.

Proponents of this view did not envision that the poor would make this transition easily or automatically. Potential homeowners would require careful counseling and guidance during the early stages of their new responsibilities. In the early 1970s, when the Section 235 program ran into serious difficulties with high foreclosure rates, many of its problems were laid at the feet of improper counseling of new homeowners, although unscrupulous behavior by builders and realtors and lax Federal Housing Administration officials had at least as much to do with the program's shortcomings as did the limitations of the buyers (Hays, 1985). Yet the basic argument remained that the act of home purchase could transform a household's entire outlook.

The transformative rhetoric of the late 1960s emerged again during the 1980s, this time employed by advocates of the sale of public housing to its tenants. A leading proponent of this viewpoint is Jack Kemp, President George Bush's secretary of housing and urban development, who said that "owning something changes behavior in ways that no amount of preaching middle-class values ever could" (Raspberry, 1990:9A) and that "the opportunity to own or control one's own shelter and living environment is probably the most basic form of empowerment" (U.S. Senate, 1990:51). Public housing tenants are viewed as a group materially and psychologically dependent on the state who will be launched toward self-sufficiency through change in tenure.

It is easy to criticize this rhetoric as overblown on its face. The assumption that cultural attitudes are the root cause of poverty has been widely criticized as a way to avoid examining the structural economic factors that generate poverty (Waxman, 1983). Moreover, the complexity of poverty gives the lie to the notion that such a narrow, specific life change as homeownership can wipe the slate clean of whatever other troubles a household may be experiencing.

A more damning critique of this rhetoric can, however, be derived from a closer examination of the manner in which homeownership programs actually operate, for their implementation is based, both tacitly and explicitly, on an assumption quite different from the notion of transformation. This is the assumption that, to be successful, homeownership programs must *select* a subset of the poor who have already demonstrated the "proper" middle-class attitudes through working and through a "stable" family life. Rather than transforming the poor, programs actually reward and reinforce those with preexisting values by helping them achieve a new and respected status.

This assumption is generally not stated in moralistic terms, as if the poor were being judged on their respective merits. Rather, it is stated as a prudent, practical principle of successful program administration, where "success" is defined as a smooth and lasting transition to homeownership. In the introduction to a publication that promotes homeownership programs by describing successful local case studies, the U.S. Department of Housing and Urban Development lists among the criteria for applicant screening in successful programs, "earned income as a portion of the family's total income; good credit, rent payment and employment histories; satisfactory house-keeping habits; and motivation and commitment to becoming a homeowner" (U.S. Department of Housing and Urban Development, 1991:7). This suggests clearly that in order to succeed, the programs have eliminated those families whose records indicate they are "unprepared" for homeownership, rather than trying to transform those with unsatisfactory outlooks.

These criteria also involve tacit recognition of two other factors. One is that not all of the poor living in public units are in need of radical transformation in order to become stable citizens with middle-class values; otherwise, the screening would yield no successful candidates. The second is that economics, not just attitudes, plays a large role in success. The families that succeed will have stable, if low, incomes and will not be saddled with large debts. This puts them at the top of the economic scale among the poor of the United States. Anything less than this degree of relative economic well-being will lead to an unsuccessful experience with homeownership, since the resources to support it are lacking.

To criticize the gap between transformative rhetoric and selectivity in action is not necessarily to dismiss the value of homeownership programs. In countries where homeownership is a definite economic plus, an argument can be made for taking more economically stable low-income families and assisting them to leap into a more favorable tenure situation. Yet such efforts must be realistically seen as an added boost to those already poised to escape poverty, not as a magic bullet that can miraculously transform all of the poor according to a middle-class model of self-sufficiency.

To question the transformative rhetoric of homeownership programs is also to call attention to another fundamental problem of efforts to sell collectively owned housing to those who occupy it. This is the question, raised by several authors in this book, of what resources will be available to those who cannot make the transition to homeownership. Will public housing remain a livable alternative for those who need subsidized accommodation, or will it be increasingly marginalized as housing of last resort for the most desperately poor? Chapters 4 and 5 by Alan Murie and Nicholas J. Williams, respectively, address concerns in the United Kingdom that Margaret Thatcher's right-to-buy efforts will marginalize public housing as it has in the United

States. In the United States, the fear is that already marginal public housing will become even more so.

This dynamic of marglinalization has two aspects. The first is physical. Although the processes are somewhat different in the United States and the United Kingdom, in both countries the most physically desirable public housing units are the ones that have been allocated to homeownership. This is a logical consequence of trying to convey to future owners properties that will have some lasting value as homes and as investments. For doctrinaire conservatives, this leads to a rather satisfying self-fulfilling prophecy in which the fact that the remaining public housing units are drab and/or in poor repair can be attributed to their public ownership and used as further justification for privatization. Yet for those concerned about the quality of housing for the disadvantaged, the fact that sales may lead to further stigmatization and disinvestment in public units is troubling. Again and again, in both countries, the question arises, Are we helping a few of the poor now, in order to cover a long-term retreat in the public commitment to help all of the poor?

The other aspect of marginalization is social and political. In the United Kingdom, as both Murie and Williams note, public housing has traditionally been occupied by persons with a broad range of incomes and occupations. This reduced the social stigmatization of the poor who lived in public units and broadened the base of political support for the program. The right to buy removes primarily those with relatively higher incomes and increases the likelihood that the remaining units will become the socially isolated domain of those with nowhere else to go. This, in turn, is likely to increase the social problems of public housing complexes, thereby again creating a self-fulfilling prophecy for privatization advocates.

In the United States, where public housing is already part of the socially isolated domain of the very poor, privatization removes the few residents with some reasonable chance for upward mobility. To remove the better off from this negative environment may be doing them a favor as individuals, but what leadership or hope does it leave among those who remain behind? If public housing complexes were to become centers for a massive infusion of public resources to deal with the multiple problems of the remaining poor, then the United States might be able to overcome the despair and violence that is bred by poverty and concentrated within the walls of the projects. Yet political support for this kind of investment is lacking in the current political climate, and it is further undermined by the notion of privatization as panacea.

Finally, in addition to its negative social and psychological impact on those left behind, the sale of public housing units potentially represents a weakening of the commitment of political leaders to provide for the physical housing needs of those with incomes too low to provide it for themselves. In the United Kingdom, a drastic reduction in the number of new public units built has accompanied privatization. In the United States, federal housing assistance currently serves less than 30 percent of those in need of such aid (Center for Budget and Policy Priorities, 1989). Despite promises to the contrary, there appears to be no strong commitment to avoid net losses to the public stock through sales, let along to provide the additional units needed to serve the remaining 70 percent of the poor who go without housing assistance.

PLAN OF THE BOOK

The organization of this book reflects the fact that the issues of ownership and control operate on several levels. With regard to homeownership, its role and significance in society as a whole and in the life of the individual must be examined. The chapters in part 1 address these fundamental issues. Marc Choko (chapter 1) examines the importance of homeownership in a number of Western societies. He traces its cultural and philosophical roots in both French-speaking and English-speaking cultures, reviews some of the current ideological and practical debates surrounding it and examines current data on the trends in homeownership in several countries. Hazel Morrow-Jones examines in chapter 2 the place of homeownership in the life cycle of families in the United States, with particular attention to the impact of differences in the opportunities between blacks and whites on their home-ownership patterns. In doing so, she raises the broader issue of the relationship between homeownership and economic opportunity.

The third chapter, by Gregory Andrusz, provides a sharp and illuminating contrast by examining the struggle in the former Soviet Union to establish the concept of private ownership, after a seventy-year effort to eliminate it from economic and social life. While Andrusz highlights the gross quantitative and qualitative inadequacy of the housing provided by the collectivist approach of the former regime, he also reveals the risks of introducing or reinforcing large disparities in housing quality through the process of conversion to private ownership.

In part 2, public policies aimed at conferring homeownership on the poor and/or all families occupying publicly owned housing are examined. Alan Murie (chapter 4) looks at the sale of public housing in Great Britain in the light of the history of British government policies toward homeownership. Nicholas Williams (chapter 5) explores in more detail who benefits and who loses from public housing sales. He concludes that public housing sales substantially diminish housing opportunities for remaining tenants who lack resources to become homeowners, and it transforms British public housing from a resource utilized by a broad spectrum of the population to something resembling the "housing of last resort" status that it has in the United States.

William Rohe and Michael Stegman (chapter 6) analyze efforts in two U.S. cities to transfer ownership of public housing to cooperatives made up of former tenants. Their chapter is placed in part 2 because it raises basic policy issues concerning the sale of public housing, such as selectivity with regard to "cooperators," the costs of transforming the units, and the marginalization of remaining units. However, their chapter also provides a bridge to part 3, in which the authors evaluate collective forms of ownership and management as routes to autonomy and control.

William Peterman (chapter 7) explores the complex roots of tenant management in both liberal and conservative efforts to change conditions in U.S. public housing. It was introduced in the 1960s as a "desperation" salvage attempt by tenants of disintegrating projects, with mixed results. Conservatives in the 1980s again took up the cause, attaching it to their own rhetoric of self-sufficiency and elimination of dependence on government aid. He concludes that it will be most successful in an atmosphere of community empowerment where the goal is an ownership arrangement beneficial to tenants rather than simply to unload an annoying public sector responsibility.

Daniel Monti (chapter 8) examines tenant attitudes toward tenant management in two U.S. public housing developments. After a detailed discussion of attitudes toward all aspects of management, he concludes that there is tension between the spirit of community empowerment that initially motivates residents to support tenant management and the ongoing role of landlord, which emerges as tenant management matures and must relate to new generations of tenants who were not part of the initial efforts.

Keith Rasey (chapter 9) examines collective control from a different perspective. The widespread development of nonprofit community housing corporations (also called community development corporations, or CDCs) in the United States has been a device through which neighborhoods take control of their housing needs. The role of private, for-profit developers of assisted housing has receded relative to that of CDCs because the former are unwilling to take the risks and make the long-term commitment to lower-income areas that community-based organizations assume. CDCs own and manage rental housing, and they support and encourage low-income homeownership.

Finally, Francine Dansereau (chapter 10) discusses the Canadian experience with cooperative ownership as a mechanism providing both financial and psychological benefits, with a special emphasis on the experience in Montreal. She discusses the forms and impacts of governmental assistance to cooperatives in Canada. She views cooperatives as a successful means of reducing costs, expanding housing opportunities, and enhancing security for both middle-class households wishing to live in the central city and lower-income families.

REFERENCES

Aaron, Henry J. 1972. *Shelter and Subsidies: Who Benefits from Federal Housing Policies?* Washington, D.C.: Brookings Institution.

Center for Budget and Policy Priorities. 1989. *A Place to Call Home: The Crisis in Housing for the Poor*. Washington, D.C.: Author.

Dean, John P. 1945. *Homeownership: Is It Sound?* New York: Harper & Row.

Dye, Thomas R. 1983. *Who's Running America? The Reagan Years*. Englewood Cliffs, N.J.: Prentice-Hall.

Elazar, Daniel J. 1969. "Are We a Nation of Cities?" In H. R. Mahood and Edward J. Angus, eds., *Urban Politics and Problems: A Reader*, 25–40. New York: Scribner's.

Hays, R. Allen. 1985. *The Federal Government and Urban Housing: Ideology and Change in Public Policy*. New York: State University of New York Press.

———. 1990. "The President, Congress, and the Formation of Housing Policy: A Reexamination of Redistributive Policy-Making." *Policy Studies Journal* 18 (Summer): 847–869.

Judd, Dennis R. 1988. *The Politics of American Cities: Private Power and Public Policy*. 3d ed. Glenwood, Ill.: Scott, Foresman.

Kemeny, J. 1981. *The Myth of Homeownership: Private vs. Public Choice in Housing Tenure*. London: Routledge and Kegan Paul.

McClaughry, John. 1975. "The Troubled Dream: The Life and Times of Section 235 of the National Housing Act." *Loyola University Law Journal* 6 (Winter): 1–45.

Raspberry, William. 1990. "Kemp at HUD Paving Path out of Dependency." *Raleigh News and Observer*, May 15, 9a.

Saunders, Peter, and Colin Harris. 1988. "Homeownership and Capital Gains." Paper presented at the Conference on Housing Policy and Urban Innovation, Amsterdam, Netherlands.

Schussheim, Morton J. 1984. "Selling Public Housing to Tenants: How Feasible?" Unpublished report. Washington, D.C.: Congressional Research Service.

Semer, Milton P., et al. 1976. "A Review of Federal Subsidized Housing Programs." In U.S. Department Housing and Urban Development. *Housing in the Seventies: Working Papers*, 82–144. Washington, D.C.: U.S. Government Printing Office.

Slitor, Richard E. 1976. "Rationale of the Present Tax Benefits for Homeowners." In U.S. Department Housing and Urban Development. *Housing in the Seventies: Working Papers*, 82–144. Washington, D.C.: U.S. Government Printing Office.

Twentieth Century Fund. 1991. *More Housing More Fairly: Report of the Twentieth Century Fund Task Force on Affordable Housing*. New York: Twentieth Century Fund Press.

U.S. Congress. Senate. Committee on Banking and Urban Affairs. 1967. *Hearings on Housing Legislation*. Washington, D.C.

U.S. Department of Housing and Urban Development. 1990. *Public Housing Homeownership Demonstration Assessment*. Washington, D.C.: U.S. Government Printing Office.

———. 1991. *Homeownership and Affordable Housing: The Opportunities*. Washington, D.C.: U.S. Government Printing Office.

U.S. President's Conference on Home Building and Homeownership. 1931. "Address by President Herbert Hoover." Washington, D.C. Proceedings. Volume XI, p. 1.

———. 1990. *Hearings on the "Homeownership and Opportunity for People Everywhere" [HOPE] Initiatives*. Washington, D.C.

Waxman, Chaim I. 1983. *The Stigma of Poverty*. 2d ed. New York: Pergamon Press.

Part 1

Basic Issues and Values in Homeownership

1

Homeownership: From Dream to Materiality

MARC H. CHOKO

In North America, homeownership has always seemed a simple matter. In addition to being financially advantageous and an obviously preferable way of life, the American dream seems to be an initiation rite—a symbol of successful entry into society. By acquiring property, these "pioneers" show they are free and independent masters of their home; they look thriftier, more responsible; they are seen as better providers and worthier citizens.

This image is reinforced by the stages of life considered typical: as a young person in transition—studying and then holding a first job—one lives downtown and rents apartments. All that is needed is a roof over one's head, a space in which to partake of good times and pleasure. Then, as one matures, one starts a family, finds a more stable job and better wages, and purchases a house, which will be well maintained, improved, and invested in. The house will be a home, the core and the patrimony of the family.

We take this image for granted, but for whom is it a reality? Is it so in countries in which homeownership is said to have grown rapidly in recent years? At a time when the American dream is said to be the world's dream, what do we know about where it comes from, how it is evolving in different geographical locations, what made it possible, and who really has access to it? Is it really universal, and does it mean the same thing to everyone?

The notion of homeownership has long been a battlefield—not so much between the proletariat and the capitalists or between tenants and owners but between intellectuals, and mostly in the English-speaking world (Barlow and Duncan, 1988). The mixing of economic, political, and moral arguments has led to great confusion between facts and a priori ideas, between interpretations based on data and opinions issuing from sheer expectations. Locally based theories that do not apply to the city next door are stated as if they were universal. Little attention is paid to history. All kinds of relevant matters are left out. Thus, although much has been written about home-ownership, there is more to add.

FROM THE RIGHT TO OWN TO THE SUPERIORITY OF OWNERSHIP

In both the American and the French revolutions, property was a central issue. When the American Declaration of Independence was formulated, there was heated discussion over whether to include the right of ownership. The Virginia Bill of Rights, written under the direction of George Mason, included it as a key element of happiness and liberty. The document also stipulated that only landowners would have a voice in government. But the final version of the Declaration of Independence, written under the direction of Thomas Jefferson and published on July 4, 1776, retains only life, liberty, and the pursuit of happiness. Most of the drafters worried that the inclusion of a universal right to ownership could be used to claim redistribution in parts of United States where land was monopolized in the hands of few. Years later, Thomas Skidmore, in *The Right of Man to Property* (1829), called for the assurance of land for everyone because he saw ownership as a crucial element of individual independence (Heskin, 1981; Attali, 1988:306–310).

In France on August 4, 1789, the Assemblée constituante abolished all privileges and feudal rights. On August 26 it adopted the Declaration of the Rights of Man, which declared ownership to be an inalienable natural right, inviolable and sacred, along with liberty, safety, and resistance to oppression (Tulard, Fayard, and Fierro, 1987:770–771).

In both nations, those in power raised the issue of the links between ownership and the rights to vote and to be elected, arguing that those who owned more had a larger stake in society and thus would be better suited to determine its destiny. These ideas were first articulated in the modern sense by John Locke in 1690. The encyclopedist Denis Diderot, as well as Voltaire and Jean-Jacques Rousseau, also pursued this debate. Diderot saw private property as a source of happiness and said that "the right to ownership is inseparable from the political, economic, and social existence of individuals." For Voltaire, private ownership was a strong incentive to "double the strength of men." Rousseau felt that the right to own was the most sacred one, in certain respects surpassing even liberty itself (Rousseau, 1758).

To some eighteenth- and nineteenth-century philosophers, property was a gift of God, thus justifying its sacred character.[1] Owners were "elected" to guide society. As rationality and the necessities of modern laws took over, ownership—previously seen as an act of God, a law of nature—became an inalienable right, from which flowed the right to govern. Owners were seen as more highly motivated, more involved, more responsible, more serious.

Private ownership became a fundamental of society, in other words, society depended on the goodwill of individual owners.[2]

In France, the close relationship between the law and the legal tradition handed down from Roman times made ownership both a simpler matter and a more radical choice than it was in England or the United States. In France, *usus, fructus, abusus* (the three fundamental rights of dominium, the full ownership of early Roman law) remained intimately linked, as they were in ancient Rome, while in England they were separate prerogatives.[3] To give this corpus of ideas a rational basis, it became common to think that ownership had a historical direction—that going from collective to individual property was progress and that individual property was the ultimate form.

Reality, in ancient as well as modern times, could not, of course, be reduced to such simple assertions, and a variety of forms of ownership were exemplified and alternatives developed by thinkers following other trends. Gabriel Bonnot de Mably (1768), Charles Fourier (1829), Victor Considérant (1848), Engels, Marx, and many others promulgated contradictory views.[4] They pointed out that in primitive societies, ownership of hunting grounds, fishing vessels, or even dwellings and domesticated animals was collective, while only weapons, clothing, and ornaments were individually owned. Levels of collective ownership varied greatly between tribes, clans, villages, extended or restricted families, and so on. Feudal tenures also multiplied the possible combinations of *usus, fructus, abusus.* All of these authors felt that people could find in themselves, or in their community, superior motivations to take care of common property (as did, for example, the Indians of South America and the monks of Europe).

Of course, roots of such utopian visions can be found in communist societies such as that of the Essenes (a Jewish sect of the second century B.C. whose members shared houses, food, goods, and clothing, which served as a model for the first kibbutzim in modern Israel) or the first Christians. St. Ambrose said, in the fourth century A.D., "It is Nature that created the right to collective property; it is violence that created the right to private appropriation." In the opinion of the historian Josèphe (first century A.D.), private ownership of land originated with a great criminal: Cain. Thus, common ownership of goods was the expression of greatest virtue (Challaye, 1967:53). In fact, collective ownership could be seen as a superior, perhaps the ultimate, ineluctable form of ownership. Some utopians even dreamed of a society without property, in which *usus* of all necessities would be available to everyone, and *fructus* and *abusus* would be irrelevant.

While philosophers deliberated, increasingly industrialized, urban societies, both in postrevolution North America and in Europe, created vast proletarian populations, comprising citizen-workers who owned nothing but the tools of their trade—their hands. Some saw an obvious contradiction between this and the will of the ruling class to rely upon private individual property and to promise it to all. Others worried that new revolutions could overthrow these societies and their predominant values. Because it was out of the question to share ownership of the means of production with the workers, the ruling classes saw property in the family sphere—the dwelling—as an interesting field to explore.

TO OWN OR NOT TO OWN: THE MAKING OF A DREAM

The credo of nineteenth-century Western capitalist countries was private ownership. But those who were growing wealthy did not necessarily see homeownership as a priority for themselves: "Most Parisian bourgeois occupied a rented flat, even if they owned buildings in the capital . . . and they often moved" (Daumard, 1987:106,107,110). In a large city such as Paris, the wealthiest saw housing as both a convenience that could be adapted to the household's changing needs or means and an investment among others. By the mid–nineteenth century, property had become a major investment, to the extent that half of the owners had no other employment. The image of the *rentier*—the respected landlord to some, the ugly "Monsieur Vautour" to others—rapidly polarized opinion. "In Paris, there is no greater title to acquire than that of landlord. It is quite pleasant to hear people say, 'This man has *pignon sur rue*'; this will grant you an assurance in society that you may not get from the most brilliant position, the most honoured title" (deJouy, 1813, in Canfora-Argandoña and Guerrand, 1976:27; Retel, 1977:48–49).

But to the workers' parties, especially the anarchists (see, for example, Pierre Kroptkin, "Déclaration des anarchistes accusés devant le tribunal correctionnel de Lyon, 19 janvier 1883," in Guérin 1976:128), landlords were the worst of exploiters; they squeezed from the poor what their jobs had not already wrung from them, interfered in their private lives, and regularly threw them and their families into the street. Some fringes of the bourgeoisie shared at least some of these opinions (as the caricaturist Honoré Daumier illustrated). Some industrialists began to worry about the pressures exerted by landlords, especially through the proportion of wages spent on rent. In 1889, the Royal Commission on Relations between Capital and Labour in Canada noted that rents constantly rose faster than wages and called for workers to own homes as the way to control this cost. In peripheral cities, such as one-industry and resource towns, housing for workers rapidly became a central preoccupation, the purpose being to control the cost of both housing and the labor force and to attract and control the movements of the latter.

After a period during which industrialists had no regard for their workers, simply replacing them as they wore out, exploitation became more rational. It was thought that workers in better physical and mental condition could produce more. The milieu of work—modern industry—was improving. The housing milieu, however, did not; it thus became the black sheep of reformers. Epidemics, loose living, alcoholism, and the spread of revolutionary ideas among workers were all said to be the fault of poor housing. "If family life does not exist among the working classes it is usually because of crowded and dirty housing. The cabaret is thus the place for meeting and leisure: there, workers become envious, greedy, revolutionary, and cynical, finally communist" (Leroy-Beaulieu, 1872, in Houdeville, 1969:56).[5] The answer was good housing and, above all, homeownership. Armand de Meulun, a member of a commission on the working class in France under the Third Republic, praised industrialists who had promoted homeownership among their workers, for "ownership has valuable qualities: it makes its owner steadier; he works harder; it keeps him from harmful distractions by keeping him home, with his family, and it keeps him busy with useful activities during his leisure time" (Journal officiel, 1875 in Guerrand, 1967:177).

It became obvious that homeownership for workers could be accomplished much more easily outside large cities. Frederick LePlay and other influential writers promoted the transfer of industries to the countryside in order to solve workers' housing problems. To these thinkers, it was a matter of salvation of societal values, among which private property was central. This was, in fact, a reinterpretation of the views of the utopians (for whom social reintegration of the working classes could be achieved only through collective ownership of land, housing, and means of production) but along an individualistic line (LePlay, 1864).

Engels had discussed the issue of workers' acquiring houses next to their place of work as early as 1887 (after receiving a letter from Eleanor Marx-Aveling, the daughter of Karl Marx, who lived in Kansas City and told him about this new issue there). He felt that this made workers even more dependent on their employers. Shackled to their homes, burdened with heavy debts, they had no choice but to accept the working conditions they were offered (Engels, 1975:32). Engels argued against the followers of Proudhon for whom homeownership was a promotion for workers. To him, it was a step backward. Engels saw collective housing as linked to collective industrial work, just as individual housing had been the norm for artisanal production.

Some of the bourgeoisie of North America who promoted individual homeownership for the working classes were the first ones to move into the new buildings rising in the core of the main cities—apartment buildings, or "French flats," as they were first called in New York (Weaver, 1987; Cohen, 1990; Dennis, 1987), thus following shared ownership of corporations with co-ownership of their living premises. However, the dominant rhetoric endowed homeowners with all the desirable qualities—"Moderation, frugality, order, honesty, and a due sense of independence, liberty, and justice," as during the debates about tenant suffrage in New York in 1821 (Heskin,

1981:184). This was used to justify exclusion of the masses: "Men who possess nothing are not held by any link to society" (d'Holbach, 1773, in Guerrand, 1967:17).

Utopians such as Robert Owen, Claude-Henri de Saint-Simon, and Charles Fourier saw collectively owned rural industrial communities as a possible means of social reintegration for the working classes. To the majority of the bourgeoisie, however, this was neither a feasible nor a desirable alternative. The means of production should be of no concern to the working classes; workers were needed in the core of large cities, and the way to homeownership should remain a private individual matter. When one works to acquire a stake in society, one does not then want to destroy it. Moreover, through homeownership, one would develop the virtues associated with it:

Home-ownership completely changes a working man. . . . With a little house and garden he becomes a real family head, which means morality and providence, a feeling that he has roots and authority over his own people. . . . Soon it is his house that "possesses" him: it makes him a moral, settled, transformed man. (Cheysson, 1881, in Guerrand, 1967:267)

As the debate continued, homeownership remained marginal among workers, who were increasingly concentrated in rapidly growing cities. And housing conditions remained very poor, or got worse. One can get an idea of these conditions through literature of the time, as well as through more specific inquiries such as Bertillon's on Paris (Bertillon, 1891), Ames's on Montreal (Ames, 1897), or Engels's on London (Engels, 1845).

For those who controlled large enterprises, dealt with unions without fearing revolution, and cared more about the availability of good labor at a reasonable cost than about morality, other arguments prevailed, and a new option opened. "Assisted housing for wage earners may be viewed as part of the necessary equipment of industry," declared the Montreal Board of Trade in 1935, arguing against the laissez-faire attitudes of governments with regard to housing. The solution offered totally contradicted the ideas current at that time:

Before the war [World War I], social idealists and industrialists alike accepted this thesis [that wage earners like to own their homes] as axiomatic. "Let the worker be a property owner. That will keep him quiet!" But today . . . the wage earner is far freer to sell his services in the best market when he is not tied to a house. (Montreal Board of Trade, 1935, in Choko, 1980:125)

This approach eventually produced massive public housing projects and state intervention to favor private investment in large apartment buildings. Later, some (among them social democrats and bankers; see Choko and Simard, 1977) even tried to promote the idea that land and housing should be considered "public utilities" (as were mass transit and electricity, both nationalized in the 1950s in Montreal).[6] But the seed had been planted: one after another, the populations of industrialized developed countries came to contain a majority of owner-occupants.

HOMEOWNERSHIP AROUND THE WORLD: THE DREAM COMES TRUE

Before discussing comparative data on the evolution of homeownership in various countries and cities, some questions about the available data must be addressed. It is not easy to measure levels of homeownership.[7] To do so, one must be able to control for the territory covered, the number of units it encompasses, and the tenure status of the inhabitants. For instance, are farms taken into account? What about second homes? There is very little concern for them even though they may play a role of some importance in tenure behavior of households and in reading situations behind figures. The issue is twofold: country houses owned by tenants living in large cities, and houses owned abroad, in the home country for immigrants.[8] How about "informal" (or illegal) occupation? Does one consider only central cities (which account for most of the agglomeration up to World War I, and even later for some) or include suburbs, which in many cases are more populous than the central city? How does one deal with annexations? The best answer should account for the total built areas that constitute urban entities, but no data exist on such territories. Does one consider the number of households or the number of families, thus taking into account the doubling-up phenomenon? Here again, there are few data (Choko and Harris, 1989:6–7; Moriconi-Ebrard, 1991).

The different ways of gathering data from one place to another and over time, the lack of data with which to establish historical background, and differences of interpretation of specific situations are also obvious questions. Nevertheless, I believe further discussion can take place on the basis of what is available, on condition that one keeps the questions I have raised in mind when drawing conclusions.

The first general observation is that homeownership increased in most countries after World War II, and censuses started systematically to include homeownership data in the 1950s or 1960s. Table 1.1 illustrates the situation in some countries according to the most recent consistent data available. These figures allow some general comments. The first surprise may be the fact that some of the wealthiest countries in Europe (and the world) have the lowest percentages of owner-occupiers. Another surprise may be the high percentages in Eastern European countries. Both rurality and the time of inception of a country's surbanization process seem to play an important role. How do these figures correlate with those for the largest cities in the countries listed in table 1.1? Table 1.2 juxtaposes the oldest and the most recent data for some major cities. Although these figures are incomplete and

Table 1.1
Proportion of Owner-Occupied Dwellings in Selected Countries

COUNTRY	EARLIEST AVAILABLE DATA	DATA FOR INTERMEDIATE YEARS	MOST RECENT AVAILABLE DATA
Australia	49.0 (1911)	63.0 (1954)	70.0 (1986)
Austria			47.7 (1981)
Belgium		38.9 (1950)	62.0 (1986)
Bulgaria			77.0 (1980)
Canada	58.0 (1921)	59.8 (1951)	63.0 (1986)
Czechoslovakia		50.4 (1961)	46.3 (1980)
Denmark		45.7 (1960)	55.5 (1988)
Finland		55.9 (1950)	64.8 (1980)
France		35.5 (1954)	54.3 (1988)
Germany (East)			46.1 (1981)
Germany (West)		29.4 (1961)	42.0 (1987)
Greece			71.9 (1980)
Hungary			71.3 (1980)
Ireland		59.8 (1961)	70.8 (1981)
Israel		51.9 (1957)	72.9 (1984)
Italy		45.8 (1961)	65.0 (1984)
Japan	68.5 (1920)	71.2 (1958)	62.4 (1983)
Luxembourg		54.7 (1960)	60.2 (1980)
Netherlands		25.7 (1956)	43.7 (1988)
New Zealand		68.9 (1966)	70.9 (1981)
Norway		52.8 (1960)	67.0 (1986)
Portugal		44.5 (1960)	58.6 (1981)
South Korea		79.5 (1960)	58.6 (1980)
Spain		49.5 (1950)	85.0 (1989)
Sweden		35.5 (1965)	55.0 (1986)
Switzerland		33.7 (1960)	29.9 (1980)
United Kingdom	10.1 (1914)	34.0 (1956)	65.4 (1988)
United States	46.0 (1921)	61.9 (1960)	63.8 (1988)
Yugoslavia		77.5 (1961)	73.0 (1980)

Sources: National censuses, European Economic Community and United
Nations publications, and various authors quoted in this essay.

These data must be read with caution, as some include rural data (farm
ownership) and some do not. Also, not all countries use the same
definition of urbanized areas.

Table 1.2
Proportion of Owner-Occupied Dwellings in Selected Cities

CITY	EARLIEST AVAILABLE DATA	DATA FOR INTERMEDIATE YEARS	MOST RECENT AVAILABLE DATA
Amsterdam		2.4[2] (1947)	7.0[2] (1987)
Athens		54.4[4] (1958)	53.9[4] (1986)
Berlin (West)		9.3[3] (1950)	11.0[3] (1985)
Boston	18.4[1] (1890)	25.7[1] (1930)	27.2[1] (1980)
Brussels		33.0[2] (1961)	14.5[1] (1981) 26.3[3] (1981) 35.7[5] (1981)
Budapest			58.0[4] (1980)
Edinburgh		46.4[1] (1966)	
Geneva		2.4[1] (1960) 10.1[3] (1960) 33.3[5] (1960)	3.2[1] (1980) 11.7[3] (1980) 20.1[5] (1980)
Glasgow		20.5[1] (1966)	
Hamburg			17.2[3] (1982)
London		40.8[6] (1961)	27.3[1] (1981) 48.6[6] (1981) 61.9[5] (1981)
Montreal	16.1[1] (1921) 29.4[7] (1921)	20.7[1] (1961) 32.6[3] (1961) 51.2[5] (1961)	22.0[1] (1981) 41.7[3] (1981) 54.7[5] (1981)
Munich		11.6[3] (1961)	
New York	20.2[1] (1930)		29.5[1] (1984)
Paris	5.0[1] (c.1870)	21.3[1] (1962) 28.0[3] (1962) 32.1[5] (1962)	24.2[1] (1984) 37.1[3] (1984) 43.0[5] (1984)
Philadelphia	50.7[1] (1930)		61.8[1] (1980)
Seoul			40.8[2] (1985)
Tokyo		25.2[3] (1941)	42.3[3] (1983)
Toronto	52.9[1] (1921) 55.6[3] (1921) 76.5[5] (1921)	56.4[1] (1961) 67.4[3] (1961) 73.6[5] (1961)	40.7[1] (1981) 56.5[3] (1981) 61.2[5] (1981)
Zurich		8.6[1] (1960) 14.0[3] (1960) 30.7[5] (1960)	6.8[1] (1980) 15.5[3] (1980) 24.1[5] (1980)

Source: National censuses and literature quoted in this essay.

Notes:
[1] Central city only (includes new annexations through time.)
[2] Probably central city only.
[3] Metropolitan area as a whole.
[4] Probably metropolitan area as a whole.
[5] Suburbs only
[6] Greater London Conurbation
[7] Four main suburbs of Montreal, comprising 67.4 % of its suburban population.

some could be disputed, the overall picture is one of great disparities, the explanation for which is not obvious.

If one keeps in mind the division between the city center and the suburbs, the radical differences in housing types and densities, the periods during which massive construction occurred, and major changes in territorial limits, it is possible to associate clearly low levels of homeownership with the older, central parts of metropolitan areas and high levels with their post–World War II peripheries. But there are exceptions—for instance, the very high levels in the center of Toronto or the much lower levels in the periphery of Zurich and Geneva, to name only the most obvious cases.

Factors such as the size, age, and level of industrialization of a city do have an impact on ownership levels but cannot be considered determining. For example, Montreal and Toronto, the two largest Canadian cities, are quite similar on these three characteristics but have always shown extreme differences in ownership levels (Choko and Harris, 1989:72). Other factors, such as general wealth, culture, and government policy, also enter into the debate.

A number of authors have attempted to explain levels of homeownership through theoretical models or through specific causal factors. It is not my purpose to make an exhaustive presentation of their propositions but rather to stress the main points and to discuss in detail the ones I feel are central. Summarizing the most common theoretical models, Duncan posits six categories of explanations: cultural (in which culture is an external structure greater than and influential upon individual decision makers who produce and consume housing); structural Marxist (in which the active force is the mode of production); modernization functionalist (in which an evolution in housing is an adaptation to industrialization and its needs); psychological and sociobiological (in which homeownership is a "universal" human need); neoclassical and behavioral (in which homeownership is a result of individual attitudes, motivations, and desires, within the context of national economic choices); and manipulated city/conspiracy (by a power elite of capitalists and government officials that intentionally manipulates the market) (Duncan, 1982:98–134).

Ruonavaara (1990a) discusses four types of explanation for homeownership levels: consumer choice (based on the preference of the population for owner occupation and improved opportunities); producer choice (in which the real choice that can be exercised by consumers is constrained by conditioning they have received at the hands of producers); housing policy (in which crucial choices are made not by consumers or producers but by politicians and other public policy makers, not necessarily in a conspiratorial manner); and a systemic explanation (something like a mix of Duncan's structural-Marxist and modernization-functionalist models). Ruonavaara also mentions the possibility that explanations may vary over time (for example, the factors behind owner-occupation growth in the 1950s could be different from those behind the rise in the 1970s).

The problem is not necessarily that all these explanations deal with different factors but that authors rank factors in different orders of importance. There is no pure explanatory model; rather, models borrow secondary factors from each other, with the central argument lying in the primacy of one factor over others. In discussing more specific causal factors for homeownership on a national level, Schmidt (1989) argues that the proportion of total government expenditures allocated to welfare is of primary importance. Topalov (1988) and Bonvalet and Lelièvre (1989) emphasize the introduction of credit facilities. Oxley (1988) adds to these the availability of second-hand houses due to the mobility of their owners. Carliner (1974) stresses the rise in incomes, government decisions about mortgage and tax rates, and suburbanization. For Chevan (1989), increasing incomes plus the changing age composition of the population primarily explain rapid growth in homeownership (see also Clark, Deurloo, and Dieleman, 1988). Schellenberg (1987) questions whether rational economic behavior guides homeowners. And the debate continues.

In fact, none of these general explanations stands up in the light of detailed analysis of specific cases. In the case of Montreal and Toronto, two Canadian cities with otherwise similar characteristics, Choko and Harris (1989) have shown there is no simple explanation for the fact that Toronto has nearly three times as many owner-occupiers as Montreal. Levels in Montreal are lower for all social classes and proportionally lower for the middle and upper classes than for workers. Comparing housing costs to incomes and ownership costs to rental costs, Harris (1986a) shows that Montrealers clearly were in the better position to become owners, and yet they did not. Collin (1986) also shows that the proportion of owner-occupants is much lower for all types of housing. Choko (1987, 1992) contradicts the main explanation for Montreal's very low owner-occupier level used throughout Canadian literature on this issue—the cultural difference between French and English—by showing that the English are more underrepresented among owner-occupiers than the French.[9]

To summarize, there are great differences in homeownership levels over time and between countries; within countries, the levels can vary greatly between locations (city center and suburbs, metropolitan and rural areas, different cities), and factors explaining these variations can change over time and by location. But what about homeowners themselves? Is there a typical homeowner?

HOMEOWNER: A CLASS OR A CLASSIFICATION?

The rising proportion of homeowners, among them people from the working classes, has stimulated debate concerning possible new ways to divide society or perhaps a superimposition of new class interests based on housing. The purpose of an early paper by Saunders (1977) was

to advance a substantially modified model of urban class relations based on the argument that the two major patterns of housing tenure—owner occupation and renting—must be understood as generating and reflecting a significant division of class interests between different sections of the urban population. (p. 1)

This went against the then-dominant approach inspired by the writings of Marx and Engels, in which only the position of individuals in the process of production determines their class membership. Short (1982) summarized it by stating that "literature on social class and capital gains suggests that inequalities arising out of the labor market are reflected and reinforced in the housing market." Forrest (1983) and Thorns (1981) agreed that "gains from the job and housing markets are in fact closely related and to some extent mutually re-enforcing" (Thorns, 1981:128).

Weber (1947) had challenged this notion, and Weberians such as Rex and Moore (1967) argued "that it was possible to occupy one class position in relation to production and another with regard to the distribution of housing" (in Saunders, 1977:1). Sociological studies in the 1950s and 1960s seemed to detect signs of a transformation of working-class values and behavior among those who had become homeowners (Chombart de Lauwe, 1956). Of course, some neo-Marxist authors resisted this point of view and stressed that "owner occupiers do not compose an homogeneous group of privileged households" (Topalov, 1987:120), that "the reality of homeownership is that it is a tenure that varies enormously—spatially, historically, and between different groups" (Forrest, Murie, and Williams, 1990:53). Thorns went even further:

The housing market functions to create a growing differentiation amongst owner occupiers. This growing differentiation means that wealth accrues to some, more rapidly than it does to others. The evidence further suggests that this process of accumulation transfers wealth to those who already have substantial assets, thus reinforcing rather than reducing existing social inequalities. (Thorns, 1981 in Forrest, Murie, and Williams, 1990:89)

One could also refer to the texts of Short (1982), Forrest (1983) and Doling, Karn, and Stafford (1986). From the quantity of material available, it can be said, in short, that many from the working classes are now homeowners, but that they are underrepresented. Most studies show great disparities among occupational and revenue groups. For Germany (table 1.3), Potter shows that since 1965, the upper three quintiles have had increasing access to homeownership. Hulchansky illustrates the same tendency for Canada (table 1.4), though access by the lower two quintiles has decreased. For France, Topalov (1987) also showed that "disparities grew wider with the growing size of the cities" (p. 310). From my own work on Montreal, from

Table 1.3
Owner Occupancy by Income Quintiles, Germany, 1965–1982

INCOME QUINTILE	1965	1972	1978	1982
1st Quintile	23.6	23.6	23.6	23.2
2nd Quintile	26.9	28.5	28.4	28.6
3rd Quintile	29.3	32.2	34.8	36.7
4th Quintile	33.0	36.3	40.0	45.7
5th Quintile	43.7	46.9	53.6	60.0
All Quintiles	31.3	33.5	36.1	38.8
Source Potter and Dreverman 1988;97				

Table 1.4
Owner Occupancy Rates by Income Quintiles, Canada, 1967–1981 (in percentages)

INCOME QUINTILE	1967	1973	1977	1981
1st Quintile	62	50	47	43
2nd Quintile	56	54	53	52
3rd Quintile	59	58	63	63
4th Quintile	64	70	73	75
5th Quintile	73	81	82	84
All Quintiles	63	62	64	63
Source: Hulchanski 1988:20				

data on Swiss cities, and from evolutionary data for West Germany, it appears that disparities also grow where owner-occupation is scarce.[10] Another source of disparities is the situation of owner-occupiers in relation to the date of purchase and their mortgage status. For example, in Paris, the occupational profile of all owner-occupiers is much more democratic than that of new purchasers, among whom employees and blue-collar workers account for only 10 percent (table 1.5; see also Massot, 1990:84). Taffin (1987) also stresses that among mortgaged owners, there are very important disparities according to when the dwelling was bought. For France as a whole, Bourdieu and Saint-Martin (1990:57) note that levels of ownership are not correlated to income but that income determines the decision to purchase (to go into debt). Thus, the portrait of all owners is totally different from that of recent purchasers alone.

Table 1.5
Percentage of Outright and Mortgaged Owner Occupancy, by Occupation of
Household Head, France, 1984

OCCUPATION	OWNED OUTRIGHT	MORTGAGED	PERCENT OWNED UNITS MORTGAGED	PERCENT ALL UNITS OWNER OCCUPIED
Farmers	52.5	21.5	(29.1)	74.0
Artisans, small business	30.3	34.7	(53.4)	65.0
Managers/ Professionals	14.2	41.9	(74.7)	56.1
Intermediate	10.5	43.2	(80.4)	53.7
Employees	11.5	22.5	(66.2)	34.0
Skilled blue collar	11.1	33.9	(75.3)	45.0
Other blue collar	12.8	19.3	(60.1)	32.1
Retired	52.5	8.7	(14.2)	61.2
No occupation	32.0	4.9	(13.3)	36.9
Source: Taffin 1987:6				

In fact, outright owners and mortgage holders seem to present two different worlds. Age, occupational, and revenue profiles, as well as localization, type, and condition of housing, vary greatly from one type to another (Topalov, 1987; Taffin, 1987; Forrest, Murie, and Williams, 1990; Bourdieu and Saint-Martin, 1990). Aside from farmers, outright owners appear clearly to be older, less active, with lower incomes, living in older and more centrally located premises (tables 1.6 and 1.7). Regarding Athens, Maloutas (1990) noted that "there is not a great social distinction between owners and tenants. However, homeownership is more common among the wealthiest, but also the poorest" (p. 1). In Finland, where condominiums account for a large share of owner-occupied dwellings, there is a clear distinction between occupational groups as far as the type of home owned. White-collar workers are much more present in condominiums than are self-employed and blue-collar workers, the vast majority of whom live in houses (table 1.8). In France, the upper classes and those with higher education own more apartment units, while others are basically oriented toward houses (table 1.9).

Clearly there is no homogeneity among owner-occupiers with regard to type and value of dwelling. But could homogeneity increase in the future? Typologically, the trend is toward diversity. Single, detached housing increasingly is being challenged by new forms of more densified structures

Table 1.6
Mode of Acquisition and Type of Dwelling, by Occupational Group, France,
1984 (in percentages)

OCCUPATION	HOMEOWNERS				APARTMENT OWNERS			
	1	2	3	4	1	2	3	4
Farmers	37.5	22.9	38.8	0.8	54.1	18.3	27.6	-
Unskilled blue collar	13.2	13.1	71.9	1.8	16.1	15.2	65.2	3.5
Skilled blue collar	7.6	4.7	84.1	3.6	8.2	10.3	75.7	5.8
Foremen	5.5	4.7	85.8	4.0	6.9	9.3	76.1	7.8
Service employees	19.4	19.0	61.7	-	22.2	22.3	53.1	2.4
Retired blue collar	21.1	35.1	39.3	4.4	17.2	42.2	35.9	4.7
Artisans	10.9	11.7	75.8	1.6	13.7	11.2	68.6	6.5
Shopowners	9.5	16.1	72.7	1.8	25.2	16.0	53.4	5.3
Retired shopowners	19.5	46.2	31.3	3.0	20.5	49.8	28.6	1.2
Police	5.3	10.1	81.4	3.2	8.0	12.4	75.2	4.4
Shop Assistants	12.1	13.8	69.7	4.4	11.8	35.7	52.5	-
Clerical	9.4	9.0	78.3	3.3	7.2	11.5	78.6	2.7
Public Services	7.4	9.8	80.8	2.0	14.2	8.3	74.9	2.6
Retired employees	20.8	37.3	38.9	3.0	7.5	49.1	40.6	2.8
Intermediate Private	5.5	5.2	86.4	2.9	6.5	6.8	85.3	1.4
Intermediate Public	5.7	7.1	85.1	2.1	7.4	10.3	78.5	3.8
Technicians	4.2	3.9	87.9	4.0	1.8	7.4	86.0	4.7
Teachers	2.9	7.5	89.0	0.6	11.6	11.5	76.9	-
Retired Intermediate	15.8	33.1	48.9	2.2	7.5	40.5	48.7	3.3
Heads of private companies	3.1	11.3	83.1	2.5	14.2	29.5	56.3	-
Private managers	2.8	8.1	88.1	0.9	7.1	9.7	81.4	1.8
Engineers	4.4	4.7	88.9	2.0	1.5	12.8	83.3	2.3
Public managers	5.5	5.5	88.4	0.6	3.2	7.9	85.5	3.4
Professors	6.8	11.4	78.3	3.5	4.1	10.8	83.2	1.9
Professionals	7.7	15.8	76.0	0.5	4.0	9.8	84.2	2.0
Artists	2.3	10.2	87.5	-	7.6	17.9	74.5	-
Retired managers	16.6	34.6	47.4	1.4	5.0	43.1	50.6	1.3
Others	28.6	37.0	31.2	3.2	21.9	34.1	42.6	1.4
All	14.1	18.7	64.4	2.8	10.8	23.6	62.5	3.1

Key   1   Heritage or donation
         2   Cash/outright
         3   Credit
         4   Others = life annuity

Source: Pierre Bourdieu and Monique de Saint-Martin, "Le Sens de la propriété," Actes de la recherche en sciences sociales 81/82, 1990: 61. Reprinted by permission.

Table 1.7
Occupational Groups and Tenure in Great Britain, 1986 (in percentages)

OCCUPATION	OWNER OCCUPANTS		PERCENT OF TOTAL	COUNCIL TENANTS
	OUTRIGHT	MORTGAGED		
Professional/Managerial	15	75	(83.3)	3
Professional/Education and Health	15	69	(82.1)	6
Professional/Science and Engineering	17	71	(80.7)	5
Literary/Arts/Sport	19	61	(76.2)	5
Managerial	22	59	(72.8)	6
Clerical	18	62	(77.5)	13
Sales	17	60	(77.9)	16
Security	8	55	(87.3)	14
Personal Services	14	45	(76.3)	30
Agricultural	19	29	(60.4)	24
Processing (excl. Metal/Electrics	15	52	(77.6)	26
Processing - Metal/Electrics	15	59	(79.7)	20
Repetitive Assembly Work	15	49	(76.6)	31
Construction/Mining	15	51	(78.5)	27
Transport/Storage	14	48	(77.4)	32
Miscellaneous	15	34	(69.4)	43
Inadequately Described	17	46	(73.0)	31
Source: Forrest, Murie, and Williams 1990				

and conversion to condominiums of existing apartment buildings in central cities. Topalov (1981:28) even showed that although living conditions of owners were better than those of tenants, the gap among owners was greater than that among tenants (see also Topalov, 1987:316; Cuturello and Godard, 1982).[11] However, regarding differentiation of owners' wealth through housing acquisition, Saunders and Harris (1988) seem to argue for homogenization: "The spread of homeownership thus reduces the relative inequality . . . between more and less affluent groups, although the absolute gap . . . is widened" (p. 29).

To reach this conclusion, Saunders and Harris argue that to calculate the

Table 1.8

Owner Occupancy by Type of Dwelling and by Socioeconomic Position of
Household Head, Finland, 1976, 1985 (in percentages)

| | FORM OF OWNER OCCUPATION | | | | | |
| | HOUSES | | CONDOMINIUMS | | ALL | |
OCCUPATION	1976	1985	1976	1985	1976	1985
Farmers	99	98	1	1	100	98
Self-Employed	64	55	16	27	80	83
Upper White Collar	20	27	37	47	57	74
Lower White Collar	21	26	27	38	48	64
Blue Collar	37	37	17	25	54	64
All Economically Active	39	39	20	30	59	69
All Economically Inactive	47	36	21	31	68	67
All Households	41	38	21	31	62	69
Source: Ruonavaara 1990b:7						

variation of economic gaps among owners, one should take into account not only absolute gains but also rates of return and that these last should be based on the original investment made by the purchaser. Forrest, Murie, and Williams (1990:138) challenge this, but perhaps their position needs further ammunition, since, in theory, Saunders and Harris's argument withstands their attack. Saunders and Harris posit that although the absolute gain differential widens, the rate of return to the poorest homeowners could be higher (even against their will, as the main problem for the cash-poor less affluent in buying a dwelling is obtaining the down payment, which is thus always as low as possible, forcing their rate of return up). But these authors forget that although housing increasingly may be seen as an investment, it cannot be bought and sold every day, so that better rates of return on smaller amounts could actually enable the poorest owners to catch up with the wealthiest. And this is without taking into account transaction and moving costs. All aspects of this issue need to be further documented before any conclusion can be drawn; the literature is full of contradictions, and housing cannot be isolated from other financial and living conditions.

Moreover, in Canada, the net value (value less debt) of real estate ownership decreased (in constant dollars) between 1977 and 1984. However, broken down per region and size of city, disparities appear. Unfortunately, the figures cannot be broken down by income group or occupational profile

Table 1.9
Tenure Status and Type of Dwelling, by Occupational Group, France, 1984 (in percentages)

OCCUPATION	OWNER OCCUPANTS			TENANTS			OTHER
	SINGLE HOUSING	APT.	TOTAL	SINGLE HOUSING	APT.	TOTAL	
Farmers	61.3	3.7	65.0	8.9	7.6	16.5	18.5
Unskilled blue collar	28.3	3.8	32.1	14.7	47.3	62.0	5.9
Skilled blue collar	39.4	6.4	45.5	10.4	38.8	49.2	5.3
Foremen	55.3	9.3	64.6	8.9	19.8	28.7	6.7
Service employees	21.7	7.6	29.3	5.3	47.6	52.9	17.9
Retired blue collar	47.4	7.9	55.3	8.7	25.2	33.9	10.8
Artisans	54.6	11.5	66.1	6.6	22.4	29.0	4.8
Shopowners	44.4	14.1	58.5	9.0	25.9	34.9	6.6
Retired shopowners	50.2	19.5	69.7	3.1	19.3	22.4	7.9
Police	25.8	4.5	30.3	8.7	37.5	46.2	23.4
Shop Assistants	21.5	6.1	27.6	5.6	57.2	62.8	9.6
Clerical	23.9	13.2	37.1	5.6	50.4	56.0	6.8
Public Services	28.4	8.4	36.8	5.0	51.6	56.6	6.6
Retired employees	39.1	13.1	52.2	4.8	34.0	38.8	9.0
Intermediate Pvt.	36.3	15.4	51.7	6.6	35.7	42.3	6.0
Intermediate Pub.	36.0	11.2	47.2	6.9	38.5	45.4	7.4
Technicians	43.4	13.7	57.1	6.0	32.2	38.2	4.6
Teachers	39.8	13.8	53.6	5.2	30.5	35.7	10.8
Intermediate Ret.	52.0	18.2	70.2	3.9	20.8	24.7	5.1
Heads of private companies	50.5	26.3	76.8	1.9	16.7	18.8	4.6
Private managers	36.1	22.4	58.5	8.8	27.7	36.5	5.0
Engineers	41.8	18.3	60.1	9.7	25.4	35.1	4.8
Public managers	32.5	17.4	49.9	10.1	29.6	39.7	10.5
Professors	33.9	15.8	49.7	6.5	32.7	39.2	11.1
Professionals	42.3	23.5	65.8	6.5	24.1	30.6	3.6
Artists	20.6	16.6	37.2	9.1	44.7	53.8	8.9
Retired managers	46.6	31.1	77.7	3.3	16.3	19.6	2.8
Others	27.2	9.5	36.7	5.8	38.3	44.1	19.3
All	39.7	11.1	50.8	7.8	32.9	40.7	8.6

Source: Pierre Bourdieu and Monique de Saint-Martin, "Le Sens de la propriété," Actes de la recherche en sciences sociales 81/82, 1990: 57. Reprinted by permission.

Table 1.10
Average Dwelling Valuation by Tenure, Montreal and Four Main Suburbs,
1921–1951 (in Canadian Dollars)

DATE	LOCATION	OWNER OCCUPANTS	TENANTS
1921	Montreal	3916	2447
	Lachine	2771	1894
	Outremont	7732	3447
	Verdun	2248	1901
	Westmount	12006	4845
1931	Montreal	3988	2637
	Lachine	3052	2362
	Outremont	8856	3916
	Verdun	2749	2189
	Westmount	13794	7179
1941	Montreal	3252	2478
	Lachine	3108	2232
	Outremont	7443	3382
	Verdun	2383	2063
	Westmount	13085	6249
1951	Montreal	4307	3108
	Lachine	4561	2306
	Outremont	8488	4090
	Verdun	2674	2178
	Westmount	12718	6245
Source: Choko and Harris 1992			

(Pastor, 1991). (Kopcke, Munnell, and Cook, 1991, show the same for the United States.) The opportunities and choices are nowhere close to equal for all. Even if everyone had the same access to information (e.g., few homeowners know how to calculate the real cost of their housing and what they gain or lose when they buy or sell it, mostly because they do not take opportunity costs of equity into account and forget to factor in the difference between current and constant dollar values), the limited maximum affordable price and the need for a down payment play against buyers with limited means getting a good deal. They are restricted to old, obsolete stock in the least desirable neighborhoods or to new, mass-produced housing in the suburbs. (Even wealthier households may rent expensive units in some preferred locations, when they could afford to buy elsewhere; see, for example, table 1.10).

But all these limitations do not negate the fact that even the poorest owners accumulate some wealth that they would not if they remained tenants. (There has been little discussion of the issue of compelled accumulation, in which one must invest time and money in rehabilitating one's property or meeting monthly payments and cut down on other vital expenses. When debating wealth accumulation among different groups of owners, one should remember to ask, "At what hidden cost?" for each group.) This wealth can be converted into available funds (not just through selling but also, for example, through new formulas for "reverse" mortgages), and these owners may even realize real gains, especially in periods of economic growth and inflation. In an article calling for housing to be considered an investment, Gaboriault (1989:21) shows that throughout Canada, this was not the case for all owners during the 1976–1987 period. The annual inflation rate was 7.4, as opposed to an average rise in value of only 5.4 for single houses. But in the largest cities—Toronto, Montreal, and Vancouver—as well as in Ottawa and Halifax, the rise in value outperformed local inflation, and gains were real. So it could be true that the gaps among owners, although very large, are surpassed by the gap between owners' and tenants' wealth.[12]

Not all owners win at this game, played first by the wealthiest and the middle class, then by skilled workers, and finally by all. Homeownership has brought increased financial problems for a growing number of households. Vervaeke (1990) notes that "home-ownership has been made possible for more and more groups with modest means . . . but they are facing the problem of an extremely high cost-to-income ratio" (p. 7). This may in part explain why increasing (although still marginal) numbers of foreclosures are detected here and there.[13] But the reality is that the vast majority of owners will withstand most problems (even drastic rises in monthly payments due to interest rate hikes, municipal tax increases, or loss of jobs) and accumulate some wealth through their housing that tenants will not. Most of them also benefit from better housing conditions. However, this does not, in my opinion, make homeowners a single class, even if they all have some common interests directly linked to homeownership, because interests can vary with what, where, and how they own.[14] As there is no longer (if there ever was) a dual society with a "race wholly apart" (Engels) of workers, there is no dual society with a race of owners wholly apart.

A TENDENCY TO OWN: FROM DREAM TO REALITY

Campaigns promoting homeownership have deep roots, and by the end of the nineteenth century, this was an important subject of public debate. To owners were, and still are, attributed all the ruling class qualities, meaning that tenants do not possess them. Struyk summarizes the arguments in favor of homeownership long used by North American governments to promote it:

• Homeowners maintain their dwellings in superior condition, saving society resources by extending the life of the housing stock. Homeowners also contribute to neighborhood stability.

• Homeowners save at a higher rate than renters, thus permitting a higher rate of national investment and greater economic growth.

• Owner occupants are more active in the local community and, in this sense, are better citizens than renters. Wider home-ownership lends political stability to a nation because of the greater economic stake owner occupants have in the existing economic and political systems. (Struyk, 1977:9–10)

The value of such arguments is questionable, especially when their application is patently absurd, as, for example, in Switzerland: "Increase in homeowners brings benefits to the entire society, such as, for example, a reduction in conflictual situations, more careful utilization of real estate . . . relative savings of public funds encouraging housing, as home buyers are generally ready to consent to higher housing expenses" (Suisse, 1979:10)— this, in one of the wealthiest countries, with the lowest percentage of home-owners, and definitely one of the least conflicted societies, with the best-maintained housing. The "fight against communism" argument seems weak, as the existence of "subversive movements" was limited at the time when the major rises occurred. Engels and neo-Marxist authors have amply contributed to the myth of "an army of small owner-occupiers" serving as a bulwark for the ruling classes against the proletariat (see, for example, Houdeville 1969:211–212, 217–218, and Trout, 1979:17, regarding the belief that owners would have something to lose if left-wing parties came to power). "Communism can never win in a nation of homeowners," declares Hoyt (1966). To Harvey (1978), a mortgaged worker is a pillar of social stability. The direct link between tenure and changes in political behavior has not been satisfactorily proved. Vitt (1990:9; see also Pratt, 1986a, 1986b; Williams, 1988) notes that among workers who became owners, although the link between ownership and general satisfaction is very strong, no correlation appears with "feeling middle-class." On the contrary, "Hugh Stretton, a leftist Australian historian . . . argues that participation in collective life may be dependent upon people feeling secure in the private sphere of home life and relates this view closely to the importance of homeownership" (Kilmartin, 1988:15–16).

The idea that workers who own homes become traitors to their class, and that if they make money this way (and not only through productive work) they even become exploiters, has sometimes caused neo-Marxist authors to misjudge this phenomenon and to minimize some of the real advantages that accompany ownership for most workers. "In a certain way, homeownership leads to turning more toward family life . . . one feels a greater desire to remain at home" (Pinson, 1988:112). Saunders and Harris (1988) also argue that "this means that owners . . . have a very real stake in the system" (p. 21) and they are right—but no more or less than do tenant workers who own a few shares of a company. The problem is not the stake itself but how much stake one gets and how much choice and control one has over it.

Table 1.11
Tenure by Annual Income, Japan, 1983 (in percentages)

ANNUAL INCOME (IN THOUSANDS OF YEN)	OWNED HOUSES	RENTED HOUSES
Less than 2000[1]	48.2	51.8
2000 - 3000	53.0	47.0
3000 - 4000	44.3	55.7
4000 - 5000	73.7	26.3
5000 - 7000	80.9	19.1
Over 7000	87.6	12.4
[1] 2000 yen equals approximately $13,300 (US)		
Source: Hayakawa and Hirayama 1990		

Other elements of the debate on homeownership promulgated by Engels have become obsolete. With housing production becoming autonomous from the workplace, workers cannot be considered more tied to their company when they become homeowners (except for the need to meet monthly payments). And now that various forms of credit are available, the same is true of the capability to liquidate part or all of the value of the property when needed. "To be a debtor—a social taboo in the Nineteenth Century—became, by the mid-Twentieth Century, a virtual social necessity for enjoying homeownership, the pinnacle of full citizenship" (Hancock, 1980:157).[15]

How was this made possible? What is certain, again in contradiction to Swiss experts, is that there has been heavy financial involvement by governments in countries where mass homeownership has been turned from rhetoric into reality. Topalov (1988) illustrated the origins of this process in the 1930s in the United States. Divay and Richard (1981:52) showed that in Quebec during the 1970s, mortgage interest rebates and tax deductions of all kinds cost governments between $1.8 billion and $4.8 billion, and stated, "The wealthiest groups of taxpayers benefit more: more of them own, the value of their dwellings is higher, and so is their rate of taxation." Forrest, Murie, and Williams (1990:108–112) illustrate the same situation in United Kingdom and Wood (1990:819–820) for Denmark, the United States, and the United Kingdom. (See also Harris and Hamnett, 1987:174.) It seems that more or less the same is true for the homeownership boom in Japan (table 1.11).

There has been much publicity touting homeownership as a good investment: money will be earned that would otherwise be given to the landlord; with a little cash one can make big money; prices will always rise.[16] Some buy dwellings meant for owner occupancy and rent them out. Some purchase a house and quickly sell it (after a short period of occupancy to avoid capital gain taxes) (Dubois, 1989:212; Hamel, Choko, and Dansereau, 1988). Today, in order to succeed in homeownership, the "king of the castle" also needs to know how to be the "boss of the enterprise." People see others around them who are wealthier and own homes, so they think that they, too, will become wealthy through ownership. To own has become a belief, a creed, a magic spell for having it all. Thus, the irrational, as well as the rational, plays a part. Somewhere in their minds, politicians and some researchers believe that becoming owners can transform the poor into model middle-class citizens, thus solving many problems of poverty.

In his philosophical essay on ownership, Attali (1988:12–13) claims that "to have and to be are nearly always merged," that "what property hides is the fear of death." Ownership is one way "to be, to last, to delay death." In ancient Greece and Rome, the dead were buried in the house; they protected the house and its grounds, thus closely associating sacred matters with the family house and property. Duby (1979) showed how, in the transfer from knighthood to nobility between the eleventh and fourteenth centuries, the central symbol was the acquisition of a castle and the addition of the castle's *lieu-dit* to the family name. Translated into more contemporary materialistic terms, owning a home gives feelings of roots, security, and duration.[17] "When asked to define the good life, owning a home is the primary component chosen by over 85 percent of [Americans] surveyed. Homeownership has been valued in such polls above an automobile, a happy marriage, an interesting or high-paying job—even above good health" (Vitt, 1990:1). Australians, Canadians, Britons, and others would give the same answer. In the United States, "the most esteemed and the predominant type of American housing has always been the detached one-family home, preferably occupant owned and separated from neighbors by extensive green space on all sides" (Hancock, 1980:157). The same opinion is expressed for France by Taffin (1987):

It is through ownership of a single detached house that buyers best realize their aspirations of "space appropriation." A condominium is less satisfying, as only the inside of the dwelling is individually owned. The single detached house allows more liberty for inside and outside interventions. It also provides the owner with a few acres of land, which is no doubt an important aspect to the rural roots that we all come from, whether recently or long ago. (p. 14)

If we follow the reasoning that we all are afraid to die and that we all, at some point, have rural roots, then we all have a tendency to own, and more precisely to own a detached house on a piece of land. But whether this is true does not really matter. After all, certain politicians incorporated the "ontological needs" theories of the "vital space" thinkers into their policies, and the results were not what we might have wished. But in a period of deep societal doubt, in good part because of the dissolution of the traditional nuclear family and the multiplication of urban problems, cocooning (creating a warm domestic environment that keeps the family at home together and protects it from invasions of various sorts) appears an attractive idea. Also, as Kemeny (1981) said, "Once a system has been established which discriminates between tenures and in favor of privatization . . . , there is a strong element of self-perpetuation involved" (p. 157).

Perpetuation of the model that equates homeownership with a single detached house is an interesting contradiction. Blind adherence to this approach must be questioned, as sooner or later societies will have to face the frustrations of those who were made to believe that they would "make it" and did not (despite heavy government assistance, ease of obtaining credit, and now possibly a lowering of housing standards) and the frustrations of those who "make it" but discover that reality does not match the dream. We know that some will not "make it" and that homeownership is not the best solution for everyone. We know that today it is not owning itself that is most likely to bring one an accumulation of money and prestige but what one owns and where:

In England it is taken for granted by the person in the street that different types of housing denote different social statuses and that it is possible to infer a lot about a person from the external characteristics of their home, provided you understand the code well enough to be able to "read" their dwelling correctly. (Darke, 1990:6)

In Great Britain, where private rental units have almost disappeared, leaving only homeownership and council flats, social cleavages have become increasingly associated with distinct tenure forms, perhaps more than anywhere else (Hamnett and Randolph, 1986). But of course, this applies anywhere. In fact, it is not dissimilar to how perceptions of apartment buildings evolved. First meant for the wealthiest, they ended up stigmatized as public housing for the poor, but today it is very unlikely that one would mistake a new condominium for a public housing project.

In addition, an approach relying totally on homeownership can directly harm tenants. Padovani (1990:3) estimated that evictions related to owner-occupancy transfers totaled about a hundred thousand in Italy between 1983 and 1986. The literature on urban renewal, gentrification through rehabilitation, and conversion to condominiums of rental buildings underlines similar problems. (See, for example, Choko, 1985, for Montreal.) Verret (1979) stated correctly that "to be an owner, or, rather, to become an owner . . . is above all not to be a tenant anymore. The working class has all the reasons in the world not to want to remain tenants" (pp. 105–106). Berry (1974) mentioned that "the major cause of the massive switch in tenure patterns (not necessarily tenure *preferences*) is that buying is often the only way to get a house at all" (p. 129).

Some may have thought that with growing homeownership among low-income households, once the dwelling is paid for, costs will drop, and so will the necessity for assistance in old age. But all the data show that ownership is decreasing proportionally among lower-income groups, thus calling such a regressive public policy into question. And most never realized that by the time the mortgage was paid off (after twenty to twenty-five years), the premises would need major renovations that would require refinancing. In developed countries, the homeownership boom has been linked with the growing proportion of double-income households, with their much higher level of real income. What if more and more households, because of deep societal transformations, are single-income ones? Dedensification and unlimited consumption of land, along with massive public hidden subsidies to homeowners and investment in transit infrastructures, have allowed unprecedented numbers of owner-occupied houses to be built at a slowly rising cost for buyers. What if necessary redensification cuts off the availability of land at a reasonable cost? These are just a few ways in which homeownership could be constrained.

Although there is much research to be done to clarify the issues, homeownership will not be the panacea for all housing ills. For governments to pretend that this is so is shortsighted and irresponsible.

NOTES

I thank Käthe Roth, who carefully edited and translated my original text, and the Univesité du Québec à Montréal, which awarded me a special grant for this purpose. Pierre J. Hamel, professor at INRS-Urbanisation, very usefully commented on my first draft. The support of the Social Sciences and Humanities Research Council of Canada is also gratefully acknowledged.

1. An extreme form of this is presented in Islam, where "the earth belongs to Allah and He chooses among His who serve Him, whom He wants as heir." *Encyclopaedia Universalis*, 1989, Paris, corpus 19:71.

2. Physiocrats, such as Dupont de Nemours, argued, "It is obvious that owners . . . are the excellent citizens of the country. Thus, by God's will, they are sovereign over their work, its nature, and its fruits . . . as well as over that of their ancestors" (*Constitution du 5 fructidor*, an III, in Allix, 1913). See also Albert de Mun, *Discours 1875*, for whom certain classes dominate not because of special prerogatives but because of special graces God granted them (Brossier, 1929:229).

3. *Usus*: "to use things"; *fructus*: "to collect the fruits of things"; *abusus*: "to dispose of things."

4. See also utopians such as Thomas More and Tommaso Campanella.

5. Leroy-Beaulieu (1896) develops four central arguments in favor of private individual property: historical (from the individual ownership of women, slaves, animals, and tools, to ownership of land, houses, inventions, and works of art); psychological (human nature needs possessions in order to feel satisfied and free);

moral (property is the result of working and saving); and societal interest (society needs the work of individuals, and ownership is the best incentive).

6. For the Montreal Board of Trade and the Improvement League of Montreal (1935:8–9), "Workers' dwellings are as much a part of the industrial plant of the country, the province, or the municipality as the mills they work in or the machinery these mills contain."

7. In a recent book, Martens (1988:127) deduced the proportion of owner-occupiers from figures on single-family housing.

8. Bonvalet (1988:5) shows that among immigrant workers living in Paris, only 16.4 percent are owner-occupiers, while 47.7 percent of those who are tenants own a dwelling elsewhere (table 1A). She adds that this is also a common behavior among provincial renters in Paris. Bonvalet and Lelièvre (1989:555) show that taking into account second homes increases significantly the percentage of owners among lower occupational groups (table 1B). Samson (1988) estimated that 12 percent of all Canadian households had a second home; that the proportion was the highest in Quebec (where owner occupancy is the lowest); that in Quebec, Montrealers counted for the highest proportion; and that lower- and middle-income groups in Montreal were more represented (thus, more likely to rent), while for suburbs it was mainly higher-income groups.

9. This does not mean that culture is irrelevant. Choko (1992) shows that if new immigrants tend to own more, those from countries with higher rates of ownership own more than those from countries with low rates (table 1C).

10. For example, Choko (1992) shows that in Montreal, in 1921 as well as in 1951, there were between 50 percent and 100 percent fewer working-class than employer, manager, and professional owner-occupiers. See also data for Geneva and Zurich in Recensement de la population, Suisse, 1960, 1970, and 1980 (tables 1D and 1E).

11. There is, however, no correlation between homeownership level in a country and its general standard of living. See Agnew (1982:66).

12. Again, there is no certitude. Pastor (1991) shows that although the gap between owners' and tenants' wealth is large (by a factor of 7.8 in 1977), it has decreased slightly (to a factor of 7.4 times in 1984). However, figures for all of Canada hide the fact that this gap increased in most cities with a population of a hundred thousand and more and decreased drastically in most rural areas. Silver (1988:20) disputes the argument of U.S. neoconservatives who favor selling public housing as a means of reducing dependence on government, increasing individuals' control over their homes, and encouraging social mobility, as the difference before and after the policy was implemented remained marginal where it was tried out.

13. See Potter and Drevermann (1988) for Germany, Saunders and Harris (1988), as well as Forrest, Murie, and Williams, (1990) for United Kingdom. Of course, extreme situations are observed in specific areas such as resource or single-industry towns when the company or subsidiary collapses. See, for example, Bradbury (1985). Among the low-income households that benefited from the special homeownership program in Canada during the 1970s, 11 percent had defaulted by 1985 (Steele, 1988:10). Also, during periods of recession, some of the very wealthy owners who bought during earlier peaks and have to sell their houses lose a great deal of money; this was also true for wealthy Anglophones who wanted to leave Quebec after the nationalist Parti Québéçois won the 1976 provincial election.

14. An interesting avenue for research is a possible "culture of property" created

Table 1A
Percentage Owner Occupancy According to Citizenship, Paris Metropolitan
Area, 1986

ORIGIN	MAIN RESIDENCE	SECOND HOMES	TENANTS OWNING "SECOND" HOME
French origin	54.7	41.0	36.0
French naturalized	48.8	30.1	29.8
Foreigners	16.4	46.7	47.7
All	49.2	42.0	38.0
Source: Bonvalet 1988:5			

Table 1B
Percentage Owner Occupancy, Main and Other Residence, by Occupational
Groups, Paris Metropolitan Area, 1986

OCCUPATION	MAIN RESIDENCE	AT LEAST ONE DWELLING
Artisans and shopowners	64	77
Private heads and professionals	69	89
Public managers	59	82
Artists	38	53
Private managers	73	88
Intermediate public	45	69
Intermediate private	62	77
Foremen	52	72
Public services	30	52
Private employees	50	62
Unskilled service	11	44
Skilled blue collar	38	61
Unskilled blue collar	13	42
ALL	49	69
Source: Bonvalet 1988:4		

Table 1C
Ethnic Groups and Owner Occupancy in Montreal, 1921–1951

	FRENCH CANADIANS	ENGLISH CANADIANS[1]	EASTERN EUROPE[2]	SOUTHERN EUROPE[3]
1921				
1	16.9	16.3	14.9	17.5
2	60.7	28.6	8.1	2.5
3	59.2	29.1	9.0	2.3
1931				
1	18.3	14.2	18.4	26.2
2	63.8	21.7	9.8	4.6
3	60.9	26.6	9.2	3.1
1941				
1	13.9	9.0	11.7	12.7
2	69.4	17.7	9.7	3.0
3	62.0	24.6	10.3	2.9
1951				
1	20.6	17.7	24.6	38.6
2	60.4	18.8	13.3	7.3
3	61.6	22.9	11.7	3.7

Key 1. Percentage of owner occupants in the ethnic group.
     2. Percentage of the ethnic group among owner occupants.
     3. Percentage of the ethnic group among all households.

Notes [1] English Canadians include Scottish, Welsh, and Irish.
       [2] Southern Europeans are mainly Italians, with some Greeks and Portuguese.
       [3] Eastern Europeans include Poles, Germans (a majority of whom are Jewish), and some Russians and Hungarians.

among homeowners, with their children more likely to become owners than others. Choko and Dansereau (1987:93–94) showed that most owners (63.8 percent) spent their childhood in a house that their parents owned. Forrest, Murie, and Williams, (1990:145 passim) argue that inheritance is very important but refer mainly to Hamnett, Harmer, and Williams (1989:148), who show that 9.2 percent of inheritances included residential property; this figure is very close to the 9.0 percent inheritance rate cited by Taffin (1987:6), who argues that inheritances are declining. The distinction should be made here between those who inherited and kept their property, the percentage of whom may be declining, and those who inherited a property and sold it, using the money to help them buy another (thus, one that is not directly inherited).

15. See, for example, the early (1919) campaigns of the Departments of Labor

Table 1D

Occupational Groups and Owner Occupancy in Montreal, 1921–1951

OCCUPATION	1921			1931			1941			1951		
	1	2	3	1	2	3	1	2	3	1	2	3
Managers	31.1	15.0	8.1	34.1	13.1	6.9	24.9	12.5	6.4	31.4	10.1	6.4
Professionals	20.8	12.3	10.0	24.0	13.0	9.6	18.3	13.0	9.1	24.8	12.6	10.2
Construction managers and artisans	44.8	1.8	0.7	53.5	1.9	0.6	*	*	*	*	*	*
Shopowners	18.8	8.6	7.7	19.1	7.8	7.3	17.9	8.0	5.7	26.0	7.1	5.5
On commission	13.6	3.1	3.8	14.0	3.5	4.5	12.7	5.5	5.5	18.3	4.2	4.6
Clerical	12.1	4.8	6.7	16.6	6.1	6.6	11.1	6.5	7.4	16.8	7.5	9.0
Skilled blue collar	15.0	18.7	20.9	18.2	19.6	19.2	10.6	17.2	20.5	16.8	22.2	26.4
Unskilled blue collar	9.8	4.4	7.5	7.7	3.5	8.3	6.3	3.9	7.7	16.0	4.8	6.1
Construction workers	14.2	17.7	20.9	13.6	16.1	21.0	8.9	14.1	19.8	16.6	12.6	15.2
Widows, retired	17.9	12.5	11.7	16.2	13.0	14.4	13.7	16.9	15.6	22.4	15.2	13.6
All	16.5			17.4			12.4			21.0		

* Insufficient number of cases

Key 1. Percentage of owner occupants in the occupational group.
     2. Percentage of the occupational group among owner occupants.
     3. Percentage of the occupational group among all households.

Source: Choko 1992

Table 1E
**Owner Occupancy by Occupational Group in Switzerland, Zurich, and Geneva,
1960 (in percentages)**

OCCUPATION	SWITZERLAND	ZURICH (METRO AREA)	GENEVA (METRO AREA)
Self Employed	63.9	32.1	22.3
Private Sector	21.4	10.6	8.9
Managers	42.2	39.0	21.2
Senior	27.2	17.7	12.8
Junior	18.9	7.2	6.6
Public Sector	23.5	13.3	8.5
Professional	35.1	33.6	22.1
Senior	28.1	20.6	10.9
Junior	23.2	11.2	7.6
Private Sector Workers	22.6	5.6	5.4
Primary/Secondary	24.5	6.2	6.2
Trans./Communic.	19.5	6.2	5.6
Commerce/Banking	13.1	4.8	3.6
Services	9.7	2.6	2.7
Public Sector Workers	24.6	6.4	8.3
Retired Workers	37.3	20.8	14.8
ALL OCCUPATIONS	33.7	14.0	11.0

Source: Switzerland, Housing Statistics, Census 1960.

and Commerce, "A New Declaration of Independence—Own Your Home," as reported in Wyatt (no date).

16. In an article about the new economic context, Minc (1991) argues that "from now on one who goes into debt grows poorer and one who owns without debt gets richer."

17. Homeownership has been associated with childbearing. Quebec's policy of the 1970s promoting a higher birthrate linked with homeownership was reminiscent of similar calls by Quebec Catholic leaders in the 1920s. It is ironic to find that, today, because of economic constraints, homeownership may play against childbearing, as women postpone it to remain in the labor force. (See Rudel, 1987, and Schellenberg, 1987.)

REFERENCES

Abrams, Charles. 1970. *Home Ownership for the Poor*. New York: Praeger.
Agnew, John. 1982. "Home Ownership and Identity in Capitalist Societies." In James S. Duncan, ed., *Housing and Identity: Cross-Cultural Perspectives*, 60–97. New York: Holmes and Meier.

Allix, E. 1913. "La Rivalité entre la propriété foncière et la fortune mobilière sous la Révolution." *Revue d'histoire économique et sociale,* 279–348.

Ames, Herbert B. 1897/1972. *City below the Hill.* Toronto: University of Toronto Press.

Attali, Jacques. 1988. *Au propre et au figuré. Une histoire de la propriété.* Paris: Fayard.

Barlow, James, and Simon Duncan. 1988. "The Use and Abuse of Housing Tenure." *Housing Studies* 3(4):219–231.

Berry, Fred. 1974. *Housing: The Great British Failure.* London: C. Knight.

Bertillon, Jacques. 1891. *Rescensement, Enquête sociale sur l'habitation.*

Bonnot de Mably, Gabriel. 1768. *Doutes proposés aux philosophes économistes sur l'ordre naturel et essentiel des sociétés politiques.*

Bonvalet, Catherine. 1988. "Le Statut de propriétaire: Analyse des différences." Paper presented to the IIIe colloque international, Association internationale des démographes de langue française, Montréal, June 7–10.

Bonvalet, Catherine, and Eva Lelièvre. 1989. "Mobilité en France et à Paris depuis 1945: Bilan résidentiel d'une génération." *Revue trimestrielle de l'Institut national d'études démographiques* 3:532–560.

Bourdieu, Pierre, and Monique de Saint-Martin. 1990. "Le Sens de la propriété." *Actes de la recherche en sciences sociales* 81/82:52–64.

Bradbury, John. 1985. "Housing Policy and Home Ownership in Mining Towns: Quebec, Canada." *International Journal of Urban and Regional Research* 9(1):1–14.

Brossier, Charles. 1929. *La Pensée sociale de A. de Mun.*

Canfora-Argandoña, Elsie, and Roger H. Guerrand. 1976. *La répartition de la population, les conditions de logement des classes ouvrières à Paris au 19e siècle.* Paris: Centre de sociologie urbaine.

Carliner, Geoffrey. 1974. "Determinants of Home Ownership." *Land Economics,* 50(2):109–119.

Challaye, Félicien. 1967. *Histoire de la propriété.* Paris: PUF.

Chevan, Albert. 1989. "The Growth of Home Ownership: 1940–1980." *Demography* 26(2):249–266.

Cheysson, E. 1881. *L'Economiste français.* August 27.

Choko, Marc H. 1980. *Crises du logement à Montréal (1860–1939).* Montréal: Editions Saint-Martin.

———. 1985. "Emergence du marché du condominium dans la restauration résidentielle à Montréal et ses conséquences." *Actualité immobilière* 9(3):18–26.

———. 1987. *The Characteristics of Housing Tenure in Montréal.* Research Paper 164. Toronto: Center for Urban and Community Studies.

———. 1992. "Mythes et réalités de la propriété d'occupation à Montréal." Unpublished.

Choko, Marc H., and Francine Dansereau. 1987. *Restauration résidentielle et co-propriété au centre-ville de Montréal.* Etudes et documents 53. Montréal: INRS-Urbanisation.

Choko, Marc H., and Hubert Simard. 1977. "La Crise du logement (1976–1977) vue par les divers groupes d'intérêts" Unpublished. Montréal: CRIU.

Choko, Marc H., and Richard Harris. 1989. *L'Evolution du mode d'occupation des logements à Montréal et à Toronto depuis le milieu du XIXe siècle*. Etudes et documents 61. Montréal: INRS-Urbanisation.

Chombart de Lauwe, Paul-Henry. 1956. *La Vie Quotidienne des familles ouvrières*. Paris: Editions du CNRS.

Clark, W.A.V., M. C. Deurloo, and F. M. Dieleman. 1988. "Modeling Tenure Choice in the U.S. Housing Market." Paper presented to the conference "Housing, Policy and Urban Innovation," Amsterdam, June 27–July 10.

Cohen, Lizabeth. 1990. "At Home in Urban America: Domestic Culture in New York and Paris in the Late Nineteenth Century." Paper presented to the conference "Modes of Inquiry for American City," Chicago Historical Society, October 27.

Collin, Jean-Pierre. 1986. "Histoire de l'urbanisation de la paroisse de Montréal, 1851–1951." Unpublished. Montréal: INRS-Urbanisation.

Considérant, Victor. 1848. *Théorie du droit de propriété et du droit au travail*.

Cuturello, Paul, and Francis Godard. 1982. *Familles mobilisées. Accession à la propriété du logement et notion d'effort des ménages*. Paris: Plan-Construction; Nice: GERM-CERCOM.

Darke, Jane. 1990. "The Objectives of Housing Policy." Paper presented to the Eleventh World Congress of the Sociological Association, Madrid, July 9–13.

Daumard, Adeline. 1987. *Les Bourgeois et la bourgeoisie en France depuis 1815*. Paris: Aubier.

Dennis, Richard. 1987. *Landlords and Rented Housing in Toronto, 1885–1914*. Research Paper 162. Toronto: Center for Urban and Community Studies.

Divay, Gérard, and Louise Richard. 1981. *L'aide gouvernementale au logement et sa distribution sociale*. Etudes et documents 26. Montréal: INRS-Urbanisation.

Doling, John, V. Karn, and B. Stafford. 1986. "The Impact of Unemployment on Home Ownership." *Housing Studies* 1(1):49–59.

Dubois, Robert. 1989. *Enrichissez-vous avec l'immobilier*. Montréal: La Presse.

Duby, Georges. 1979. *La Société Chevalresque*. Paris: Champs/Flammarion.

Duncan, Nancy G. 1982. "Home Ownership and Social Theory." In James S. Duncan, ed., *Housing and Identity: Cross-cultural Perspectives*, 98–134. New York: Holmes and Meier.

Engels, Friedrich. 1845. *Die Lage der Arbeitenden Klasse in England*.
———. 1887/1975. *The Housing Question*. Moscow: Progress Publishers.

Forrest, Ray. 1983. "The Meaning of Homeownership." *Society and Space* 1:205–216.

Forrest, Ray, Alan Murie, and Peter Williams. 1990. *Homeownership: Differentiation and Fragmentation*. London: Unwin Hyman.

Fourier, Charles. 1829. *Le Nouveau monde industriel et sociétaire*.

Gaboriault, Robert. 1989. "Le financement de la propriété résidentielle." *Actualité Immobilière* 13(3).

Guérin, Daniel. 1976. *Ni Dieu ni Maître. Anthologie de l'anarchisme*. Paris: Maspéro.

Guerrand, Roger H. 1967. *Les Origines du logement social en France*. Paris: Les éditions ouvrières.

Hamel, Pierre J., Marc H. Choko, and Francine Dansereau. 1988. "La spéculation foncière." Unpublished. Montréal: INRS-Urbanisation.

Hamnett, C., M. Harmer, and P. Williams. 1989. *Housing Inheritance and Wealth: A Pilot Study*. London: Economic Social Research Council.

Hamnett, Chris and Bill Randolph. 1986. "Socio-Tenurial Polarisation in London: A Longitudinal Analysis." Paper presented to the Housing Policy Conference, Gävle, June 10–13.

Hancock, John. 1980. "The Apartment House in Urban America." In Anthony D. King, ed., *Buildings and Society*, 151–189. London: Routledge and Kegan Paul.

Harris, Richard. 1986a. "Housing Affordability and Working-Class Homeownership across Canada in 1931." *Histoire sociale/Social History* 19(37):121–138.

———. 1986b. "Homeownership and Class in Modern Canada." *International Journal of Urban and Regional Research* 10(1):67–86.

Harris, Richard, and Chris Hamnett. 1987. "The Myth of the Promised Land: The Social Diffusion of Home, Ownership in Britain and North America." *Annals of the Association of American Geographers* 77(2):173–190.

Harvey, David. 1978. "Labor, Capital, and Class Struggle around the Built Environment in Advanced Capitalist Societies." In Kevin R. Cox, ed., *Urbanization and Conflict in Market Societies*. Chicago: Mearoufa.

Hayakawa, Kazua, and Yosuke Hirayama. 1990. "Housing and Related Inequalities in Japanese Society." Paper presented to the Eleventh World Congress of the Sociological Association, Madrid, July 9–13.

Heskin, Allen David. 1981. "The History of Tenants in the United States, Struggle and Ideology." *International Journal of Urban and Regional Research* 5(2):178–204.

Holbach, Baron d'. 1773. *Système social*. Vol. 3.

Houdeville, Louis. 1969. *Pour une civilisation de l'habitat*. Paris: Editions ouvrières.

Hoyt, Homer. 1966. *According to Hoyt*. Washington, D.C.: Homer Hoyt.

Hulchanski, John D. 1988. "New Forms of Owning and Renting." Unpublished paper. Vancouver: University of British Columbia.

Journal officiel du 14 août 1875, no. 222, annexe no. 3283, 6788–6792.

Kemeny, Jim. 1981. *The Myth of Home-Ownership*. London: Routledge and Kegan Paul.

Kilmartin, Leslie. 1988. "Housing: An Antipodean Perspective." Keynote address to the conference "Housing Policy and Urban Innovation," Amsterdam, June 27–July 1.

Konadu-Agyemang, Kwadwo. 1990. "Home Ownership in Urban West Africa: A Mirage of Increasing Proportions." *Ekistics* 57:205–213.

Kopcke, Richard W., Allicia H. Munnell, and Leah M. Cook. 1991. "The Influence of Housing and Durables on Personal Saving." *New England Economic Review* (November–December):3–16.

Krohn, Roger, and Hunthy Duff. 1971. "The Other Housing Economy: Self-Renewal in a Central Montreal Neighborhood." Unpublished.

LePlay, Frederic. 1864. *La réforme sociale*. 2 vols.

Leroy-Beaulieu, Paul. 1872. *La question ouvrière au 19e siècle*.

———. 1896. *Traité théorique et pratique d'économie politique*. Paris: Guillaumin.

Linneman, Peter, and Susan Wachter. 1989. "The Impacts of Borrowing Constraints on Homeownership." *AREUEA Journal* 17(4):389–402.

Maloutas, Thomas. 1990. "Statut d'occupation, mode d'acquisition du logement et

choix de localisation résidentielle à Athènes." Paper presented to the conference "Housing Debates-Urban Challenges," Paris, July 3–6.
Martens, Maartje. 1988. "Owner-Occupied Housing: A Tenure in Transition." In Michael Ball, Michael Harloe, and Maartje Martens, *Housing and Social Change in Europe and the USA*. London: Routledge.
Massot, André. 1990. "Qui achète des logements à Paris?" *Cahiers de l'IAURIF* 93:81–88.
Minc, Alain. 1991. "Si la gauche était au pouvoir." *Le Nouvel Observatuer* (June).
Montreal Board of Trade and City Improvement League. 1935. *Housing and Slum Clearance for Montreal*. Montreal.
Moriconi-Ebrard, François. 1991. "Les 100 plus grandes villes du monde." *Economie et Statistique* 245:7–18.
Oxley, Michael. 1988. "Tenure Change in Western Europe." Paper presented to the conference "Housing Policy and Urban Innovation," Amsterdam, June 27–July 1.
Padovani, Liliana. 1990. "New Relationship between Public and Private Sectors in Italian Urban Renewal and Housing Policy." Paper presented to the conference "Housing Debates—Urban Challenges," Paris, July 3–6.
Pastor, Marie-Hélène. 1991. "L'Habitation: Source de richesse." Ottawa: CMHC.
Peil, Margaret. 1976. "African Squatter Settlements: A Comparative Study." *Urban Studies* 13(2):155–166.
Pinson, Daniel. 1988. *Du logement pour tous aux maisons en tous genres*. Paris: Ministère de l'équipment et du logement, Plan construction et architecture.
Potter, Philip and Marlis Dreverman. 1988. "Home Ownership, Foreclosure and Compulsory Auction in the Federal Republic of Germany." *Housing Studies* 3(2):94–104.
Pratt, Geraldine. 1986a. "Housing Tenure and Social Cleavages in Urban Canada." *Annals of the Association of American Geographers* 76:366–380.
———. 1986b. "Why Canadian Homeowners Are More Conservative Than Tenants." *Urban Geography* 7(3):187–209.
Raymond, Henri, et al. 1966. *L'Habitat Pavillionnaire*. Paris: Centre de recherche d'urbanisme.
Retel, Jacques. 1977. *Eléments pour une histoire du peuple de Paris au 19e siècle*. Paris: Centre de sociologie urbaine.
Rex, John, and Peter Moore. 1967. *Race, Community and Conflict*. Oxford: Oxford University Press.
Roistacher, E., and J. S. Young. 1979. "Two Earner Families in the Housing Market." *Policy Studies Journal* 8(2):227–240.
Rousseau, Jean-Jacques. 1758. *Discours sur l'économie politique*.
Rudel, Thomas K. 1987. "Housing Price Inflation, Family Growth, and the Move from Rented to Owner Occupied Housing." *Urban Studies* 24(4):258–267.
Ruonavaara, Hanna. 1990a. "On Explaining the Growth of Homeownership." Paper presented to the conference "Housing Debates—Urban Challenges," Paris, July 3–6.
———. 1990b. "Recent Trends in the Access of Owner-Occupation in Finland," Paper presented to the Eleventh World Congress of the Sociological Association, Madrid, July 9–13.
Samson, Marcel. 1988. "La résidence secondaire et la région métropolitaine de

Montréal. Essai d'interprétation." Ph.D. dissertation, Université d'Aix-Marseille.

Saunders, Peter R. 1977. *Housing Tenure and Class Interests.* Working Paper 6. Brighton: University of Sussex, Urban and Regional Studies.

Saunders, Peter, and Colin Harris. 1988. *Home Ownership and Capital Gains.* Working Paper 64. Brighton: University of Sussex, Urban and Regional Studies.

Schellenberg, Kathryn. 1987. "The Persistence of the Homeownership Norm and the Implications of Mortgage Debt." *Journal of Urban Affairs* 9(4):355–366.

Schmidt, Stephan. 1989. "Convergence Theory, Labor Movements, and Corporatism." *Scandinavian Housing and Planning Research* 6(2):83–101.

Short, John. 1982. *Housing in Britain.* London: Methuen.

Silver, Hilary. 1988. "Privatization, Self-Help and Public Housing Homeownership in America: A Preliminary Appraisal." Paper presented to the conference "Housing Policy and Urban Innovation," Amsterdam, June 27–July 1.

Steele, Marion. 1988. "The Demand for Home Ownership." Unpublished paper. Toronto: University of Toronto.

Stegman, Michael A. 1984. *Housing in New York: Study of a City.* New York: City of New York.

Struyk, Raymond J. 1977. *Should Government Encourage Home-Ownership?* Washington, D.C.: Urban Institute.

Suisse, Département fédéral de l'économie publique. 1979. *Rapport de la Commission d'experts pour l'encouragement de l'accession à la propriété de logements.*

Taffin, Claude. 1987. "L'Accession à tout prix." *Economie et statisque* 202:5–15.

Thorns, David C. 1981. "Housing Policies and the Influence of the Growth of Owner Occupation in a Social and Political Change." Paper presented to the conference "Comparative Urban Research," Essen, October 3–5.

Topalov, Christian. 1981. *Tous propriétaires! Propriété du logement et classes sociales en France depuis 1950.* Paris: Centre de sociologie urbaine.

———. 1987. *Le logement en France: Histoire d'une marchandise impossible.* Paris: Presses de la Fondation Nationale des Sciences Politiques.

———. 1988. "Régulation publique du capitalisme et propriété de masse du logement: La révolution hypothécaire des années 1930 aux Etats-Unis." *Economie et sociétés* 22(5):51–59.

Trout, Kilgore. 1979. "Construction de logements et crise économique: Quelques éléments d'analyse." *Critiques de l'économie politique,* no. 9.

Tulard, Jean, Jean-François Fayard, and Alfred Fierro. 1987. *Histoire et dictionnaire de la Révolution française, 1789–1799.* Paris: Robert Laffont (Déclaration des droits de l'homme et du citoyen, 26 août 1789, introduction et article 2).

Verret, Michel. 1979. *L'Ouvrier français: L'espace ouvrier.* Paris: Armand Colin.

Vervaeke, M. 1990. "Ségrégation sociale: L'accès au logement dans un espace régional connaissant une désindustrialisation." Paper presented to the conference "Housing Debates–Urban Challenges," Paris, July 3–6.

Vitt, Lois A. 1990. "The Social Psychology of Homeownership in U.S. Society." Paper presented to the conference, "Housing Debates–Urban Challenges," Paris, July 3–6.

Weaver, John. 1987. "The North American Apartment Building as a Matter of Business and an Expression of Culture: A Survey and Case Study." *Planning Perspective* 2:27–52.

Weber, Max. 1947. *The Theory of Social and Economic Organization*. New York: Oxford University Press.

Williams, Nicholas J. 1988. "Housing Tenure, Political Attitudes and Voting Behavior." Paper presented to the conference "Housing Policy and Urban Innovation," Amsterdam, June 27–July 1.

Wood, Gavin, A. 1990. "The Tax Treatment of Housing: Economic Issues and Reform Measures." *Urban Studies* 27(6):809–830.

Wyatt, Graham S. "Home in America: Early Alternatives to the Single-Family House." Unpublished.

2

Black-White Differences in the Demographic Structure of the Move to Homeownership in the United States

HAZEL A. MORROW-JONES

Housing and changes in housing are woven into the fabric of American life (Perin, 1977; Adams, 1984; Hayden, 1984). A home of one's own is seen as a major part of the American dream, a symbol that one has achieved success (Ong and Grigsby, 1988). This symbolism defines part of the implicit social contract under which American society functions (Sternlieb and Hughes, 1982). The distinction between owning one's home and renting it is "arguably the central divide in most housing markets" (Kendig, 1990:133). Because of the social importance of homeownership, U.S. federal policy has emphasized ownership as the tenure of choice.

Although the social and psychological importance of homeownership in the United States is immense, owning a home also has other benefits. First, the physical structures associated with ownership are larger on average and often located in better neighborhoods and school districts. Interest payments made on a mortgage (a very large proportion of the monthly costs in the early years of the mortgage) are tax deductible, as are the property taxes. No part of rents is deductible. Capital gains tax on the profits made from the sale of one's residence may be deferred by reinvesting them in another house. Once during one's life, an owner can take advantage of a capital gains exclusion on the profits made on the sale of a residence. Historically, home prices have appreciated in the United States so that owners have profited on the sale of houses or have been able to take out home equity loans on the increased value of properties. This has helped pay for vacations, home improvements, college educations, and comfortable retirements. In general, those who do not become owners are at an economic disadvantage and may also suffer social disadvantages. We must be concerned, then, with equality of access to owner occupancy (Bullard, 1979) and with the fairness of the distribution of its benefits (Lake, 1979, 1981). Race constitutes one of the major divisions within American society and consequently plays an important role in access to all housing, including owner-occupied housing.

BLACK-WHITE DIFFERENCES

Blacks and whites in the United States have dissimilar life chances and experiences in all areas. For example, between 1980 and 1990, the black population grew by 13.2 percent, while the white population increased by only 6 percent. In 1990 83.7 percent of blacks and 76.4 percent of whites lived in metropolitan areas, with blacks more than twice as likely to live in central cities (56.7 percent versus 26.2 percent). The 1988 median net worth of black households was $4,169 and for white households $43,279. In 1988, 21 percent of blacks 18 to 24 years old and 31 percent of whites 18 to 24 years old were enrolled in college (O'Hare et al., 1991). (For more examples of nonhousing issues, see Farley, 1984, and O'Hare et al., 1991.) Some of these differences and the reasons for them have been studied in depth, including some aspects of housing and residential segregation (see, for example, Pettigrew, 1980; Kain and Quigley, 1975; Lake, 1981; Laurenti, 1960; Rose, 1976; Frey, 1985; Bianchi and Farley, 1979; Brown, 1981). Differences in the demographic structure of residential mobility have attracted less attention, though life cycle effects on housing have been noted (e.g., Burns and Grebler, 1986).

Much is known about differences in the housing-life experiences of blacks and whites. We know, for example, that discrimination continues to play an important role (Galster, 1990). Blacks and whites have different migration rates (Rose, 1985), including different experiences with retirement migration (Longino and Smith, 1991). White and Mueser (1988) have also shown differences in residential mobility. We do not yet have detailed information on differences at a variety of ages, differences between kinds of moves, or whether differences remain stable over time. This information is what I refer to as the demographic structure of movement. Knowledge of racial differences in housing lives will help us predict future asset positions of blacks and whites and understand the housing impact of these relative positions. In addition, we will be able to focus policies on actual rather than apparent differences. For example, it is apparent that blacks and whites have different ownership rates. Added knowledge of movement to ownership at specific ages will help target programs specifically at the ages where they might have the most impact.

Homeownership is one way in which black and white housing lives differ (Galster, 1990; Lake, 1981), and it remains a major fair housing issue (Clay, 1989; Boyer, 1989). Many authors have discussed the gap in black and white ownership rates (Adams, 1987; Jackman and Jackman, 1980; Amin and Mariam, 1987), and several provide evidence of increasing black ownership rates

(Bianchi, Farley, and Spain, 1982; Hughes and Sternlieb, 1987) or at least discuss reasons why we might expect increasing black ownership (Frey, 1985; Farley, 1984). We also know something about the location of local moves and the interplay between central city and suburban locations (Stahura, 1990; Frey, 1978; James, McCummings, and Tynan, 1984).

The information we need in order to understand the demographic structure of movement includes the within-group age-specific and origin/destination-specific rates of movement, particularly movement to and from homeownership; how these rates compare between racial groups; whether there have been changes in the rates or the relationship between groups over time; what characteristics of the two groups are different between different kinds of moves; whether the differences (if any) indicate that the two groups have different life cycles (Ong and Grigsby, 1988) or whether there are other explanations; and what effect changes in the economic context of housing have on the two groups and on the relationship between their movements.

METHODOLOGY AND DATA

The approach taken in this chapter is based on the importance of the life cycle concept in the analysis of mobility (Rossi, 1955). This life course conceptualization (Kendig, 1990) is operationalized using data from the American (formerly the Annual) Housing Survey and the techniques of multistate demography.

Multistate Demography

Multistate demography is a life-table-based analysis ideally suited to examining changes over an individual's life course. The emphasis is on individuals because the analysis uses each person's age, and it is awkward to assign an age to a household. We use cross-sectional data on individuals, the housing in which they live, and the moves they make at specific ages to examine the larger national patterns in hypothetical life courses. That is, we develop housing-life tables for the data from a specific year. We can then compare the statistics generated by each year's specific rates to examine change over time. These life tables provide the answer to the question: What would happen if an individual lived his or her life at the rates extant in a given year? (Details on the mathematics of the technique may be found in Keyfitz, 1979; Rogers, 1980; Land and Rogers, 1982; and Willekens and Rogers, 1978. For a discussion of the application of multistate demographic methods to housing issues, see Morrow-Jones, 1988. A similar, though not identical, approach to analysis of the same data set for urban areas is taken by Moore and Clark, 1986, 1990.)

There are a variety of problems, constraints, and compromises associated with this combination of data and technique. We will detail the most important of these in the following discussion.

Data

The American Housing Survey (AHS) is a national sample of between sixty thousand and eighty thousand housing units each year that the survey is done. Our data set covers the years 1974 through 1987. The survey follows housing units rather than households and asks a variety of detailed questions about the structure and its inhabitants. (For more on the AHS in general, see HUD Data Access Description 43, Goering, 1979; Hadden and Leger, 1990.)

For present purposes, the most important aspect of the AHS is that it asks whether members of the household have moved into the unit within the last year. If the answer is yes, several questions about the former unit are asked, allowing us to compare previous and current housing for recent movers. One immediately apparent problem is that we know only about the most recent move for a person within the past year. Fortunately, this is likely to be a particular problem with people moving between rented units and less of a problem for those who moved from a rented to an owned unit or from an owned to a rented unit, the focus of this chapter. The calculated rates of movement are thus always underestimates, but the amount of underestimation is lowest for moves ending in ownership and highest for moves ending in rentership (especially those between rented units) (Moore, 1985).

In the earlier years of the data set (through 1983) if the respondent moved, the rest of the household was assumed to move with that person. In order to report consistently for all years, it was assumed that a moving respondent meant a moving household for all of these analyses. The characteristics of the former home are also assigned to all of the current household members.

Procedure

The analysis proceeds by defining a set of housing states. Because of the importance of tenure, the housing states used in this analysis are based on tenure (figure 2.1). A third dimension for ages is added to the matrix in figure 2.1. We can estimate occurrence/exposure rates (how many people made a specific move divided by those who were at risk of making it) for each racial group.

These occurrence/exposure rates (Ledent, 1980) are then combined with age-specific birth and death rates for the appropriate year and racial group to perform the multistate analysis. Life tables are calculated, including probabilities of dying or moving, as well as life expectancies and projections. We will focus on a few of the measures produced by the analysis and compare the results obtained for blacks and for whites.

Figure 2.1
Housing States Based on Tenure

CURRENT STATE |

		OWN	RENT
PREVIOUS STATE	OWN		
	RENT		

THE STRUCTURE OF MOBILITY

Figure 2.2 shows the age-specific rates of movement between different tenures for blacks and whites in 1987. First, notice that the magnitude of the rates differs a great deal between kinds of moves. Movement between rented units is highest, and movement between owned units is lowest. Remember also that these are estimated rates and that the rent-to-rent moves are probably significantly underestimated. Second, notice the general shape of the curves. There is usually a peak in the young adult years, with a gradual decline to the older ages. A secondary peak often appears in childhood (the children of the people in the young adult peak moving with their parents) and a tertiary peak at older ages. This reflects the classic shape of a migration curve, with the largest amount of movement between the ages of 18 and 30 and a decline thereafter to a small retirement peak.

In terms of a stereotypical American life cycle, one might expect moves between rental units to be made largely by young adults. As people age, marry, and raise families, rent-to-own movement should become more important. After obtaining one owner-occupied unit, a household may trade up to a larger, more expensive one. In old age, one might prefer to sell an owner-occupied unit and move to a rented unit. This "ladder of housing" is a widely accepted part of our collective mythology (National Association of Realtors, 1990; Perin, 1977). Figure 2.2 is organized in this way, with rent-to-rent moves in figure 2.2a, rent-to-own moves in figure 2.2b, own-to-own moves in figure 2.2c, and own-to-rent moves in figure 2.2d.

Of course, this idealized housing progression has many flaws. People make own-to-rent moves at times other than old age, for example, a young person setting up his or her own renting household upon leaving an owned parental home. People who are transferred or take new jobs at a distance from the old one might sell a house, rent for awhile in the new location, and then buy (an own-to-rent move followed by a rent-to-own move, both at the "wrong" ages). Disruptions in the normal life cycle, such as divorce or separation, often also produce an own-to-rent move.

Turning to the figure for 1987, we can see that at almost all ages, blacks have lower rates of movement. Since these age-specific rates are standardized for differences in population size, we are looking at the estimated probability of a certain kind of movement for a person of specific characteristics. For example, a white renter between the ages of 20 and 24 has a chance of .472 of moving to another rented unit in a one-year time period. A black renter of the same age has a chance of .344. The number of white or black renters does not matter; the rates are strictly comparable. The 20 to 24 age group has the largest difference on the rent-to-rent age rate schedule. In fact, except for ages 10 to about 29, the shapes and levels of the two schedules are remarkably similar.

Figure 2.2b indicates a much larger racial difference in the movement from renting to owning. Many of these moves are made by first-time home buyers. Blacks are less able or willing to make this move at all ages (the jump at age 80 is probably a result of relatively small numbers), and the size of the gap is a matter for concern, especially if later analysis indicates that this is the pattern across all years. Notice the multiple peaks for both blacks and whites, but especially for blacks, and the lack of a child peak for blacks. This implies that black households without children are more likely to buy, and that for black adults, there is not one clear home-buying age. We have no way to judge from these numbers to what extent the difference reflects differences in income, differences in taste, discrimination, or some other factor. Lake (1981) has shown that blacks benefit less from homeownership, so it is possible that this results in a lower preference for that tenure among blacks. In addition, blacks have generally lower mobility rates of all types. One the other hand, the benefits of homeownership are so numerous that one doubts that a difference in tastes alone is the explanation. Other possible factors will be examined later in this chapter.

Since movement rates between owned units are independent of the number of black and white homeowners, the difference in this category of moves does not simply reflect the lower rate of homeownership among blacks. It reflects the likelihood that an owner will move to another owned home in a given year. In 1987 this move was much more probable for white home-owners at all ages (except the age 85 and older group). In addition to the wide gap between races, the peak for this kind of move among blacks is significantly older than for whites. The white peak is between ages 25 and 34 (with the child peak under age 4). For blacks, the peak is between ages 35 and 39 with children between ages 5 and 9. Since the black move to ownership from renting has multiple peaks over the adult years, it may be that only somewhat older blacks are able to move from one owner-occupied home to another. Because there is less of a typical home-buying age for blacks, there is an older move-up age.

Figure 2.2
Age-Specific Rates of Movement, 1987

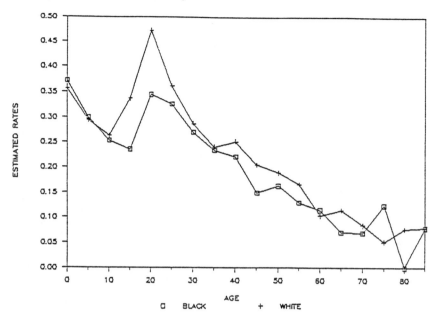

a. Rent-to-Rent

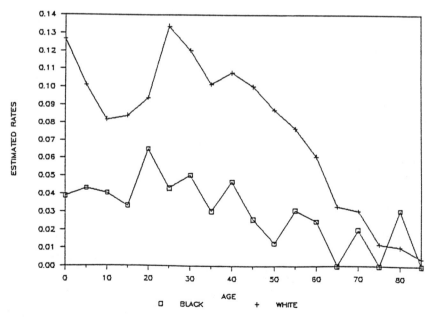

b. Rent-to-Own

Figure 2.2 (continued)

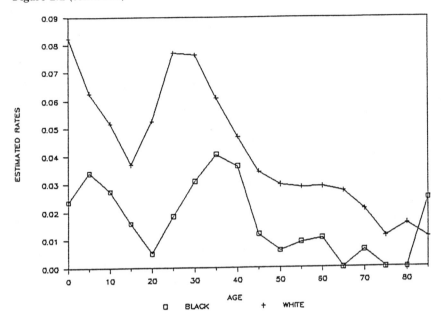

c. Own-to-Own

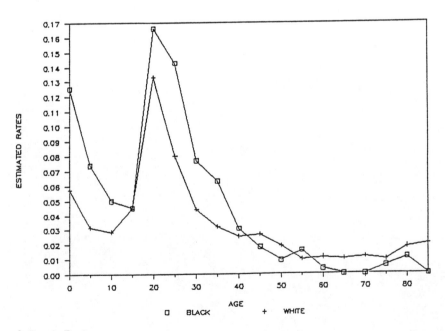

d. Own-to-Rent

Finally, the own-to-rent curve in figure 2.2d is the only age-rate schedule in which black rates dominate white rates over multiple ages. This may indicate lower tastes for homeownership (more willingness to leave the tenure), more formations of separate households (leaving a parental home, divorce, or separation), and/or more negative impacts of problems in the wider economy on blacks than on whites. The peak ages are similar for the two groups, and the child peak appears to reflect the higher young adult peak (between the ages of 20 and 29). Information on the characteristics of people making this move should help to clarify possible explanations.

CHARACTERISTICS OF MOVERS

One benefit of the multistate conceptualization of housing transitions is that it encourages examination of moves by combined origins and destinations. Rather than looking at all moves ending in owner-occupied units, for example, we can examine moves that start in rented units and end in owner-occupied units separately from those that begin and end in owner-occupied houses. It is likely that this kind of disaggregation will be important in understanding mobility.

Economic Factors

Rent-to-Own Moves

The levels in the rent-to-own move (figure 2.2a) illustrate one major distinction between black and white mobility in the United States: the lower rates of black movement. This lower movement from renting to owning (combined with the higher movement from owning to renting discussed below) causes an individual homeownership rate (in 1987) of 48.5 percent for blacks and 71.5 percent for whites. I suggest several reasons for the observed differences in rent-to-own movement between racial groups. A formal test of these possibilities is beyond the scope of this chapter, but we can examine some ideas.

Differences in economic indicators are an obvious first factor to consider. The 1987 AHS allows an examination of several of these (table 2.1). In 1987 black rent-to-own mover households had average incomes more than $10,000 lower than their white counterparts. Not surprisingly this led to the purchase of homes more than $20,000 lower in average value. The resulting mean value-to-income ratio of the two groups is almost exactly the same (2.03 for whites and 2.05 for blacks). Both groups buy houses in a similar ratio to their incomes, but white buyers have more income to work with. One outcome is that white rent-to-own movers benefit more from tax deductions available to people with mortgages. First, their tax bracket will be higher, so deductions mean more. For example, the 28 percent versus the 15 percent

Table 2.1
Mean Incomes, Values, and Rents of Movers, by Race and Type of Move

	WHITE	BLACK
INCOME		
Own to Own	$ 42,544	$ 34,701
Rent to Own	$ 37,690	$ 27,300
Own to Rent	$ 21,633	$ 14,806
Rent to Rent	$ 20,879	$ 15,074
SALE VALUE		
Own to Own	$ 96,628	$ 70,768
Rent to Own	$ 76,664	$55,870
VALUE/INCOME RATIO		
Own to Own	2.27	2.04
Rent to Own	2.03	2.05
MONTHLY RENT		
Own to Rent	$ 408	$ 306
Rent to Rent	$ 404	$ 330
RENT AS PERCENT OF INCOME		
Own to Rent	22.64	24.77
Rent to Rent	23.20	26.27
INCOME AS PERCENT OF RACE'S OWN-OWN INCOME		
Own to Own	100	100
Rent to Own	88.59	78.65
Own to Rent	50.85	42.66
Rent to Rent	49.08	43.43
BLACK INCOME AS PERCENT OF WHITE INCOME		
Own to Own		81.59
Rent to Own		72.43
Own to Rent		68.44
Rent to Rent		72.20

bracket brings about a difference between 28 cents and 15 cents of the mortgage interest dollar deducted. Second, white households' mortgages will probably be larger, so there is more interest to deduct.

The table also indicates that white rent-to-own households' average income was 88.5 percent of white own-to-own households' average income, while for blacks, the figure was 78.6 percent. Black own-to-own movers come closer to their white counterparts than any other black group (an average income 81.59 percent of white own-to-own movers).

Black households that moved between rental units had incomes only slightly greater than half of the black rent-to-own movers. Rent also consumed the highest proportion of their monthly incomes of any of the other renter groups studied (26.7 percent) so that their ability to save a down payment is reduced.

The number of people the household income must support differs between black and white households. In every move type, black households contain more people both before and after the move than white households do. The final rows of table 2.2 indicate that for rent-to-own movers, the per capita income among blacks is $7,358 and among whites it is $12,733 (the white figure is 73 percent higher than the black). Black households stretch more to purchase a house that is two times their household income than whites because of the different number of people to be supported on that income, and this further limits their ability to save for a down payment.

The age-rate schedule for the rent-to-own move indicated a lower child peak that was taken to imply fewer children in black rent-to-own households. Since black households making this move are larger than their white counterparts, perhaps there are more adults in the average household. That is, more adult incomes are necessary for blacks to move than for whites.

Figure 2.3a shows the reported change in costs due to the move for rent-to-own movers. Costs increased for both races. In both cases slightly fewer black households reported this change. Black households are more likely to report not knowing whether their costs changed, and almost the same proportion in each race report no change.

Own-to-Rent Move

The own-to-rent move is the other part of the equation determining how many owners there are at any time (figure 2.2d). This is a move that upsets the stereotype of the ideal housing life cycle because it is a move down the ladder. We can accept it for older people who have already owned at least one home and want to have smaller, lower-maintenance units. We can also accept it for job-related long-distance moves and for people just starting out and leaving their parents' homes. Otherwise, its effect can range from unpleasant to tragic.

The age-rate schedules in figure 2.2 show that this is the only kind of move for which black mobility rates are higher than those for white rates.

Table 2.2
Household Size before and after Moving, by Race and Move Type

	Rent to Own	Own to Own	Own to Rent	Rent to Rent
PERSONS / HOUSEHOLD (ORIGIN)				
White	2.75	3.23	3.60	2.85
Black	3.39	4.40	4.26	3.08
PERSONS / HOUSEHOLD (DESTINATION)				
White	2.96	2.97	2.20	2.49
Black	3.71	3.50	2.31	2.87
PERCENT CHANGE				
White	+7.6	-8.0	-38.0	-12.0
Black	+9.4	-20.0	-45.0	-6.8
WHITE HOUSEHOLD SIZE AS PERCENT OF BLACK (ORIGIN)				
	81.1	73.4	84.5	92.5
WHITE HOUSEHOLD SIZE AS PERCENT OF BLACK (DESTINATION)				
	79.7	84.8	95.2	86.7
INCOME PER PERSON				
White	$ 12,733	$ 13,325	$ 9,833	$ 8,385
Black	$ 7,358	$ 9,917	$ 6,410	$5,252

I suggest a variety of possible reasons for this, and we can look at some of the indicators available in the data set. Figure 2.3b shows the reported changes in costs for these movers. The largest portion of each race reports cost increases, but blacks are much more likely to indicate an increase and much less likely to indicate a decrease. Neither race has many households who do not know what had happened to their costs.

Turning again to table 2.1, we see that black households making this move had average incomes about two-thirds those of white households. They ended the move paying less rent than black rent-to-rent households and $100 less than white own-to-rent households (which actually pay more than white movers between rented units). This rent is almost 25 percent of the household income. Apparently black own-to-rent movers are in a very weak economic position, with the lowest average incomes of any of the other moving groups, black or white, that I have examined. This group also has the smallest household size of all other black mover households, even smaller than most

Figure 2.3
Change in Costs Due to Move, 1987

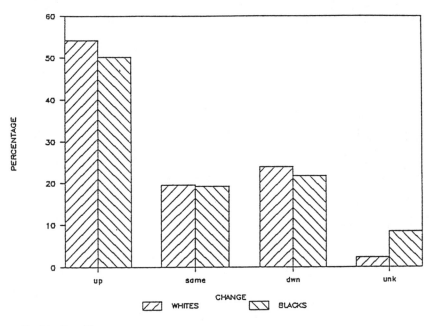

a. Rent-to-Own Move

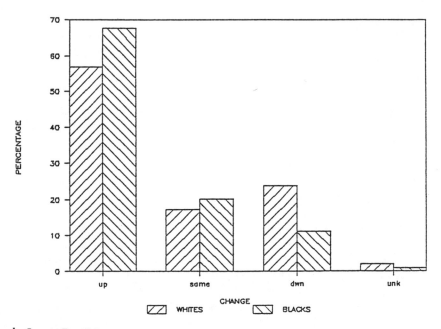

b. Own-to-Rent Move

of the white movers. As a result, its per capita income ($6,410), while lower than its white counterpart ($9,833), is higher than black rent-to-rent movers and a higher proportion of the white counterpart than any other move type except own-to-own. Economic differences alone do not seem to be a complete explanation. Let us turn to the reasons people give for their actions for further information on the differences between groups.

Reasons for Moving

Rent-to-Own

The AHS allows us to look at a household's stated reasons for moving, its reasons for selecting a particular neighborhood, and its reasons for selecting a particular house. Figures 2.4, 2.5, and 2.6 show the results for the two types of moves with which we are most concerned. People who make the rent-to-own move are far more likely to indicate that the move was made strictly because they wanted to own a home than for any other reason. This is especially true for whites. It is also the main reason for black households, but it is not nearly as dominant. Blacks also often cite improvements in the quality or size of the unit and the desire to form their own household as major reasons for ownership. This may indicate a difference in preferences for owning per se and suggests that for black households owning a home may be a means to other ends, while white households appear to value it for its own sake.

Both racial groups give similar reasons for selecting the neighborhood in which they bought a home (figure 2.5a). For both groups (but more so for blacks), the house, not the neighborhood, was most frequently the deciding factor. This and the fact that "other" is the second most important reason for both races indicates that we do not know much about why people choose neighborhoods; it does not seem to be for the reasons we expect. As to reasons for selecting a given house (figure 2.6a), the primary one for both races is financial (affordability, quality of investment). This is more important for whites than for blacks. Reasons that are more important to blacks than whites include the design and layout of the house and its size. (Considering the larger black household sizes, this makes sense.)

Own-to-Rent

Once again, white and black households in this category have similar priorities in the reasons given for moves, but they differ in the proportion of the households citing each reason (figure 2.4b). Both groups give forming one's own household as the most important cause of the own-to-rent move, but well over 50 percent of blacks cite this reason, while for whites it is under 40 percent. The second reason is a job change, but this is more important for whites (almost 30 percent) than for blacks (under 20 percent).

Figure 2.4
Reasons for Moving, 1987

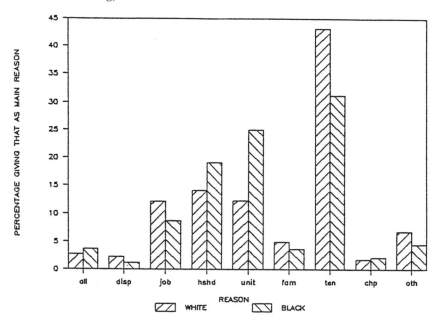

a. Rent-to-Own Move

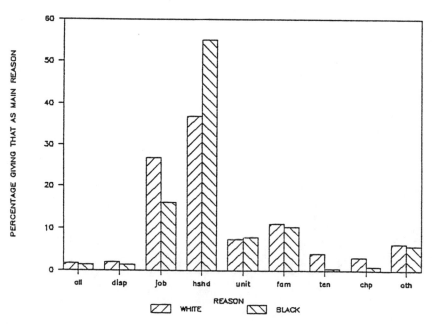

b. Own-to-Rent Move

Figure 2.5
Reasons for Selecting This Neighborhood, 1987

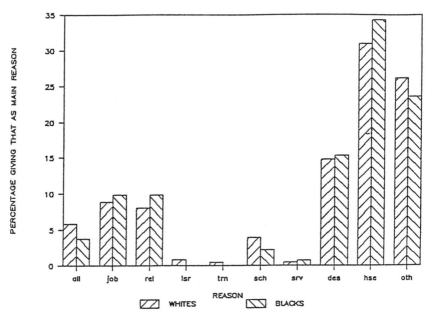

a. Rent-to-Own Move

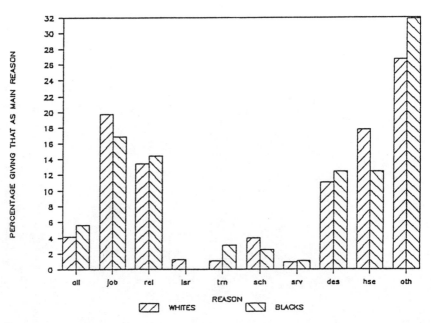

b. Own-to-Rent Move

Figure 2.6
Reasons for Selecting This House

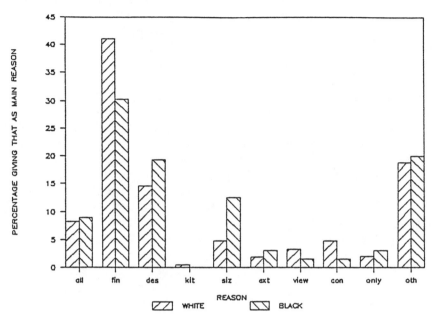

a. Rent-to-Own Move

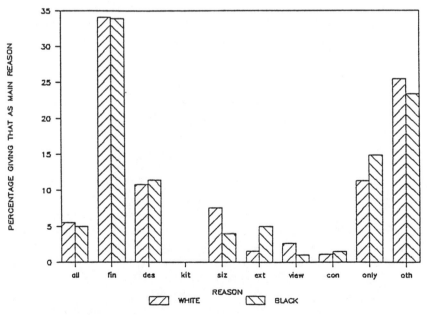

b. Own-to-Rent Move

Other responses garnered less than 10 percent of households. Neither group gives lowering costs as a particularly important reason, although the white level is somewhat higher than the black level.

Forming one's own household by making an own-to-rent move can take place in two ways. One is to leave the parental home as a young adult. The other is to undergo a divorce, separation (including the separation of room-mates), or widowhood. Both entail leaving a home that the former household (or some member of it) owned to create a new household in a rented unit. Both moves would be associated with a decrease in household income and probably an increase in individual costs. We expect that the young adult just starting out would have a low income level, but half of the households formed by marital dissolution are female headed, and they are also likely to have low incomes. Both households should see a decrease in household size, though young adults would probably see a greater decrease. The young adult household would be significantly younger than a household created through marital dissolution.

According to the characteristics reported in tables 2.1 and 2.2, households making this move, no matter what their race, have low incomes after the move (we have no information on income prior to the move), and black income as a percentage of white income is lowest for this move (68.4 percent). Black and white households in this category are the smallest sizes of their racial groups. More important, both show very large declines in size from their former households (38 percent decline for whites and 45 percent decline for blacks). As a result, black per capita incomes after the move are a relatively high proportion of white per capita incomes (65 percent—the second highest proportion). Finally, the median age of the age-rate schedule for the own-to-rent move is 31.8 years for whites and 23.8 years for blacks.

The data suggest that black households making an own-to-rent move are more likely to be young adults starting out in their own (renting) households by leaving their parents' (owned) homes or that black divorces occur at far younger ages. It would be worthwhile to examine the idea that once black households obtain ownership, they are less likely to leave the house as a result of economic factors or marital dissolution and more likely to move on as part of the process of developing lives independent of parents.

Own-to-rent movers chose their neighborhoods differently than did rent-to-own movers. While the house itself was reasonably important, it was not overriding consideration (after all, a rental unit is not an investment for the renter). Instead, convenience to jobs and to relatives were more important, with jobs slightly more important to whites and relatives slightly more im-portant for blacks. "Other" is still the main category, especially for black movers.

Although decreasing the cost of housing was not an important reason for deciding to move, it was a very important reason for selecting the unit moved to. "Other" was again reasonably important. The third most important reason for both races (larger proportion for blacks) is that this was the only unit available, an indication of fairly sudden moves, discrimination (against households with children, against female-headed households, or against blacks, all of which would affect blacks disproportionately), or other constraints.

CHANGE OVER TIME

We have explored the structure of mobility and the characteristics of movers of different types in some detail. This yields a cross-sectional comparison of blacks and whites and their housing transitions in 1987. Let us now examine changes in the relationship between black and white mobility over time. We will focus on the multistate analysis and its outcomes.

Figure 2.7 is analogous to figure 2.2 except that it shows a comparison by first and last year of the data set, as well as by race. It is organized in the same life cycle order as figure 2.2. For both races, the shapes of the 1974 and 1987 rent-to-rent graphs are quite similar. The primary difference is that the rates increased between the two years for both races. The black rates are generally lower than the white rates.

Rent-to-own movement is somewhat lower in 1987 for both races, and the peak is at a younger age. Those individuals who become owners do so earlier in 1987 than in 1974. The truncated child peak appears in both black curves. It is, in fact, a characteristic of all of the years of the black rent-to-own age-rate schedule. The lack of a single dominant young adult peak in this transition is also typical for all of the years of black movement, as are the consistently lower levels of movement at all ages than among whites. Own-to-own movement shows little difference in the two years for the white movers. Black movers between owned units exhibit the later child and adult peaks in most years (including these two). There are some differences between 1974 and 1987 for both races, including a later peak and less spread over the adult years. Apparently, if one has become an owner, the ability to move between owned units is not much different over time. Of course, the probability of making this move is lower for black owners than for white.

Finally, the own-to-rent shift shows large increases in rates over all ages under 50 for both races. There is a much higher probability of making this move in 1987 than in 1974, and the black probability is higher than the white.

Comparing the beginning and ending points of the time period is useful, but it hides trends and changes occurring over the period and can lead to incorrect interpretations. In order to examine trends without being overwhelmed by age-rate schedules, figure 2.8 charts changes in the overall gross rate of each kind of movement over time. The gross rate is one measure resulting from the housing-life table analysis. It is the number of moves of this type that a person would make if he or she lived an entire life according

Figure 2.7
Comparison of 1974 and 1987 Rates

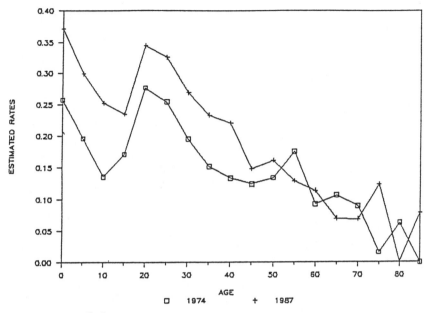

a. Rent-to-Rent, Blacks

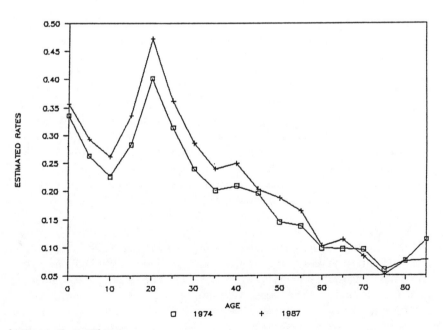

b. Rent-to-Rent, Whites

Figure 2.7 (continued)

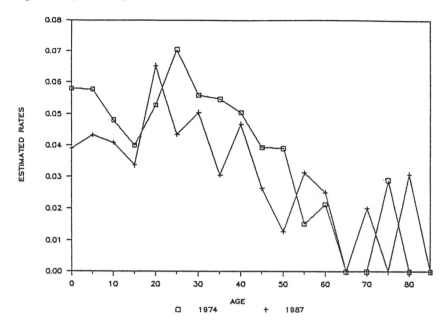

c. Rent-to-Own, Blacks

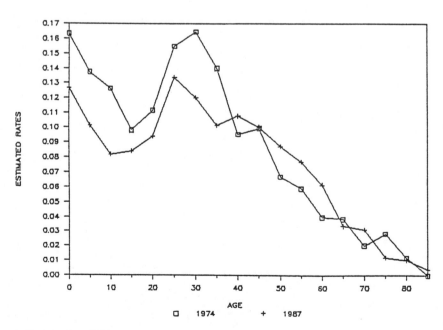

d. Rent-to-Own, Whites

Figure 2.7 (continued)

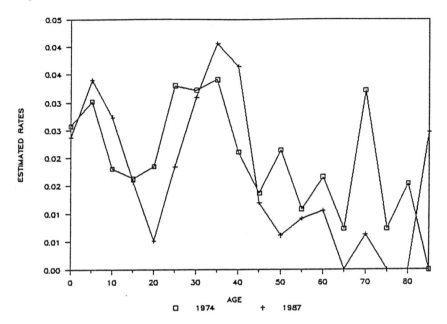

e. Own-to-Own, Blacks

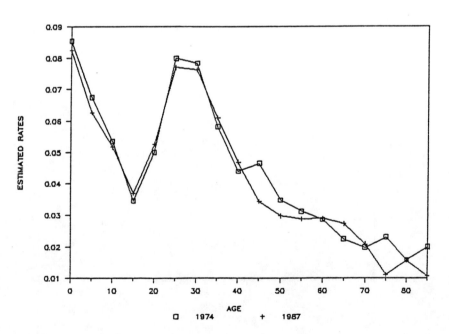

f. Own-to-Own, Whites

60

Figure 2.7 (continued)

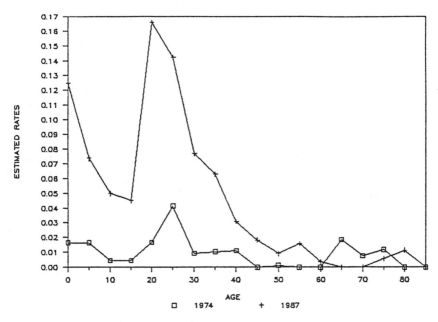

g. Own-to-Rent, Blacks

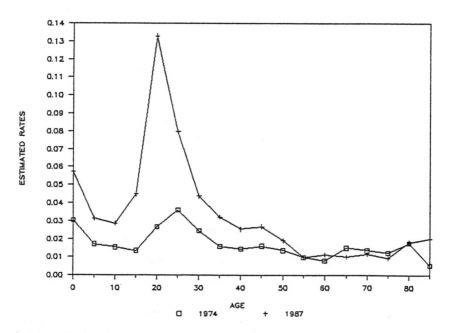

h. Own-to-Rent, Whites

to the rates extant in this particular year. For example, in 1974 a white individual could expect to move between owned units almost four times in a lifetime, if he or she lived that lifetime at the 1974 rates.

Figure 2.8a begins the life cycle with rent-to-rent movements. The number of moves of this type that a hypothetical person would make appears quite large, but it is not unreasonable since it includes all moves from birth on and incorporates moves between rented apartments with young parents, moves as a college student, and so on. In any case, the important thing is not the absolute rates but the comparison between the two races and the changes over time.

The gross rent-to-rent rate is fairly consistent throughout the 1970s. After the recession of the early 1980s, however, it rises dramatically for both races, although black rates remain lower than white rates (possibly as a result of fewer choices). The gross rent-to-own rate shows a relationship to economic cycles: it rises in good times (as in 1976–1978), falls during bad times (the early 1980s), and rises again, though not as high, in the mid–1980s. The black rate is always below the white rate and does not seem to respond as much to improved economic conditions. The own-to-own gross rate shows the same response to economic cycles that the rent-to-own rate shows and the same apparent constraint on the increase in black rates in good times.

As we would expect from the analyses, the gross own-to-rent movement rate has risen fairly steadily over time for both races. No consistent relationship with economic cycles appears; in the early years, this rate increases in bad times and decreases in good times, but the mid–1980s were good times, and the rates rose faster than ever and to new levels. At the times when this rate rises, black rates rise faster than white rates and to higher peaks. We have already discussed the apparent black interest in forming new households, but the gross rates indicate some pressures that push blacks into own-to-rent moves more than whites. The post–1983 increase in own-to-rent movement is difficult to explain. The economy was growing at the time (unlike the times of the earlier peaks in this rate). The complete restructuring of housing finance in 1980 might have had some effect, although one would expect the effect to be larger on moves ending in ownership rather than a move out of ownership. Possibly these are people who obtained mortgages in the early 1980s just after the changes, and the subsequent increased movement out of owned homes indicates an inability to continue with the high payments or to refinance. If these are people who are forming their own households by leaving an owned home (either their parent's or former spouse's), perhaps in an earlier time more of them would have immediately bought homes (an own-to-own move), and the changes in mortgage financing made this more difficult. None of these possibilities is currently testable.

Focusing on moves that change tenure, since that is our primary interest, figure 2.9 graphs the black rate of movement as a proportion of the white

Figure 2.8
Gross Rate of Movement over Time

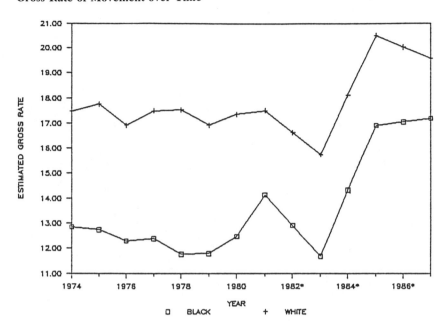

a. Rent-to-Rent

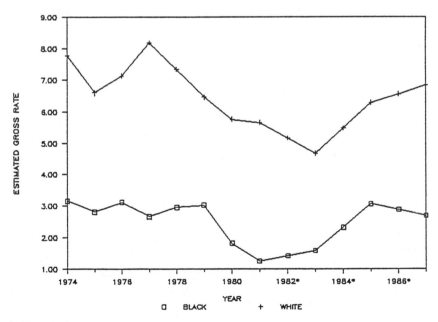

b. Rent-to-Own

Figure 2.8 (continued)

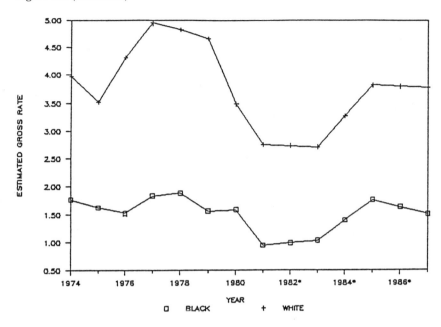

c. Own-to-Own

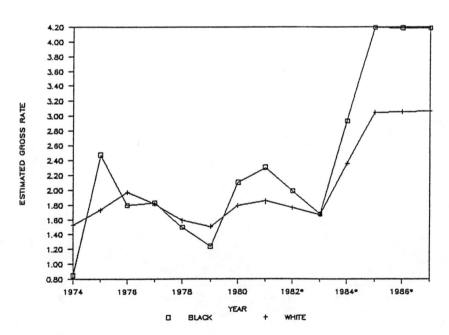

d. Own-to-Rent

Figure 2.9
Black Rate of Movement as a Proportion of White Rate

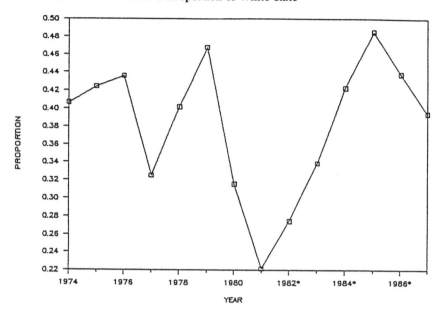

a. Gross Rent-to-Own Rates

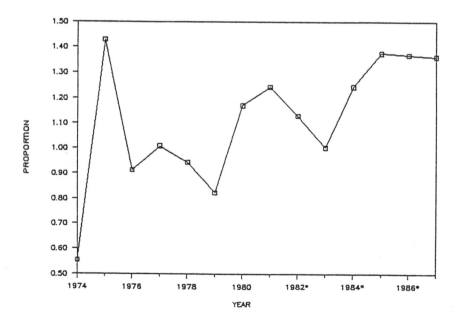

b. Gross Own-to-Rent Rates

rate for the rent-to-own move and the own-to-rent move. The gross rates of rent-to-own movement fluctuate with the economy, but the relationship between black and white gross rates indicates that black rates follow white rates out of recessions (e.g., 1979 peak and 1985 peak) and that black rates fall further during recessions (e.g., 1981 trough).

Since 1976, black own-to-rent rates have tended to rise as a proportion of white rates, and for every year since 1979 they have been higher. If the restructuring of housing financing has had an impact on this measure, then it appears that blacks have been more affected than whites. Meyerson (1986) argues that the increasing reliance of mortgage lending on the secondary mortgage market has reduced the importance of local lenders with community ties and more flexibility to lend to local people. A mortgage sold on the secondary market requires a home buyer who meets a fixed set of criteria. A locally oriented lender that plans to hold the loan rather than sell it can be more flexible and operate on a case-by-case basis. Thus, local control rather than secondary market control should benefit lower-income and marginal buyers, a group that would be disproportionately black. Refinancing of owned homes would operate under these same constraints, and difficulty with refinancing a relatively high interest rate loan might also help to explain the high own-to-rent rates.

The net impact of movement to and from home ownership is shown in figure 2.10. There has been a general decline in net movement to ownership since 1974 (in spite of a recovery in the later 1970s). White net movement dipped below zero in one year (1985), but black net movement has been below zero every year since 1980 (except 1983).

The effect of these movements on the overall proportion of homeowners for each race is shown in figure 2.11. There was an almost continuous rise in the percentage owning from 1974 through 1980 for whites and through 1983 for blacks. The white rate rose from about 72.6 percent to about 75.5 percent, the black rate from 48.5 percent to 51.4 percent. A few ups and downs reflect economic cycles before 1980. Since the early 1980s, there has been a sharp drop in the proportion owning homes, so that in 1987, the white percentage was about 71.6 and the black percentage was about 48. These changes do not sound large, but consider that the post–1980 period is the only time since World War II that homeownership has not increased and that the drop came at a time of economic growth. There appears to be a problem for both races and an extra burden for blacks.

CONCLUSIONS

The results reported in this chapter indicate that black and white Americans have similar life cycle patterns and make moves for similar, though not identical, reasons. Blacks do not move into homeownership as readily, and they are more likely to move out of it. We have examined some possible

Figure 2.10
Net Movement to Homeownership over Time

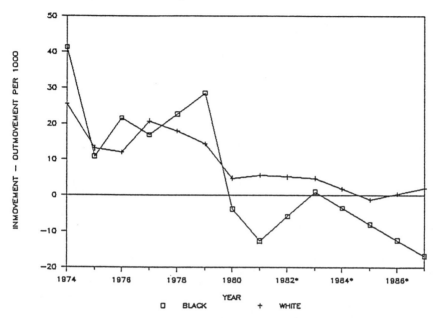

explanations and have noted surprisingly little change over time in the relationship between the housing-life chances for the two races. Possible reasons for the differences in rates of movement to and from homeownership include differences in tastes, differences in benefits from owning (which could then affect tastes), differences in income, and discrimination. We are not able to test these explanations, but it seems likely that all contribute.

Incomes of the two races differ even within mover groups. The push of the black rent-to-own group into owning in spite of lower incomes seems to argue against the difference-in-tastes explanation. The later peak for buying and the lower child peak imply that blacks wait longer, and those with fewer children are more likely to buy. Both of these factors are tied to income (Kendig, 1990; Rudel, 1985).

We have seen possible differences in the benefits of owning, especially getting less benefit from tax breaks. Blacks may see owning more as a road to improved housing quality than as a tenure with great economic benefits. The post–1980 situation may indicate that changes in the housing finance industry have adversely affected all potential home buyers and some current owners but have been especially hard on blacks. This is an excellent example of the point that "racial inequality is perpetuated through the 'normal' operations of the society's key institutions" (Allen and Farley, 1986:303). This perpetuation of inequality seems to be one outcome of the changes in housing

Figure 2.11
Homeownership Rates

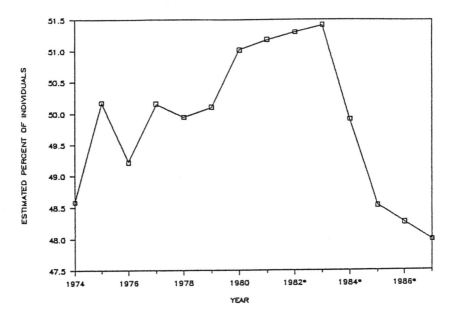

a. Percentage of Black Individuals Owning Households

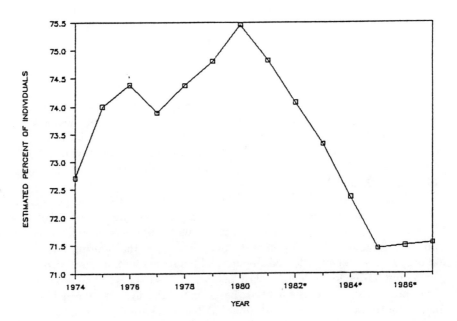

b. Percentage of White Individuals Owning Households

finance. The differences between blacks and whites in terms of the institution of homeownership also have implications for continuing inequality.

Black Americans have lower ownership rates, and their lower representation in a tenure favored by policy and with so many other economic advantages is likely to create long-term problems. One problem may be paying for a comfortable retirement, especially with the strains the baby boom will put on the social security system. Historically, Americans have relied on their homes as a major source of savings and as an important cushion for retirement (Kendig, 1984). In order for one's home to be as valuable as possible, one should have paid off the mortgage (that implies having lived in the home for a long time, possibly thirty years) and/or lived there long enough for it to appreciate significantly and/or have been able to trade up several times to more costly, and faster appreciating houses.

As Kendig (1990) points out, "The time spent in a particular tenure . . . can have a major influence on the financial ability to move on to other housing" (pp. 139–140). This is true whether that housing is one's first owner-occupied unit (more time in a relatively high-cost rental unit with no tax advantages will make it more difficult to obtain), a trade-up unit (a large amount of equity in the first owned home makes moving to a more expensive home easier), or a retirement home financed with the equity from a formerly owned home. Accrued equity can also be used for college tuition and to help adult children with home purchases. Thus, not taking advantage of homeownership's benefits or membership in a group that does not benefit as much from homeownership will perpetuate the gap between blacks and whites into succeeding generations (Kendig, 1990).

If blacks have a lower preference for ownership, resulting from the fact that they do not benefit as much from it, then the solution lies in helping people to buy in better areas or to buy houses with a better chance of appreciating. Changing the income tax deduction for mortgage interest to a tax credit (Dolbeare, 1986) would also be more advantageous to lower-income groups with lower value houses. If lower ownership rates are not a result of preferences but of discrimination or income differences, then the solutions must be approached from a different direction.

Income differences result in part from discrimination. They also result from differences in access to good education, including training at higher levels. In this case, parental ownership of homes in good school districts will help the next generation of black Americans. If those homes appreciate so that the parents are able to help the children with college or other advanced training, ownership will be even more important. Sternlieb and Lake (1975) suggest assisting minority home purchase in the central city as a step in helping people build equity. The difficulty with this solution is that it does not address the issue of fewer benefits to black households from homeownership and may actually exacerbate the problem by encouraging black households to buy in submarkets that do not appreciate as fast.

Discrimination is a continuing fact of life in the United States, and differences in homeownership are only one of its manifestations. This is a large problem that requires much broader and deeper solutions than a relatively simple change in the tax policy. It is impossible, however, to overestimate the importance to our entire society of finding a solution to the problem.

When housing opportunities are freely available, there will be little concern if one group chooses to have different ownership patterns. The issue is choice, and it is doubtful that the existing patterns of homeownership among black Americans actually result from free and equal ability to choose among comparable opportunities.

NOTE

The research reported in this chapter was sponsored by the Geography and Regional Science Program of the National Science Foundation (NSF SES–8605613) and by the Population Processes Program of the Institute of Behavioral Science at the University of Colorado at Boulder. The computer programs were supplied by the Population Processes program and rewritten for use with housing data by John F. Watkins and Charles R. Morrow-Jones. They were altered for the Ohio State University computer system by Charles Morrow-Jones and Dae Sic Yun. I also thank the editor of this collection, R. Allen Hays, for his helpful comments on an earlier draft of this chapter. Additional work was performed by Julia Chen and Mary Wenning.

REFERENCES

Adams, John S. 1984. "The Meaning of Housing in America." *Annals of the Association of American Geographers* 74, 4:515–526.
———. 1987. *Housing America in the 1980s*. New York: Russell Sage Foundation.
Allen, Walter R., and Reynolds Farley. 1986. "The Shifting Social and Economic Tides of Black America, 1950–1980." *Annual Review of Sociology* 12:277–306.
Amin, Ruhul, and A. G. Mariam. 1987. "Racial Differences in Housing: An Analysis of Trends and Differentials, 1960–1978." *Urban Affairs Quarterly* 22, 3:363–376.
Bianchi, Suzanne M., and Reynolds Farley. 1979. "Racial Differences in Family Living Arrangements and Economic Well-Being: An Analysis of Recent Trends." *Journal of Marriage and the Family*, 537–551.
Bianchi, Suzanne M., Reynolds Farley, and Daphne Spain. 1982. "Racial Inequalities in Housing: An Examination of Recent Trends." *Demography* 19, 1:37–51.
Bowyer, Elizabeth Ellen. 1989. "Social Issues and the Future of Fair Housing: Comment." In *Housing Issues of the 1990s*. Edited by Sara Rosenberry and Chester Hartman. New York: Praeger.
Brown, Kevin. 1981. "Race, Class and Culture: Towards a Theorization of the 'Choice/Constraint' Concept." In *Social Interaction and Ethnic Segregation*. Edited by P. Jackson and S. J. Smith. London: Academic Press.
Bullard, Robert D. 1979. "Housing and the Quality of Life in the Urban Community:

A Focus on the Dynamic Factors Affecting Blacks in the Housing Market." *Journal of Social and Behavioral Sciences* 25, 2:46–52.

Burns, Leland S., and Leo Grebler. 1986. *The Future of Housing Markets: A New Appraisal.* New York: Plenum Press.

Clay, Phillip L. 1989. "Social Issues and the Future of Fair Housing." In *Housing Issues of the 1990s.* Edited by Sara Rosenberry and Chester Hartman. New York: Praeger.

Dolbeare, Cushing. 1986. "How the Income Tax System Subsidizes Housing for the Affluent." In *Critical Perspectives on Housing.* Edited by Rachel Bratt, Chester Hartman, and Ann Meyerson. Philadelphia: Temple University Press.

Farley, Reynolds. 1984. *Blacks and Whites, Narrowing the Gap?* Cambridge, Mass.: Harvard University Press.

Frey, William H. 1978. "Black Movement to the Suburbs: Potentials and Prospects for Metropolitan-Wide Integration." In *The Demography of Racial and Ethnic Groups.* Edited by Frank D. Bean and W. Parker Frisbie. New York: Academic Press.

———. 1985. "Mover Destination Selectivity and the Changing Suburbanization of Metropolitan Whites and Blacks." *Demography* 22, 2:223–244.

Galster, George. 1990. "Racial Discrimination in Housing Markets during the 1980s: A Review of the Audit Evidence." *Journal of Planning Education and Research* 9, 3:165–176.

Goering, J. M. 1979. *Housing in America: The Characteristics and Uses of the Annual Housing Survey.* Annual Housing Survey Studies, no. 6, U.S. Department of Housing and Urban Development. Washington, D.C.: U.S. Government Printing Office.

Hadden, Louise, and Mireille Leger. 1990. *Codebook for the American Housing Survey.* Cambridge, Mass.: Abt Associates.

Hayden, D. 1984. *Redesigning the American Dream: The Future of Housing, Work and Family Life.* New York: W. W. Norton.

Hughes, James, and George Sternlieb. 1987. *The Dynamics of America's Housing.* New Brunswick, N.J.: Center for Urban Policy Research.

Jackman, Mary R., and Robert W. Jackman. 1980. "Racial Inequalities in Home Ownership." *Social Forces* 4:1221–1234.

James, Franklin J., Betty L. McCummings, and Eileen A. Tynan. 1984. *Minorities in the Sunbelt.* New Brunswick, N.J.: Center for Urban Policy Research.

Kain, John F., and John M. Quigley. 1975. *Housing Markets and Racial Discrimination.* New York: National Bureau of Economic Research.

Kendig, Hal L. 1984. "Housing Careers, Life Cycle and Residential Mobility: Implications for the Housing Market." *Urban Studies* 21(3):271–283.

———. 1990. "A Life Course Perspective on Housing Attainment." In *Housing Demography.* Edited by Dowell Myers. Madison: University of Wisconsin Press.

Keyfitz, N. 1979. "Multidimensionality in Population Analysis." In *Sociological Methodology 1980.* Edited by K. Schuessler. San Francisco: Jossey-Bass.

Lake, Robert W. 1979. "Racial Transition and Black Homeownership in American Suburbs." *Annals of the American Academy of Political and Social Science* 441 (January): 142–156.

————. 1981. *The New Suburbanites: Race and Housing in the Suburbs.* New Brunswick, N.J.: Center for Urban Policy Research.

Land, K. C., and A. Rogers (eds.). 1982. *Multidimensional Mathematical Demography.* New York: Academic Press.

Laurenti, Luigi M. 1960. *Property Value and Race.* Berkeley: University of California Press.

Ledent, Jacques. 1980. "Multistate Life Tables: Movement versus Transition Perspectives." *Environment and Planning A* 12:533–562.

Longino, Charles F., and Smith, Kenneth J. 1991. "Black Retirement Migration in the United States." *Journal of Gerontology: Social Science* 46, 3:125–132.

Meyerson, Ann. 1986. "Deregulation and the Restructuring of the Housing Finance System." In *Critical Perspectives on Housing.* Edited by Rachel Bratt, Chester Hartman, and Ann Meyerson. Philadelphia: Temple University Press.

Moore, Eric G. 1985. "Mobility Intention and Subsequent Relocation." Paper presented at the annual meetings of the Association of American Geographers, Detroit.

Moore, Eric G., and Clark, W.A.V. 1986. "Stable Structure and Local Variations: A Comparison of Household Flows in Four Metropolitan Areas." *Urban Studies* 23:185–196.

————. 1990. "Housing and Households in American Cities: Structure and Change in Population Mobility, 1974–1982." In *Housing Demography.* Edited by Dowell Myers. Madison: University of Wisconsin Press.

Morrow-Jones, H. A. 1988. "The Housing Life Cycle and the Transition from Renting to Owning a Home in the United States: A Multistate Analysis." *Environment and Planning A* 20:1165–1184.

National Association of Realtors. 1990. *The Housing Ladder: A Steeper Climb for American Households.* Washington, D.C.: National Association of Realtors.

O'Hare, William P., Kevin M. Pollar, Taynia L. Mann, and Mary M. Kent. 1991. "African Americans in the 1990s." *Population Bulletin* 40, 1.

Ong, Paul M., and J. Eugene Grigsby III. 1988. "Race and Life-Cycle Effects on Home Ownership in Los Angeles 1970 to 1980." *Urban Affairs Quarterly* 23, 4:601–615.

Perin, Constance. 1977. *Everything in Its Place: Social Order and Land Use in America.* Princeton, N.J.: Princeton University Press.

Pettigrew, Thomas F. 1980. "Racial Change and the Intrametropolitan Distribution of Black Americans." In *The Prospective City: Economic, Population, Energy, and Environmental Developments.* Edited by Arthur P. Solomon. Cambridge, Mass.: MIT Press.

Rogers, A. 1980. "Introduction to Multistate Mathematical Demography." *Environment and Planning A* 12:489–498.

Rose, Harold. 1976. *Black Suburbanization: Access to an Improved Quality of Life or Maintenance of the Status Quo?* Cambridge, Mass.: Ballinger.

————. 1985. "The Evolving Spatial Pattern of Black America: 1910–1980." In *Ethnicity in Contemporary America: A Geographical Appraisal.* Edited by Jesse McKee. Dubuque: Kendall/Hunt.

Rossi, Peter H. 1955. *Why Families Move.* Glencoe, Ill.: Free Press.

Rudel, Thomas. 1985. "Changes in Access to Homeownership during the 1970's." *Annals of Regional Science* 19, 1:37–49.

Stahura, John M. 1990. "Rapid Black Suburbanization in the 1970s: Some Policy Considerations." *Policy Studies Journal* 18, 2:279–291.

Sternlieb, George, and James Hughes. 1982. "The Evolution of Housing and Its Social Compact." *Urban Land* 41, 12:17–20.

Sternlieb, George, and Robert W. Lake. 1975. "Aging Suburbs and Black Home-ownership." *Annals of the American Academy of Political and Social Science* 422:105–117.

White, Michael, and Peter Mueser. 1988. "Race and Residential Mobility in the U.S. 1940–1980." Paper presented to the Population Association of America, April.

Willekens, F., and A. Rogers. 1978. *Spatial Population Analysis: A Methods and Computer Programs*. Report 78–18. Laxenburg, Austria: International Institute for Applied Systems Analysis Research.

3

Housing Reform in Russia: The Limits to Privatization

GREGORY D. ANDRUSZ

Historically, societies in transition to capitalism have experienced intense conflicts. In contemporary Russia, these are visible in the production, distribution, acquisition, and consumption of housing.[1] A commonly expressed view is that attitudes produced by paternalistic Soviet-type societies, where accommodation is granted (as a benefice) rather than purchased, are conducive to "begging, dependency and neglect of the home" (Bessonova, 1992). Accompanying these traits has been ever more bureaucracy, whose functionaries in a situation of housing shortage are capricious and corrupt in their allocation policies. Privatization of housing is regarded by some as an antidote to the endemic bureaucratic abuse of privileged access to housing. Some allege that even the caricatured nefarious private landlord is preferable to the public landlord.

This poses a key question: Is the apparent movement in Russia toward private homeownership a manifestation of "liberalism triumphant" (in the sense popularized by Fukuyama)? Is it an expression of the two forces—the economic logic of modern science and the human struggle for recognition—that impel societies toward establishing capitalist democracies as the end state of the historical process (Fukuyama, 1992)? The grand events initiated by perestroika naturally engender such grand, metaphysical responses. An answer has to be couched in more modest, agnostic terms.

The notion of an "economic logic," reminiscent of the functionalist and structural imperatives found in Parsonian sociology and of the "convergence thesis" of the 1960s, does merit consideration. The same cannot be said of the other "force." Russia is still at the stage where personal struggles are more for survival (basic shelter) than for personal recognition. Nevertheless, the motor of change is to be found in the interaction between institutional structures and individual demands, needs, and expectations. This chapter could be read as suggesting that the first force is pushing toward privatization of housing, while the second opposes it.

Since the mid–1960s, the evolution of international organizations within Europe, such as the United Nations Economic Commission for Europe (ECE), has brought together civil servants and specialists from member states. As transnational think-tanks, they have encouraged debate on policy initiatives of common concern. Even before perestroika, delegations to ECE meetings were composed of members of the Soviet "hackocratia," with their origins in the nomenklatura and younger, well-qualified specialists. Both the feeble and the quick of mind were influenced by the similarity of some of the housing problems experienced by the Soviet Union and the range of alternatives available to deal with them. Above all, they were brought face to face with a rejection in much of Western Europe of the postwar consensus on the necessity of planning and state intervention in areas such as housing, which until recently had been the sacrosanct domain of the caring state. It was this criticism of Maynard Keynes that presaged the revolt against Karl Marx.

So years before the advent of perestroika, there were calls for more detailed studies on housing issues. On one occasion the Soviet delegate, declared that the state would retain its dominant role as housing provider into the foreseeable future. However, the correlation between rising incomes and the level of interest in the development of cooperative and individual housing was also duly noted. This meant that the Soviet Union was not immune from a global trend toward growth in the non–state housing sector accompanying the rise in national gross domestic product (GDP). However, such a rational technocratic solution to the housing problem was countered by ideological rigidities, ensuring that policy moves in this direction by the central government were hesitating. More important was the refusal of local authorities to implement these policies; they used ideology to defend their own material interests, which lay in controlling access to this most valuable property.

The mounting pressure of housing on the budget in the late 1970s ended the period of expanding state housing construction. Building fell from a peak of 110 million square meters in 1975 to a low of 102 million in 1979. After stagnating in the early 1980s, it rose to 113 million in 1985 and to 120 million in 1986, peaking at 132 million in 1988. By 1988–1990, it was acknowledged that the economic crisis required radical restructuring of the housing system. Because of economic and political chaos, house-building plans were not fulfilled, and people were beginning to doubt whether the 1986 goal was achievable. By 1990, output had declined to 115 million and was continuing to fall in 1991 (Goskomstat, 1987, 1990a, 1990b).

It is widely recognized, even outside the circle of housing specialists, that housing reforms in Russia are integral to macroeconomic stabilization, especially since housing subsidies are a major burden on the central government's budget. Current housing policies seriously constrain labor mobility and the mobilization of household savings. However, housing reforms require radical transformations of the financial system, the legal framework, and the laws governing the ownership of property. These changes are integral to restructuring the economy, which includes movement away from the combination of low cash wages and heavily subsidized housing. In policy terms, the reduction in government revenue and expenditure requires that greater assistance has to be directed to household-financed and self-build housing programs.

This chapter begins by outlining the structure of housing ownership and control (which applied to all the constituent republics of the former Soviet Union), followed by a summary outline of the magnitude of the housing crisis. At the heart of the crisis is the question of rent, the subject of the next section. Housing reform entails reorganizing the construction industry which itself has contributed to existing problems. This provides the context in which new policy has been formulated. This includes the establishment of a real estate market whose emergence symbolizes a fundamental political clash over the subject of property. These developments are components of the privatization policy, which is discussed and critiqued.

THE STRUCTURE OF HOMEOWNERSHIP

Legal texts and commentaries on housing law continue to deal with the management and distribution of accommodation, eviction, and tenants' rights in terms of tenure classification. In 1991 the four tenure categories that had emerged by 1924 continue to be the pillars of homeownership: (1) local soviet (municipal housing); (2) state ministries, enterprises, and trade unions ("departmental sector"); (3) house-building cooperatives; and (4) individual homeownership (Andrusz, 1984, 1990b). Although subletting existed, private housing built or acquired specifically for renting has not been tolerated since 1937. The 1989 census revealed that 1,525,000 urban families were inhabiting "part of a private house," and 535,000 families were living in rooms in "privately rented quarters." These figures are almost certainly conservative. Globally, from 1960 until 1988, the state sector (publicly rented) grew at the expense of the private sector (owner-occupier), both relatively and absolutely. As late as the mid–1980s, government officials continued to declare that the trend toward greater state prominence would continue. In 1990 the housing stock was divided among the state (57 percent), the private sector (39 percent), and cooperatives (4 percent). (In towns the state owns 73 percent of the housing stock, owner-occupiers 21 percent, and cooperatives 6 percent.) State property was divided among local soviets (25 percent), firms, ministries (29 percent), and social organizations (3 percent). (Zhilishchnye usloviya . . . ,1990; Goskomstat, 1990b.) This typology of tenures, in which the state sector predominates, conceals a different reality. Although state-owned flats are rented, in practice, families tend to pass them to their children. Moreover, since it is virtually impossible to evict tenants, public property is de facto private. Nevertheless, the determining trait of private ownership—that the object owned can be freely disposed of by the processor—has been lacking.

The departmental sector remains the main commissioner of new construction (80 percent in towns and 68 percent overall) and the main allocator of newly constructed housing (Kosareva, Ronkin, and Pchelintsev, 1990). It was initially established and has subsequently sought to maintain this preeminence in order to meet manpower requirements. Enterprises building less accommodation suffered from unstable work forces, since those on the housing waiting list had a strong incentive to find employers with shorter waiting times. Such a system creates a quasi-housing market in which the individual shops around for accommodation on the basis of marketable skills, not spending power.

Another attribute of the housing system, even more ubiquitous in its control over the population, is the residential permit (*propiska*). This plays a pivotal role in blocking residential choice and in impeding geographical and occupational mobility. The feudalistic relationships generated by this system are actually referred to as "enserfing" the population. According to one *apparatchik*, "We are tied by our flats, as by a rope, to our place of residence (through the *propiska*), to our place of work (which often is the provider of accommodation) and to many other 'pillars' (*stalby*) of the System" (*Delovaya Sabir*, 1991).

Following legislation in 1962, house-building cooperatives began to play a role in meeting demand. For over twenty years, the cooperatives, although ideologically acceptable to some, were considered heretical by others, and the sector underperformed in terms of both government policy and popular demand. By the mid–1980s, more voices were suggesting that more of the population might be expected to use their own resources to finance house building (Andrusz, 1992). This long-term trend in housing policy has been accompanied by another. Since 1957, decrees had been passed on the need to transfer accommodation controlled by industry and institutions into the jurisdiction of the local soviets. This was regarded as a technically rational way to improve management and maintenance of the state stock. It was an administrative solution to escalating costs (Andrusz, 1986, 1990b). Decentralization and the greater autonomy being accorded to local soviets may lead to concentration of housing in the hands of municipal authorities, thus filfilling a thirty-five-year-old government objective. However, this is itself probably a transitional phase: the 1988 Decree on Cooperatives clearly encourages establishment of housing associations and housing trusts, similar to those in Western Europe. These will be smaller, self-managing tenants' and residents' associations.

The Twenty-seventh Congress of the Communist party in 1986 passed a resolution to provide each family with its own separate flat or house by the year 2000. In doing so, it acknowledged both the enormous shortage and the importance of overcoming it as part of a reform program. In order to reach its objective, 40 million new flats and individual houses would have to be erected in the fifteen-year period 1986–2000, thereby doubling the housing stock. But even this utopian goal had to be revised upward in 1988 when the foremost housing research institute in the Soviet Union concluded that 2.8 billion square meters were needed in order to provide an average of 19.5 square meters of living space per person, in flats averaging 66 square meters. It was deemed that at this level of need satisfaction, housing would no longer adversely affect infant mortality, birth and death rates, and morbidity (TsNIEP, 1988). In 1989, another specialist revised the figure upward again, to 54 million flats (Kolotilkin, 1989a).

The state will inevitably play a role in achieving these targets, but its investment in the housing sector will decline from 50.2 percent to 20.5 percent (Boiko, 1991:41), with investment by cooperatives and individuals rising from 18.3 percent to 40.3 percent. The enterprise social development fund must increase its share from 22.9 percent to 31.8 percent; in 1989, 80 percent of households on waiting lists were registered for enterprise accommodation (Kalinina, 1992). In July 1991 the minister of construction candidly told an interviewer that in Moscow at least, the pledge to provide each family with a separate flat could not be met (Resin, 1991), no matter who assumes responsibility.

THE MAGNITUDE OF THE PROBLEM

In 1990, 14.5 million households nationwide (23 percent of all urban households) were on housing waiting lists. This figure rises to 33 percent in Moldavia, 32 percent in Turkmenia, 28 percent in Belorussia, and 25 percent in Russia (Boiko, 1991:40). These figures are best seen as indicating the magnitude of the problem while underestimating the need. Moreover, the omission of figures for other Central Asian and Caucasian republics does not mean no overcrowding exists there. Many factors, including cultural norms, keep people off waiting lists. In fact, waiting lists are actually closed after the (low) minimum living space norm per person has been attained. (The amount of living space accepted as indicating the need for improved accommodation varies from city to city but generally ranges from 5 to 7 square meters per person.)

Of the 14.5 million in the queue, roughly 15 percent live in communal (shared) accommodation and hostels (often at densities of four to six persons to a room). Eighteen percent have been waiting for over ten years, a figure that almost certainly underestimates the number deserving to be rehoused. The 1989 population and housing census revealed that 17 percent of urban

Table 3.1
Dwelling Space Available

SPACE (SQUARE METERS PER PERSON)	PERCENTAGE OF FAMILIES
Up to 5	10.6
5.1 to 7.0	18.2
7.1 to 9.0	20.4
9.1 to 11.0	21.3
11.1 to 13.0	8.9
13.1 to 15.0	8.6
15.1 and over	12.0
Source: Ob obespechennosti 1990	

households in self-contained accommodation and 16 percent of those in communal flats had 7 to 9 square meters of space per person, with no fewer than 4.5 million having less than 5 square meters per person (Boiko, 1991:41). Table 3.1 shows the distribution of urban households by dwelling area.

Planners do not consider as in need of housing individuals in the age range of 20 to 30 years old, since they still live with their families (Khodzhaev, 1990). This is another way in which housing demand is underestimated. One scholar concluded that by the year 2000, the country will have 119 million households in contrast to Gosplan's estimate of 97 million. So instead of the projected 40 million new homes needed in the period 1986–2000, the figure is actually 54 million. The lack of information on the growth in the number of households made it impossible to match the impressive annual increments to the housing stock against new household formation (Kolotilkin, 1990).

The acute shortage has led to informal subletting. However, the number of people renting a room (or a shared room) in a private house or in a state or cooperative apartment has never been published and probably will never be known. Even today, data on this issue are extremely incomplete. Anecdotal information on private renting and the extortionate prices charged by landlords exists, as do occasional exposés in newspapers. But while individual exploitative landlords are pilloried, the phenomenon itself has never been systematically explored.

Considerable intrarepublican disparities in housing standards persist. For instance, in the three Baltic republics, the average per capita living space was 17.4 square meters in 1988, while it stood at 11.4 square meters in the Central Asian republics and Azerbaidzhan. Even greater differences are found in the countryside: rural families in the Baltic republics enjoy over

24 square meters of living space per person compared with 11 square meters in the Central Asian republics and Azerbaidzhan. These disparities were perpetuated by the fact that nationwide over 1981–1985, 1.8 square meters of housing were erected for each rural inhabitant. However, in Tazhikstan and Azerbaidzhan, the figure was 0.7 square meters and in Estonia 2.9 square meters, differences attributed to underinvestment by the state in these poorer regions. During Estonia's struggle for independence in 1989–1990, housing output fell to half that achieved annually between 1981 and 1987. Inflation caused 1991 prices of newly built housing units to be 220 percent higher than in 1987. This increase is partly explained by the fact that from 1991, no new housing construction receives direct subventions from the central state budget. Regional and republican differences in housing standards are considerable and constitute a sore in ethnic relations.

RENT

For a long time, the price paid in the Soviet Union for accommodation by those living in their own homes or cooperative apartments has been at least seven to eight times greater than rents for state housing. Unlike in Western countries, those living in owner-occupied housing, rather than those in public housing, are generally worse off in terms of housing quality, provision of amenities, and access to shopping and services. Moreover, privileged groups live in highly subsidized state apartments and yet pay the same rent as those living in dilapidated state housing. The fact that rent is calculated on the actual dwelling area, which excludes kitchen, bathroom, hallway, and storage space, creates an additional inequity, for it is precisely such useful space that has increased as a proportion of the actual dwelling area with newer housing designs.

In order to ensure housing access for low-income groups, rents have been kept very low and are unrelated to household income and ability to pay. Since the basic tariff for calculating rent has not changed since 1928, rents have long since ceased to bear any relationship to the costs of either construction or maintenance. The average urban industrial family continues to spend 2.8 percent of its monthly income an accommodation (Goskomstat, 1989:88). A breakdown of the charge for accommodation reveals that a tenant's annual outlay on 1 square meter of dwelling space is a follows: rent, 19 percent; central heating, sewage, water, and gas, 33 percent; electricity, 18 percent; telephone, 12 percent; Television aerial, 2 percent; and general maintenance, 16 percent (Kolotilkin, 1990). The 13 to 16 kopeks per 1 square meter rent charged at present cannot possibly cover increasing running and maintenance costs. Yet despite the low public sector rents, in 1989, arrears amounted to 307.9 million rubles (equal to 13.7 percent of total rents for that year).

Moreover, since rental income does not influence the supply of new construction, which depends solely on budgetary allocation, the government has sought to minimize expenditure by erecting low-cost units. Unfortunately, low cost has been purchased at the expense of quality, which has meant that buildings quickly fall into disrepair. In the absence of adequate maintenance, they become dilapidated and generate demands for new accommodation. This poor quality is one reason cited by tenants for not paying higher rents. The huge housing account deficit and accumulating arrears notwithstanding, rent reform is taking place but in a remarkably disconnected way. One common scheme is to surcharge households for inhabiting living space above a locally defined norm.

In L'vov in the Western Ukraine, for instance, each person is entitled to 20 square meters of living space per person, with each additional square meter being charged at five times the top rate. However, few people will be so fortunate. On the other hand, in Alma Ata, the per capita norm has been set at 18 square meters plus a further 9 square meters for the whole family. Here the tariff is 10 kopeks per square meter, but while the first 10 square meters of "additional" space is charged at five times the 10 kopek rate, the next 10 square meters are charged at ten times the rate. Nevertheless, even under less inflationary conditions, the total charge remains small in relation to income. Rents charged on a progressive scale are intended to discourage households from "consuming" so much space. The introduction of this policy has been accompanied by a simplified procedure for exchanging larger flats for smaller ones (Boiko, 1991:45).

It is generally recommended that rent and service charges be increased for everyone without exception, regardless of social class. Afterward, low-income families can be compensated from the local budget, social security, and other sources. However, these suggestions have already come under attack for failing fully to take into account the low rates paid by privileged social groups, especially for extra living space (Boiko, 1991:46). Moreover, built into the old policy was considerable inequity, for the rent formula disregarded the age of the property. Although location and availability of utilities were taken into consideration, the fact that the maximum charge was 13.2 kopeks per square meter meant that variations were negligible.

The issue of rent reform is linked with the notion of the social guarantee. Since unemployment, homelessness, and the numbers in poverty are increasing, the state has to establish minimum subsistence levels. These comprise the social guarantees (Kalinina, 1992). However, the actual definition of the minimum varies. According to radical reformers, the state will be spurred to increase housing construction and improve its management and distribution if it has to bear financial responsibility for not meeting its pledge to the population. For instance, for every year that a family remains on the waiting list, it has to receive compensation—in the form of money if it joins a cooperative or in the form of higher space and quality standards if it accepts public housing. In addition, public housing not exceeding the prescribed minimum should be granted to tenants free of charge, thereby ensuring access of all to housing up to that level, regardless of economic circumstances (Kalinina, 1990).

It should be stressed, however, that apart from Mikhail Gorbachev's mention of the rent issue in 1986, when he hinted that they were too low, rent reform has not really figured on the housing agenda (Gorbachev, 1990:58). Until recently, maintaining rents at the 1928 level seemed politically benign and economically inexpensive. It offered some compensation for the hardships endured during the industrialization campaign of the 1930s when housing conditions deteriorated and was a moral imperative in view of the suffering and destruction of the meager housing stock during World War II. Then, during Khrushchev's relatively brief interregnum, the new party program projected the abolition of rents by 1980 (*Programma*, 1961:95). An amalgam of political expediency, utopianism, and propagandistic necessity, which cultivated popular expectations, elevated the notion of low rents to the plane of myth, a symbol of building of socialism, and an important source of legitimation.

By the time Gorbachev came to power, housing finance was in deep crisis. Now, drinking from the font of Western experience and economic theory, policy advisers speak openly of painful remedies for the housing problem, noting that low public sector rents inhibit demand for cooperative and owner-occupied housing. If rents are raised, tenants will take refuge in the private sector. There has been a temporary readjustment in the focus of attention, from increasing the supply to financing it.

CONSTRUCTION INDUSTRY

Despite significant advances during the 1930s, it was not until the mid–1950s that, in order to expand house building rapidly, prefabricated technology was introduced on a large scale in construction. A series of decrees from 1955 to 1980 resulted in multistory, large panel blocks of flats' becoming an increasing proportion of new accommodation. The calamitous legacy of high-rise policies—from four- to five-story walk-ups to sixteen-story blocks—and highly centralized design institutions is conspicuous in an aesthetically unpleasing environment and slum residential estates.

In 1980, 51 percent of all new public and cooperative dwellings built in towns were of nine or more stories. In Moscow, Kiev, and Leningrad, construction is virtually all in blocks of nine, sixteen, or more stories. Almost all flats in cities of fewer than a hundred thousand inhabitants are five-story walk-ups. On the whole, the last will remain the norm in all towns with fewer than 500,000 inhabitants. According to some forecasts, the 1990s will see a shift from buildings of nine stories and over to those of nine or ten stories and less, with greater use of one- to four-story blocks in high-density complexes.

In 1987 the government passed one of its periodic votes of censure of the architectural profession, but the party exonerated it on this occasion, explicitly acknowledging that building production was dictating the activities of architects. The establishment of private construction and architectural cooperatives and the greater prominence accorded to architecture, signified in the renaming the government agency responsible for overseeing housing the State Committee for Architecture and Town Planning (*Goskomarkhitektury*), could have a positive effect on the built environment (Postanovlenie, 1987). The first head of this new state committee was Boris Yeltsin.

Compelling building contractors and others in the building trade to become self-financing should improve the industry. The decision to expand the private and cooperative housing sectors has required legislation to increase the flow of building materials produced in the state sector to the market and to create a private building materials industry. Gorbachev's presidential edict (*ukaz*) of 1990 marked the tentative beginning of reform in the construction industry (Gorbachev, 1990), a process in which building firms in the West should find it profitable to participate. There is considerable interest within the new republics in the formation of small firms to manufacture construction materials and to set up as building contractors.

In terms of economic viability, cultural desirability, and social acceptability, a more technically advanced form of self-build has considerable prospect. It could achieve such longstanding objectives as containing the growth of large cities and the dispersal of industry to smaller towns. If housing (and infrastructural) standards improve in small towns, this will probably have a more positive impact on restricting migration to large cities and reducing congestion than directive, administrative measures have had in the past. From the point of view of cultural and political desirability, a well-planned self-build program could be of greater benefit to the people and government than merely the provision of good accommodation.

Unemployment is rising, and the Russian government is reducing its budget. The immense trauma of change, exacerbated by what is virtually a national apostasy, has left many people discontent, anomic, and alienated. Self-build might have a therapeutic, as well as material, benefit by helping to break the state dependency bond and offering a sense of pride, dignity, and achievement.

The greater stress now being placed on modernization and conservation work requires retraining of the work force, which, because of the widespread use of students and soldiers and high labor turnover in this branch of the economy, is lacking in skills. An army of building workers, operating as individual tradesmen or in groups (known in Russian as *shabashniki*), has existed for many years. In the past they contracted work clandestinely (for it was illegal) for either private clients or public organizations, and their earnings were three to four times greater than the average industrial worker's wage (Shabanova, 1985). Many are now forming legal construction cooperatives. Very little research has been conducted by Western scholars and consultants on the Russian construction industry, yet this sector is critical for the restructuring and development of the Russian economy.

THE NEW POLICY

Three important housing decrees were published in February, March, and December 1988, and all marked, in the consistency of their prime objectives, a major change in direction. The first decree came in February 1988: On Measures to Accelerate the Development of Individual Housing Construction (Postanovlenie, 1988a). At that time, it was the most radical of all postwar government promulgations on housing policy. It stated that much greater reliance would be placed on the population's using its own labor, income, and savings to provide accommodation. Savings deposits were an obvious target for the government, and in a period of inflation and economic insecurity, it makes sense for citizens to invest in property. In comparison with 1985, when the self-build sector erected 16.3 million square meters of living space (14.4 percent of all housing construction), by 1995 the figure should be 60 million. By the end of the century, "housing erected by the population" will comprise 29.3 percent of all accommodation built and 19.7 percent of that erected in urban areas. This compares with 17.1 and 8.8 percent, respectively, in 1988. Thus, the new legislation signals a reversal of the thirty-year decline in building for private ownership.

Bank credit was made available to enterprises starting or expanding production of building and decorating materials. They could also make advances of up to 20,000 rubles, repayable over twenty-five years in towns and fifty years in the countryside. The decree increased the size of the loan from 3,000 rubles and extended the repayment period. The same favorable terms were offered to people wishing to purchase individual homes, an important means of fostering an open housing market.

The development of a housing market was enhanced by allowing enterprises and organizations to sell houses to their workers. The latter were asked to pay them "no less" than 40 to 50 percent of the value of the house over a period of twenty-five to fifty years. The corresponding figures for urban dwellers were 50 percent and twenty-five years. This was the nearest the Soviet Union ever came to the U.K. policy of selling council housing.

Insofar as encouraging the population to use its resources to expand the housing supply has in recent years been directed at least as much to the cooperative as the owner-occupied sector, it was to be expected that the increased benefits accruing to the latter would soon be accompanied by amendments to legislation governing cooperatives. This occurred in March 1988 in the decree On Measures to Accelerate the Development of Housing Cooperatives (Postanovlenie, 1988b). The decree stated that cooperatives would become "one of the main ways for expanding housing construction

. . . so that by 1995 they will contribute no less than two to three times more than at present to the overall volume of construction." In the period 1996–2000 this could mean 20 to 30 percent of new building in towns compared with 9.5 percent in 1988.

The legislation defined two types of cooperative. The first are house-building cooperatives specifically created for the purpose of constructing and running dwellings for the benefit of their members. They are allowed to acquire buildings in need of major repairs, renovate them, and then occupy them. The second type are set up to acquire existing housing, either newly erected or renovated, from enterprises and local municipal authorities (soviets). These properties are offered at a huge discount, since the purchaser has to pay "not less than 20 to 25 percent of the property's assessed value," with the balance to be paid off over twenty-five years. The creation of cooperatives to purchase older and newly erected buildings from the state was symptomatic of the shift toward acceptance of the principle that at least part of the state housing stock might legitimately be privatized.

Third, in December 1988 the logic of these developments culminated in local soviets and enterprises being allowed to transfer dwellings controlled by them into private ownership. Local authorities were given considerable discretion in their sales policies and in their rules for service and maintenance charges for individuals who want to buy their flats.

The low density of automobile ownership and a deteriorating public transport system mean that housing policy will continue to be based on erecting high-rise prefabricated flats in towns and allowing people to engage in self-build activities in the countryside. Nevertheless, the decision to expand automobile production will see a gradual conversion to lower-density development associated with suburbanization and small towns. It seems to me that the Group of 7 countries, when considering practical ways of assisting the Russian economy (and other states in the region), should pay careful attention to the development of the house-building industry. Aid to this sector would both stimulate the economy and subdue social unrest.

The failure of output forecasts to be translated into reality and the slow implementation of the above decrees prompted Gorbachev to issue a presidential edict (*ukaz*) in May 1990, On New Approaches to the Solution of the Housing Problem in the Country and Measures for Their Practical Implementation. The edict required an "expansion in the sources of finance by drawing upon: state, leasing and cooperative enterprises, share societies (*aktsionernye obshchestva*), voluntary organizations, bank loans and personal savings." The edict envisaged a shift toward building more houses for sale with low monthly repayments spread out over a long period. This in turn necessitated the establishment of a network of commercial banks, building cooperatives, and firms dealing with the sale and renting of accommodation.

In this regulated market phase, which emphasizes solving the problem through private individuals, cooperatives, and work collectives, the state's role is to concentrate on increasing aid to a range of disadvantaged social groups. As far as the problems of younger people in obtaining housing are concerned, the edict recommended that young families and young adults be helped to build their own homes, housing complexes, cooperatives, and hostels. This extensive reliance on self-build by young people is still attractive, for although the heroic period of the metaphoric building of socialism has passed, the concrete construction of one's home is the only way most young persons can acquire a place of their own. At present much of this self-build uses the same materials as state and cooperative builders to erect the same type of multistory apartments. The principal aim of edict is to create a housing market in which every individual may freely acquire a flat or house through purchase or lease in the public and private sectors. This will impel removing all unnecessary restrictions on redistribution and exchange. Individuals with more living space than they require must be given financial compensation to transfer to a smaller flat.

Some sitting tenants might exercise their right to buy and then sell in order to reap a quick gain and use the money to build a house in the country. This could stimulate the whole house construction industry. The prudent might accept the gift and then hold onto their asset as a hedge against inflation. These are, however, only speculative scenarios, for there has been growing hostility among tenants toward, on the one hand, the propriety of "selling tenants their own flats" and, on the other, the charging of higher rents. Many people still adhere to the belief in a universal housing norm.

The environment within which these policies are being formulated is in flux. First, production control is being decentralized to enterprises, including the manufacture of building materials and dwellings, which now have to be responsive to the forces of supply and demand. Second, the tax structure is being refashioned in the direction of higher levels of progressive income and corporation tax. The latter includes concessions and exemptions as incentives to increase house building. Third, major budgetary changes are being introduced in order to increase the powers and functions of local governments. Last, greater wage differentials are being applied as part of a wide-ranging wage reform. This is essential if the aim is to establish a housing system where the majority pay the full cost of their accommodation, obtained in competitive markets, and only special needs' groups receive public sector assistance.

REAL ESTATE TRANSACTIONS

The Soviet Union had a quasi-housing market for decades. A bulletin on personal housing exchanges has been published regularly in Moscow, Kiev, and in other cities for over twenty years. This supplemented notices attached to boards, trees, and lampposts announcing that someone wished to exchange their accommodation, specifying both the size and type of unit they had and the location and type of housing they required. Exchanges are frequently unequal in that a large flat might be offered in exchange for a smaller one. This expresses the value attached to another location; moreover, a price had to be paid for the difference in value (*Ekonomicheskaya*, 1986:18). To date, no one has examined these valuable data to reveal the cognitive maps that people have of cities that determine the differential housing values set in local housing markets.

The spring of 1991 witnessed a major step toward the commodification of housing and the land on which it stands. On April 22, 1991, Moscow held its first auction of flats. The ten properties offered sold for a total of 3.3 million rubles, with proceeds going into the Moscow City Council (Mossovet) budget. The properties, in aggregate comprising 670 square meters, were located in large residential districts. Attracting the greatest interest was a three-room flat of 111.8 square meters in a modern block on the Roublevskoe Shosse. The opening price was 164,000 rubles; it sold at 1.1 million rubles. In another instance, a single-room flat of 36.7 square meters started at 26,000 rubles and finished at 120,000 rubles. (The average size of a three-room flat in 1986 was 66.7 square meters and that of a single-room flat 34.4 square meters. See Goskomstat, 1987: 513.) These prices probably represent the market price for accommodation in Moscow (Pervyi, 1991). In June it was announced that the Babushkinskii district of Moscow was offering eight properties for the lease of which Soviet and foreign legal entities could bid (V Moskve, 1991). However, it was not the actual ownership or lease of flats that was offered but a certificate to the *right to lease it*. Thus, the auction was testifying to the legality of selling residential permits (*propiski*).

This highlights both the uniqueness of Soviet institutions and the contradictoriness of introducing markets into this environment. According to experts, the auctioning of personal residential permits will bring two benefits. First, it will help rich Moscow enterprises solve their labor problems. Second, it will generate a new type of business activity: firms registered in Moscow will be able to invite specialists living outside the capital to work in Moscow. These firms will then obtain *propiski* for the specialists that they need through this legal auction. In doing so, they will come into conflict with the (illegal) private sector, which arranges fictitious marriages in order to obtain a *propiska*, the cost of which in June 1991 was about 20,000 rubles (Moskovskaya propiska, 1991). The auctioning of residential passes is, in the context of a city with a radical government set on implementing the marketization objectives of perestroika, bizarre and absurd; a quintessential feature of capitalism is the free mobility of labor.

The first auction was considered unsuccessful, with only two licenses sold. Nonetheless, actual sales of licenses certifying the right to tenant flats in the Severnyi Butovo district point to the high value placed on obtaining *propiski*: two single-room flats with a dwelling area of 20.7 square meters sold for 220,000 rubles against a starting price of 63,000 rubles; three two-room flats of 30.4 square meters sold for 330,000 rubles when the starting price was 81,000 rubles. Finally, four three-room flats, one with 48.5 square meters and the others with 48.2 square meters, had starting prices of 130,000 rubles; one went for 600,000 rubles, two at 700,000, and one at 900,000 (Kharnas, August 1991a; Dva kuska, 1991). The lack of success was attributed to the high starting prices set by the mayor and deputy mayor of Moscow, who seemed to be out of touch with commercial reality. Again, although referred to as the "first land auction in the USSR," the subject of auction was the *future rent to be received from the first ten years of the lease* of two plots of land in the October district of Moscow. Another short note in the same edition of this newspaper indicated that auctions of land and property are not confined to Moscow and St. Petersburg. Two organizations in Sverdlovsk were offering thirty-three lots for sale, including private flats, houses in the countryside, and twenty flats in an uncompleted block of cooperative housing. Another property in the July auction in Moscow was an old log house with a garden (of 15.8 sotki, or 0.158 hectaves). "It did not attract much attention and was acquired at its starting price of 990,000 roubles" (Propetsko, 1991).

These sums prompted one *Izvestiya* correspondent to pose two questions. First, Who can afford to pay such "mad" prices for ordinary houses and flats? Second, "Where, in a country in which private ownership does not exist, do private dwellings come from?" To the first question he said there can be no full answer "because that is a commercial secret and it is necessary to accept that there are rich people, even legal millionaires." The only consolation is that individuals were not party to these transactions, which were confined to representatives of state organizations, small enterprises, and cooperatives, some of whom during this transitional (mercantile) period, can make money easily. For such firms, even a log hut is an investment, "and real estate has always been the best way of investing capital."

Those who sell their "extra" (*lishnyi*) space, which might be an inherited flat or house, become rich, "but not for long, since the purchasing power of the rouble continues to fall." Unless the beneficiary of this windfall puts the money to good use, conceivably by purchasing a property outside the capital, it will soon vanish. The lesson that the correspondent was transmitting to his readers was simple: first, the individual worked and joined a waiting list for accommodation; then in 1988 he was offered the opportunity to buy his home from the state. "Some people invest their savings in square meters. Now they know how to conduct a business."

At the same time Leningrad (St. Petersburg) was holding its first real estate auction in which the objects of transaction were the receipts payable from the *first five years of a lease*—not the right to a leasing contract. Real estate prices in Leningrad are considerably lower than in Moscow, reflecting Moscow's status as capital city. (A lot in Leningrad sold at 5.4 million rubles, and one of comparable size in Moscow reached 35 million.) Moscow's higher prices reflect the demand of large businesses for land and residential and nonresidential properties, not for immediate use but for future resale. This phenomenon is soon likely to occur in Leningrad, especially with the creation of free economic zones (Koptyaev, 1991).

The Russian Real Estate Exchange, based in Moscow, has opened branch offices in Kaluga, Rostov-on-Don, Penza, Sverdlovsk, Tomsk, and Novosibirsk and maintains foreign representatives in Budapest and London. When it began operation, dealers purchased apartments, land, uncompleted construction projects, industrial concerns, and buildings designated for demolition, with residential trade being particularly brisk. The seventeen properties sold were valued at 107 million rubles. The largest acquisition, an office building of 670 square meters located 20 kilometers from Moscow, sold for 37 million rubles (Morozov, 1991).

A whole new economic sector is developing rapidly. Apart from those already mentioned, auctions have been arranged by the Housing Initiative Association and by BANSO, which in July 1992 held the first televised auction of private flats and houses in Moscow. This is now acknowledged as a lucrative commercial activity, yielding returns of 5 to 17 percent on the property sold, reflecting the high commissions charged (Kharnas, 1991b).

PROPERTY

At the heart of the economic and political changes inaugurated by perestroika, indeed their underlying premise, is the creation of a totally new set of property rights. The latter require a new legal framework within which state property, leasing arrangements, and cooperative and private ownership may coexist. Not only does this fatally undermine the ideological foundation of Soviet Marxism, but it is the basis for a reconceptualization of the relationship between class and property. Furthermore, as various writers have noted, the very notion of private property is almost wholly alien to the culture (Pipes, 1974).

Its importance for housing policy derives in part from the relationship of housing to land. The transformation of property in land into a legal relationship becomes a necessity only when it is suitable for becoming a commodity, that is, when it has a value, thus making its private appropriation profitable.

An axiom of Soviet theory was that under socialism, land had lost its commodity status. At the same time, the ideology acknowledged that land had scarcity value, which enabled differential rent to be calculated. Thus, according to Soviet legal experts and economists, the commodity character of land had not been abolished; rather, its circulation had been restricted. From its inception in 1986, perestroika contained in its agenda, written in invisible ink but known to all, the question of the extent to which restrictions on the circulation of land (as one form of property) were to be removed.

The absence of rights to landownership constitutes an obstacle to the emergence of a legal land market and an effective land pricing mechanism. Even the creation of a leasehold tenure, let alone freehold, is problematic.

The Soviet Law on Ownership of July 1990 is a step toward creating a framework for private property ownership (O sobstvennosti, 1990). The aim is "to put property in the hands of owner-producers." This means that property can be in the hands of individuals (foreign as well as Russian), joint stock companies, mixed companies in which the state has a stake, and cooperatives.

The most recent step toward a regulated land market is the Russian republic's Law on the Payment for Land, which came into force on January 1, 1992. Its principal aim is to "stimulate the rational use of land." For agricultural land, the average annual tax for the whole of Russia will be about 50 rubles per hectare of arable land, ranging from 10 rubles in poor areas to 184 rubles in the fertile Krasnodar region. The average annual tax in urban areas will be from 0.5 rubles to 4.5 rubles per square meter (Voronetskii, 1992:2). This legislation should be seen in the context of the ratification in April 1992 by the Sixth Russian Congress of People's Deputies of the constitutional ban on the private sale of agricultural land. An analysis of the voting behavior of the deputies revealed that 35 percent of those voting against the proposal to permit the sale of agricultural land were members of the senior administrative echelons (that is, political and economic leaders at the republican and provincial [oblast'] levels) (Kto ne dal, 1992).

This is one aspect of the lack of respect for property rights generally in both Soviet political culture and institutional and individual behavior. This disrespect cannot be underestimated. It permeates the whole society, from the pinnacles of power down to the completely powerless. One moment's contemplation of Yeltsin's unseemly treatment of Gorbachev after August 1991 compels the conclusion that Gorbachev's attempt to lay the foundations of a Rechtsstaat and to emphasize the rule of law has not been understood by even the president of Russia. One step further down the hierarchy, when Mossovet confiscates newly erected housing commissioned and paid for by state enterprises, it not only infringes the ownership rights of that enterprise, but it actually underwrites the "requisitioning" carried out by members of the squatters' movement (dvizhenie samozakhvaty).

Two other points regarding property rights merit contemplation. First, the sequestration of buildings, printing presses, and other property belonging to the Communist party by different public bodies resembles the "illegal" seizure of property by the Bolsheviks after October 1917. Second, the transfer of housing from public bodies (ministries, enterprises, institutes) to local soviets assumes a completely different significance to the agents involved now, when property is being privatized (purchased for use or disposal by private individuals), than previously when all property was state property so that all transfers were between state bodies.

PRIVATIZATION

The property rights enjoyed by tenants in public sector housing are frequently more protected and valuable than those of owner-occupiers. Insofar as these tenants virtually control the right of transfer, public property is de facto converted into private property. This is one reason that sitting tenants in public housing are adamant that they should not have to pay large sums for the purchase of "their" flats.

Actual need, although an important criterion for being allowed to join a legal queue, is not the sole determinant of whether a person will be provided with housing. Since the early 1930s, the government has issued decrees and circulars defining which citizens may be given priority in the allocation process. However, in a situation of acute shortage, rules conferring entitlement have been far less important than contacts in the distributional system.

The *propiska* system restricts people's ability to settle in republican capitals, large cities, and other categories of settlement. Those who evade this procedure effectively deny themselves the rights of citizenship. For instance, they are unable to go to court over extortionate rents that they are compelled to pay as "illegal immigrants." This practice, together with the constraints placed on private homeownership and legal regulations on the quasi-housing market, have all served to intensify bribery and corruption both within and outside the bureaucratic allocatory system. The term *mafia* is used to describe institutionalized corruption in both spheres.

In order to eradicate these endemic problems, the Russian parliament has decided to privatize the existing housing stock. Little thought has been given to whether the new owner-occupier should pay tax on the increasing value of this property arising from any modernization of the building. No answer has been provided to the question of whether the sale is taxable and if so, at what level of taxation. No decision has been made on whether a tax will be imposed on the property itself. Since 1989, discussions have centered on privatization of the state housing stock. Suggestions on the form it should take have been thoughtful, innovative, and, at times, bizarre. Most fail to deal with the fact that, in the short term, privatization will perpetuate preexisting inequalities.

The costs to the government of the existing system provide sufficient reason for privatization. But other factors also led to this choice. The notion of a nation of "property-owning democrats" ("nothing is so conservative as the possession of property") represents a potent ideology, much appreciated by social democrats of the late nineteenth century (Hole, 1866:109) and criticized by socialists (Engels, 1962:578ff.) because of its ability to "draw the teeth of the dragon of revolution."

Supply and demand for rented and owner-occupied accommodation can be channeled in a government-chosen direction by changing the regulations governing rents. This could entail, for instance, the government's using carrot-and-stick methods to force higher-income groups out of the publicly rented sector by substantially raising rents. This would encourage better-off tenants to exercise their right to purchase. Others might prefer to live in a family house and be obliged to pay higher rent until a supply of new properties becomes available. In either case, the government would generate revenue to subsidize low-income groups, whose numbers will increase with rising unemployment and inflation.

One advantage to the sitting tenant purchaser is that real estate prices will rise more rapidly than other prices. Hence, investing in housing provides a higher return than from buying stocks and shares or receiving interest. Other factors might also motivate such purchases. For instance, they might want to use the proceeds to build a cottage in the country. However, in a situation of a chronic shortage of building materials and contractors, it would appear better to stay put. Purchasing in order to bequeath is possible but not in order to register relatives who live in other cities. That is still not permissible in large cities, as the *propiska* system is being maintained in order to regulate growth. However, this system is an anomaly that is likely to become increasingly unworkable in the future.

On July 4, 1991, the Supreme Soviet of the Russian Soviet Federated Socialist Republic (RSFSR) ratified a new law, On Privatization of the Housing Stock in the RSFSR (O privatizatsii, 1991). In principle, the law envisages free transfer of state-owned units to sitting tenants. However, if the estimated value of the property exceeds the average, the new owner must pay the difference. Where the property is below average (in standard and therefore in value), the state is not obliged to pay any compensation.

Flats that are transferred free of charge cannot be less than 18 square meters per person plus an additional 9 square meters for the family. Since the average flat size in Moscow is 16.4 square meters per person, up to three-quarters of the population will not have to pay compensation to the local government. Setting the norm at the 18 square meter level would mean that local soviets would receive too little from privatization to enable them to improve their generally lamentable financial state (Artem'ev, 1991). The evaluation of the stock to be privatized will be undertaken by a privatization committee set up by the local soviet.

Another variant of privatization was to compensate those whose shelter fell lower than the local norm by giving them money or a "housing promissary note" (*veksel'*) that obligates the local soviet to compensate the family when it moves out of its accommodation. This suggestion, though difficult to calculate and open to abuse and "bureaucratic perversion," commands support in Mossovet, Lensovet, and elsewhere (Kuplyu, 1991). However, the RSFSR has opted for an intermediate solution.

At present, housing will be transferred free of charge within the limits of the average-sized apartment in that particular settlement or city district at an average selling price per square meter. For every square meter above the socially guaranteed norm, buyers will pay on a progressive scale. Individuals whose units are below the norm will be put on a list for special compensation by the bank, which will ensure that it is spent only in the housing market. So far there has been no decision on whether the number of years that an individual has worked and contributed to the social consumption fund will be taken into account. Some specialists working in the National Academy for the Housing and Communal Economy have recommended that the transfer of average size living space to a household should be free where there is an aggregated fifteen-year period of work service, with pro rata charges for those with shorter lengths of service (Boiko, 1991: 48).

The procedures by which privatization will be introduced have not yet been clarified. Thus, it is unclear whether it will be by apartment or apartment block on the principle, "one house, one owner." (In this case, "house" [*dom*] can mean "apartment" or "apartment block.") Although popular discourse focuses on the first alternative, housing managers favor the second, on grounds that the owner, whether the local soviet, a firm, housing association, or private person, must take responsibility for the block as a whole.

ARGUMENTS AGAINST PRIVATIZATION

The reality of privatization is in reverse proportion to the heated debate that it has generated. Since December 1988, when the decree permitting the sale of state-owned housing was published, only a tiny proportion of the total stock has been sold. Between January and September 1990, 19,300 flats (of which 65 percent belong to local soviets and 35 percent to enterprises) were sold, although this was four times more than for the whole of 1989. Between December 1988 and the end of 1990, according to different estimates, only seven hundred to fifteen hundred flats in Moscow were "privatized." In Leningrad, 0.01 percent of the city's public stock was sold off, although there were twelve times as many applications (Boiko, 1991:42). The discrepancy between application and sale can be explained partly by bureaucratic delays and partly by loss of interest when applicants discover the true (future) costs they will incur with the loss of subsidy for the property's repair and maintenance.

If the intention is to lease the property to derive an income, then it is better to remain a tenant and rent out space, which is perfectly legal, although prices are theoretically fixed by the local authority. If the aim is to purchase in order to run and maintain the property at a higher standard, then a moment's reflection reveals this to be unachievable, for the individual owner in a multistory block has little chance of effectively organizing management and repairs.

It is estimated that only 3 to 5 percent of the population actually possesses sufficient money to buy their units outright, a figure that compares well with other countries. The rest require some form of subsidy. In St. Petersburg, where, admittedly, house prices are higher than elsewhere, only 0.2 to 0.3 percent of the population are able to purchase outright (Boiko, 1991: 42). The problem is that where privatization takes the guise of sitting tenants' purchasing their existing homes, resources are diverted from stimulating the house-building industry. However, if the government wants to stimulate the production of materials and house building, it will have to continue its low-interest-loan policy. Unfortunately, this will fuel inflation even further.

Many believe that since state accommodation has already been paid for by tenants through their rent (and because much of it is in serious need of repair), housing should simply be given to them free of charge. At the global level, this position may be sustainable on the grounds that the population has paid for its accommodation through past rental payments and taxation (Bessonova, 1988; Andrusz, 1990b). On the other hand, at the household level, there are families who live in appalling conditions despite having paid rents and taxes over a long period, while better-housed families may have made smaller contributions. The tangled issue of which households have paid what for which housing becomes further confused and conflict generating when, as has happened, members of cooperatives began to demand that if state tenants receive their accommodation free of charge, then those in cooperatives should also be compensated. This raises the question of who should pay so that others can receive their accommodation free of charge.

Because state housing has in the past been allocated according to criteria that are now said to have breached the canons of social justice (a key notion in the political lexicon of perestroika) and because different space standards and quality of amenity are provided in different types of accommodation, the granting of state property as a gift to sitting tenants may unleash strong egalitarian impulses within the lower echelons of society and give rise to demands for the expropriation of the expropriators (Bessonova, 1992). Families differ in terms of their demands, needs, and actual living conditions, while accommodation differs in terms of its various characteristics. For this reason, the interests of those directly or indirectly involved in the privatization process vary, and this suggests that no single variant on privatization can meet everyone's needs.

At the end of 1990, the recently created All-Union Association for the Housing Economy convened a seminar on privatization and the management of the housing stock (Pynochnye, 1991:4). Participants were asked to reflect on the absence of demonstrators on the streets carrying banners demanding, "Give Us Housing and We Will Repair Them Ourselves!" The question focused attention on the fact that privatization, as a policy, emanates from above, not from the people. Various delegates working in the field of housing management spoke against privatization. This could be an expression of unadulterated self-interest on the part of middle management faced with a loss of status and comfortable jobs. As Zaslavskaya observed in the pre-perestroika days: "The reorganization of production relations promises a substantial narrowing and simplification in responsibilities for workers in departmental ministries and their organs." It implies the reduction in the economic influence of bureaucrats and even the closure of some offices. Not surprisingly, "Such a prospect does not suit the workers who at present *occupy numerous 'cosy niches' with ill-defined responsibilities but thoroughly agreeable salaries*" (Novosibirsk Report, 1983/1989).

Privatization could indeed threaten officials in housing departments who control the allocation of state accommodation. On the other hand, their lack of support for privatization may be founded on more altruistic (or at least practical) grounds. For instance, tenants who buy a dilapidated property are unable to repair and maintain it because of scarce building materials. In the end, the conference concluded that privatization would occur and could only condemn the haste in which the government was seeking to implement it. This complaint of undue haste has not, however, been wasted on political decision makers who have not universally favored its implementation.

The theoretical and moral dimension of privatization revolves around the topic, Who *financed* the building of the housing in the first place? One view is that "since housing was built with our money and, since investment in public housing is the same as investment in cooperative or owner-occupied housing, there can be no discussion of *selling*, but only of *transferring* it as a gift (*darenie*) from municipal into private ownership." The head of the Housing Repair Department in Novosibirsk asked in whose name privatization was occurring and who benefited from it. The policy was manifestly designed to reduce the budget deficit, and so "the cheaper accommodation is for us, the dearer it is for them." The writer's analysis and lexicon seem remarkably like those of a (Western) Trotskyist: he is dismayed at the prospect of "the people" paying more for housing, which will benefit only "them," an undefined class or bureaucracy whose vehicle is "an active market—or more accurately, a *bazaar of barefaced extortion*" (*Delovaya Sibir'*, 1991).

Perceptions of a dominant and manipulative state remain deeply engrained. Yet at the same time, this state is expected to be "paternalistic" so that the proposed tactic of shifting "all the worries onto the shoulders of tenants is [regarded as] wholly unjust (*neblagorodnyi*), even more so since the subject responsible for the transfer is the State."

Privatization is regarded by some critics as less a radical housing reform than as a way to preserve the inequality created by the administrative system (Bessonova, 1991a). For those in good-quality units, the advantages of buying are greater, as is the opportunity for speculation, thus amplifying the injustice (of inhabiting a better-quality dwelling). Legislation or regulations could diminish the effect of these injustices, for instance, by forbidding elites to sell their public accommodation or by insisting that the receipts from such sales face progressive levies. A pervasive objection to the use of such regulatory devices is that they rekindle the bureaucracies that are being rejected.

The principal thrust of privatization is to sell to those members of the population who have resources to invest. This investment, however, does not create new accommodation. To the extent that it reduces the flow of personal finance into the house-building market, it impedes the buildup of demand, which stimulates the formation of new building firms and the development of a private building materials industry. The more appropriate focus of housing reform is privatization of production. This allows small contractors to build high-quality, single-family dwellings and larger property companies to erect new multistory blocks, which they would let at market rents.

The logic behind this argument, understood and adhered to by a minority of the population, leads to the conclusion that the best, and possibly only, way to employ personal savings in an economically beneficial manner is to channel them into building for owner occupation. Housing reform along this path constitutes a crucial first step to reforming the economy as a whole. If, on the other hand, the "reform" is based on selling off the existing stock, the construction industry will continue to stagnate, and market prices for a commodity in short supply will continue to soar. The acuteness of the shortage will see speculative buying and selling, leading to even steeper price rises. The social conflicts that this situation will generate could be exacerbated by tensions arising from the creation of antagonistic groups of owners and nonowners living in the same blocks of flats. Even without open conflict, the coexistence of different types of resident—owners and tenants—could be socially divisive to the extent that life for individuals would be intolerable.

Even within these housing classes, there are wide fluctuations in housing conditions: some live in poor conditions despite their contributions to housing construction through taxation, while others enjoy a standard of comfort far higher than that to which they have contributed. The potential conflict engendered by these different living conditions (and subsequent life chances) is compounded by the fact that better flats and their associated subsidies tend to be allocated to individuals well placed in the status hierarchy. Thus, privatization will further disadvantage those large sections of "ordinary (*prostye*) people" who are without homes or inhabiting inferior accommodation (Bessonova, 1991b:53–59).

It is difficult to assuage the fear that in Russia today, because of growing social differentiation, economic crisis, rising prices, social anomie, and the collapse of political control, the underlying social tensions could be aggravated by housing policies and "place a revolutionary mine under future stability" (Bessonova, 1991a). This view is shared by senior Russian government ministers.

In a question-and-answer session with a member of the RSFSR Committee on Economic Reform and Ownership, the correspondent asked whether price rises for accommodation, which are part of the general inflationary process in the transitional period, will "threaten a social explosion." The reply was brutally clear. Surveys show that the majority prefer that everything remain as it is, with accommodation being provided free of charge. Unfortunately, the man in the street (*chelovek na ulitse*) is far from understanding not just the complexity of various cause-and-effect linkages but also the "simple truth that there is no such thing as 'free'; we all pay for everything out of our pockets through taxation" (Kuplyu kvartiru, 1991). This poses the question, "How can homeownership be introduced quickly without inspiring popular protest (*protesta naseleniya*)?" So in order to satisfy the public, the proposal of the deputy prime minister of the RSFSR, which is the simplest solution, should be adopted: each household should be given the property it already occupies. Of course, this would be acceptable to those in large, well-equipped flats but not to those in shared, communal flats.

Such matters may be problematical, but they are largely technical and resolvable. Much more fundamental is the answer given to an interviewer by a senior Russian government official in August 1991. The interviewer asked: "Why do we need to change from a system of publicly owned and free (*besplatno*) accommodation to paid and private accommodation?" His reply was the same as that applied to explain the paradigmatic change to the market in all spheres: public ownership means that there is "no owner." And since, as a result, no one, neither tenants nor state officials, has an interest in looking after it, the state spends on the repair of one property alone as much as it does on the erection of three new blocks.

Another justification for the change in ownership was more novel: the existing system "prevents technological progress." In order to stimulate the introduction of modern technology, corporate taxation must be reduced and wages increased. Firms will then find it advantageous to substitute machinery for hired slave labor (*rabskii trud*) (Kuplyu kvartiru, 1991). The capital-labor ratio is extremely important and merits a major cross-national comparative study of the construction industry. The case for privatization does not, however, rest on economic considerations alone.

The level at which decisions on housing matters are taken is far from being resolved. Although there is a strong case for granting greater autonomy to officials at the point of distribution, the conservatism of the provinces must be considered, for most cities have not yet drawn up plans for transferring ownership, nor have steps been taken to make commercial credit and insurance available to buyers or builders.

Many decisions are still needed at the center if privatization and housing reform more generally are to be achieved. In their desire to reject most (if not all) forms of centralized control and decision making, many radicals want to leave as many decisions as possible to the local level. Since the 1960s the columns of *Izvestiya* have been filled with pleas for decisions to be taken at the local level (*na mestakh*), on the grounds that local people and their representatives "know better." By the same token, today, "the struggle against speculators should be determined by the actual situation prevailing in a particular town." This, unfortunately, can also lead to arbitrariness and injustice. Therefore, to ensure the equal treatment of all citizens, the central government must set basic parameters of legal and illegal action.

CONCLUSION

The high levels of overcrowding, the universally low space standards, and the often poor quality of external design and interior layout will not be remedied overnight by raising rents or by selling state units to sitting tenants or cooperatives. This can be done only by increasing the housing supply. It is difficult to predict whether current economic reforms will have a positive effect on housing production. As in other advanced industrial countries, a revitalized private sector will have to coexist with a public sector. The latter will serve as a social guarantee for those on low incomes unable to compete in the market. The exact nature of the public sector remains to be determined but will certainly vary from republic to republic.

But it is not just a question of increasing the supply. Reform policies reflect a profoundly felt disapprobation for the way in which individuals have in the past gained access to this vital commodity, the self-contained family home. Greater wage differentials and the simultaneous removal of fringe benefits, such as closed shops, are necessary concomitants of the demise of "the distributor" in the field of housing. In this way, Soviet housing policy might be seen as a handmaiden of the bourgeois revolution and of the restructuring of the class system.

The important thing is that subsidies will cease to be universal and become means tested. Not only will this remove the corruption and injustice so typical of the state sector in the former centrally planned economies, but it could lead to more efficient use of central government assistance, which could go to those engaging in self-build. Private sector prices will no longer be forced upward by unfair competition between the public and private sectors.

The fear of predatory speculators may be genuine. This, however, must be distinguished from paranoia toward profit-motivated behavior. The shift toward the market, which expresses an intense political struggle, demands that a clear distinction be made between the different forms of capitalist behavior.

The prescription preferred by many housing specialists is a system comprising a municipal sector, providing low-cost housing for low-income families, and owner-occupier, cooperative, and privately rented sectors. Following practices in other European countries, the owner-occupier and privately rented tenures are regarded as sources for profitable capital investment, while cooperatives will, like British housing associations, enable households on average incomes to satisfy their housing needs at a reasonable level of expenditure.

NOTE

1. It is difficult to find an appropriate name for the territory that used to be called the "Soviet Union." Because such a short period of time has elapsed since the beginning of the Soviet state, a strong case exists for referring to it as the "former Soviet Union" (FSU). However, the Baltic States have detached themselves completely and, following the attempted coup in August 1991, the remaining constituent republics of the Soviet Union renamed themselves as members of the "Commonwealth of Independent States" (CIS). This is such a unstable, short-term political arrangement that it is already anachronistic! What remains as a historically identifiable entity is Russia. The name adopted in April 1992 by the Russian Congress of People's Deputies for their state is *Russian Federation–Russia*. In this chapter, the simpler and understandable name *Russia* alone is used. However, the text still uses statistics for the whole Soviet Union.

REFERENCES

Andrusz, G. D. 1984. *Housing and Urban Development in the USSR*. London: Macmillan/SUNY.
———. 1986. "Sowjetische Wohnungspolitik: Das Ende einer Epoche." *Osteuropa. Zeitschrift fur Gegenwartsfragen des Ostens*, no. 4.
———. 1990a. "A Note on the Financing of Housing in the Soviet." *Soviet Studies* 42, no. 3.
———. 1990b. "Housing in the USSR" in J. Sillince (ed.), *Housing in Eastern Europe and the USSR*. London: Routledge/Croom Helm.
———. 1992. "Housing Co-operatives in the Soviet Union." *Housing Studies* 7, no. 2 (Spring).
Artem'ev, R. 1991. "Privatizatsiya zhil 'ya: bez anneksii i kontributsii." *Kommersant*, no. 27: 1–8.
Bessonova, O. 1988. "Fenomen besplatnogo zhil'ya v SSSR." *IzvestiyaSibirskogo Otdeleniya Ak.Nauk SSSR*. Seriya ekonomiki i *prikladnoi sotsiologii*, vypusk 3.
———. 1991a. "Mina zamedlennogo deistviya." *Delovaya Sibir'*, no. 2.
———. 1991b. "Zhilishchnaya strategiya: Kak uiti ot gorodov Khrushchob." *EKO*, no. 5:53–59.
———. 1992. "Reform of the Soviet Housing Model: The Search for a Concept." In B. Turner et al. (eds.), *Housing Reforms in Eastern Europe and the Soviet Union*. New York: Routledge.
Boiko, T. 1991. "Posmotrim v zuby 'darenomu' zhil'yu," *EKO*, no. 5: 41.
Delovaya Sibir'. 1991. no. 2, January: 3.
"Dva kuska moskovskoi zemli vpervye poidut s molota." 1991. *Kommersant*, July 17–24.
Ekonomicheskaya gazeta. 1986. no. 36:18.

Engels, F. 1962. "The Housing Question." In K. Marx and F. Engels, *Selected Works*, vol. 2. Moscow.

Fukuyama, F. 1992. *The End of History and the Last Man*. London: Hamish Hamilton.

Gorbachev, M. 1986. *Political Report of the CPSU Central Committee to the 27th Party Congress*. Moscow: Novosti Press.

———. 1990. "O novykh podkhodakh k resheniyu zhilishchnoi problemy v strane i merakh po ikh prakticheskoi realizatsii." *Izvestiya*, May 20.

Goskomstat. 1987. *Narodnoe khozyaistvo SSSR za 70 let*. Moscow.

———. 1989. *Narodnoe khozyaistvo SSSR v 1988 g*. Moscow.

———. 1990a. *Narodoe khozyaistvo SSSR v 1989 g. Statisticheskiisbornik*. Moscow.

———. 1990b. *Zhilishchnye usloviya naseleniya SSSR. Statisticheskii sbornik*. Moscow.

Hole, J. 1866. *The Homes of the Working Classes with Suggestions for Their Improvement*. London.

Kalinina, N. 1990. "Privatising Public Housing in West and Eastern Europe." Unpublished paper. Washington, D.C.

———. "Housing and Housing Policy in the USSR." In B. Turner et al., *Housing Reforms in Eastern Europe and the Soviet Union*. Routledge.

Kharnas, V. 1991a. "Prodazha moskovskoi propiski: zhadnost' fraera sgubila." *Kommersant*, July 29–August 5.

———. 1991b. "Going Like Hotcakes." *Commersant*, July 22.

Khodzhaev, D. 1990. "Novye pokhody k resheniyu zhilishchnogo voprosa." *Planovoe khozyaistvo*, no. 10.

Kolotilkin, B. 1989a. "Kazhdaya sem'e—otdel'naya kvartira. Raschety i proschety." *Argumenty i Fakty*, no. 22 (June):4.

———. 1989b. "Kvartplata i koshelek." *Argumenty i fakty*, no. 29 (July).

———. 1990. "Kvartirnaya plata: khozraschet i sotsial'naya spravedlivost." *Voprosy ekonomiki*, no. 8:91–94.

Koptyaev, A. 1991. "Nedviszhimost' v Leningrade okazolas' deshevle." *Kommersant*, July 29–August 5.

Kosareva, N., N. Ronkin, and O. Pchelintsev. 1990. "Na puti k zhilishchnoi reforme: analiz i prognoz." *Voprosy ekonomiki*, no. 8.

"Kto ne dal zemlyu narodu." 1992. *Argumenty i fakty*, no. 15 (April):2, 8.

"Kuplyu kvartiru." 1991. *Demokraticheskaya Rossiya*, August 2.

Morozov, M. 1991. "Success First Time Around." *Commersant*, July 22.

"Moskovskaya propiska: syashchennaya korova poshla s molota." 1991. *Kommersant*, July 8–15.

Novosibirsk Report. 1989. Reprinted in M. Yanowitch (ed.), *A Voice of Reform: Essays by Tat'iana I. Zaslavskaya*. London: M. E. Sharpe.

"Ob obespechennosti zhil'em semei rabochikh, sluzhashchikh i kolkhoznikov RSFSR." 1990. *Argumenty i fakty*, no. 7 (February):3.

"O privatizatsii zhilya v RSFSR." 1991. *Novaya stroitel'naya gazeta*, August 6.

"O sobstvennosti v SSSR." 1990. *Novy Zakony*, Issue 1, Yuridicheskaya Literatura, Moscow.

"Pervyi auktsion kvartir v Moskve: million za rublevku." 1991. *Kommersant*, April 22–29.

Pipes, R. 1974. *Russia under the Old Regime*. London: Weidenfeld and Nicholson.

Postanovlenie TsK KPSS i Soveta Ministrov SSSR. 1987. "O dal'neishem razvitii sovetskoi arkhitektury i gradostroitel'stva." *SP SSSR 1987*, September 17.

———. 1988a. "O merakh po uskoreniyu razvitiya individual'nogo zhilishchnogo stroitel'stva." *SP SSSR 1988*, no. 11, art. 28.

———. 1988b. "O merakh po uskoreniyu razvitiya zhilishchnogo kooperatsii." *SP SSSR 1988*, March 31.

Programma Kommunisticheskoi Partii Sovetskogo Soyuza. 1961. Moscow: 94.

Pravda. 1986. June 10.

Propetsko, A. 1991. "Normal'naya nedvizhemost' zashal'nye den'gi." *Izvestiya*, July 18.

"Pynochnye zhil'ya: budet li nyneshnee pokolenie sovetskikh lyudei zhit' vsvoikhdomakh." 1991. *Delovaya Sibir'. Rossiiskii kommercheskiiezhednevnik*, no. 2 (January): 4.

Resin, V. 1991. "Deshevo khrosho ne byvaet." *Kurant*, July 20.

Shabanova, M. 1985. *Sezonnye sel'skie stroiteli: kto onu i kakoviikh problemy.* Novosibirsk.

TsNIIEP zhilishcha. 1988. *General'naya skhema opespecheniya k 2000 godu kazhdoi sovetskoi semi'i otdel'noi kvartiroi ili individual'nom domom.* Moscow.

"V Moskve predlagaet nedvizhimost'. Snachala ee nado vyigrat', a potom zaplatit'." 1991. *Kommersant*, June 24–July 1.

Voronetskii, V. 1992. "Nalog na maluyu zemlyu i bolshuyu." *Argumentyi Fakty*, no. 1 (January):2.

Zhilishchnye usloviya naseleniya SSSR. 1990. *Statistichesteii sbovnite.* Moscow.

Part 2

Public Policy and Homeownership

4

The Changing Face of Homeownership in Britain: Divisions, Interests, and the State

ALAN MURIE

At the turn of the century, the housing market in Britain, like that of other developed European countries, was dominated by the private rented sector. Its development since has had some remarkable features. The privately rented sector has declined further and faster than elsewhere; the rental market or social rented sector has been directly owned and controlled by the state through local authorities rather than voluntary organizations, and this state housing sector grew to account for almost one in three properties— much more than in Eastern Europe; and the homeownership sector has become among the largest in proportionate terms in Europe. Britain has represented the contradictory position of a well-developed mature home-ownership sector alongside an abnormally important state housing sector.

This chapter is concerned with the growth and nature of the homeown-ership system that has emerged. It is particularly concerned with three major elements in debates and understanding of homeownership: accounts of homeownership that present it as demand led; presentations of homeown-ership as a uniform tenure and homeowners as having common interests and obtaining common benefits; and presentations that equate homeown-ership with the private sector and imply that growth has been independent of, or in spite of, the state. These are related themes in presentations by politicians and academics (Saunders, 1990). They relate to euphoric views of the social and economic benefits of homeownership—views that tend to be contrasted with the social, economic, and moral dangers associated with state housing. Just as home ownership has been part of the "American dream," it has been a key element in conservative images of a property-owning democracy in Britain. And the merits of homeownership were particularly associated with stability and conservatism. For example, home-ownership has variously been referred to as:

"A revolution which of necessity enlisted all of those who were affected by it on the side of law and order and enrolled them in a great army of good citizens."

"People find satisfaction and stability in the ownership of property, especially of their own homes and gardens."

"Property ownership is valuable in itself, encourages independence of character, acceptance of responsibility as well as the savings habit."

"A home owner can get his roots down and get his roses planted. Ownership and responsibility advance hand in hand."

"It satisfies a deep and natural desire on the part of the householder to have inde-pendent control of the home that shelters him and his family." (quoted in Murie, 1975; Merrett, 1982)

The reality of homeownership in Britain is more complex. Its origins are more variable, and its growth has not always been driven by individual desire for ownership. The nature of homeownership and the demand for it have been partly formed by public policy and the framework of taxation, subsidy, and welfare state institutions within which it operates. Spatial and social variations are such that homeowners gain differentially from owner-ship. The material and political interests of homeowners are not all the same. The nature of homeownership is spatially and historically specific and is affected by a wider environment.

These issues are the subject of active debate in Britain. The experience of the period 1988–1992 has eroded the euphoric uniform view of home-ownership. However, because of this active debate, it is important to state at the outset what views of homeownership are not being advanced in this chapter. The alternative to the euphoric uniform view is not one that is concerned to show that homeownership damages individuals, communities, or societies or uniformly represents false promises and devices to dupe and divert the energies of households. Indeed, at one level, a key element in debate is about whether homeownership does anything or whether it is the product of other processes (Barlow and Duncan, 1988).

THE ORIGINS OF HOMEOWNERSHIP IN BRITAIN

Much contemporary debate refers to recent policies bringing homeown-ership within the reach of lower-income groups. The inference that could be drawn is that homeownership developed initially among the most affluent, but this is not the case. In 1910 homeownership in Britain as a whole was around 10 percent, but in some working-class districts, homeownership lev-els exceeded this considerably. This was particularly true in single-industry communities and areas where the building society movement was better

Table 4.1
Housing Tenure in Great Britain, 1914–1990 (percentage of all dwellings)

YEAR	OWNER OCCUPIED	PUBLIC RENTED[1]	PRIVATE RENTED AND OTHER[2]
1914	10.0	1.0	89.0
1938	25.0	10.0	65.0
1951	29.0	18.0	53.0
1964	45.6	28.1	26.3
1981	55.8	30.8	13.1
1990	67.1	22.4	10.5

NOTES [1] Local authorities and new towns and other public bodies.
       [2] Includes housing associations.

SOURCES Boddy, 1980
         Housing and Construction Statistics(HMSO)

developed. This movement had grown as a movement through which working-class households sought to develop independence from employers and obtain good housing. The South Wales Coalfield appears to have had very high levels of working-class homeownership, and working-class homeownership was reported to be common in a number of areas (Forrest, Murie, Williams, 1990:56–62).

Accounts of the growth of homeownership from these early origins embrace factors producing a complex pattern of growth. Rentier landlords withdrew from an active investment role in housing because of better investment opportunities in other markets. Consequently, those seeking housing, and especially those seeking new, modern houses, were increasingly likely to look toward the homeownership sector. The development of building societies facilitated an alternative route to housing and one that was increasingly attractive to the more affluent.

Table 4.1 presents the basic statistics of the changing structure of the housing market in Britain. As homeownership has grown, however, it has also changed in other ways.

CHANGING TENURES

Arguments that homeownership has certain intrinsic or essential features that hold true irrespective of time or place are difficult to reconcile with the long history of growth and the variety of factors that have influenced it. As with the other housing tenures, the nature of homeownership has changed

Table 4.2
Homeownership in Britain: Early, Middle, and Late Stages

DIMENSION	EARLY STAGE	MIDDLE STAGE	LATE STAGE
Households	Established upper and working class families	White, affluent families with incomes and jobs enabling them to live in suburbs.	Increasingly mixed ages, incomes, and family structures; skilled, and semi-skilled workers and those outside labor market.
Dwellings	Small-scale, new build and self-build	Mass suburban new build and transfers from private renting.	Declining importance of new build. Mixed age, quality and location. Substantial transfers from public and private renting.
Organizations	Terminating organizations, small investors, mutual organizations.	Speculative builders and permanent building societies.	Rationalized structure of building societies and builders with closer corporate links with government. Increased competition and integration with financial markets.
Production	Small firms and self-build to contract	Wide range of speculative builders.	Rationalized structure of larger speculative builders, less dependent on house-building and catering to specialized markets.
Market Structure	Very localized, new build.	Stock transfers and regional/local new build.	Predominantly second-hand market. National but highly segmented.
Relationship to Renting	Junior partner in parallel development of private renting.	Replacing private renting. Public renting developing alongside.	Replacing renting generally as public renting becomes increasingly residual.
Risk	Borne by investors in building process.	Borne by depositors / savers.	Borne by users / owners.
Role of State	Passive / minimal	Establishing and guaranteeing legal rights of owners and status of credit institutions.	Regulation, sponsorship, subsidy. Encouragement through intervention and privatization of public housing.

in significant ways. Table 4.2 summarizes key features of these changes in Britain.

Its nineteenth-century origins are associated with newly formed working-class organizations or with the wealthy employer class. Small-scale, purpose-built (sometimes self-built) housing was not state subsidized and was financed through mutual organizations (the terminating building societies are the best example) or in the same manner as other investment. The sector was restricted to new building largely by small builders in urban areas. No second-hand or mass market existed.

Homeownership developed into a mass tenure between the wars. In this middle phase, additions were largely through new development but as detached and semidetached homes with gardens in leafy suburban areas. These middle-class suburbs derived their characteristics partly from who was able to become a homeowner. With limited state subsidy, access was restricted according to income and credit status. In a period of high unemployment, it was white-collar and skilled workers' families and those in stable employment who were most likely to become homeowners. Building for this market was no longer organized on a small scale through mutual organizations but predominantly involved speculative building ahead of purchase and for profit. Credit institutions had, in the same mold, developed into permanent building societies, sometimes with very close links to builders (Craig, 1986).

In some cases, the terms and rights associated with the emerging form of homeownership bore a close similarity to renting. Builders and investment organizations were developing homeownership on a renting model. The unsatisfactory nature of this model resulted in mortgage strikes and other action and, in turn, in changes in legislation to change significantly the rights of homeowners and the legal relationship between them and their building societies or mortgagor. At this stage, homeownership was still a new tenure, growing mainly through new building and transfers from private renting. There was a limited second-hand market and little resale accumulation.

The postwar period has seen the transition from a middle to a late stage. New building became less important than second-hand transactions, and estate agencies handling the increasingly complex chains of transactions grew with the number of these transactions. Growth of the tenure continued to involve transfers from private renting but, increasingly, from older, working-class and inner-city neighborhoods. Recently, growth has been dominated by substantial transfers from public sector renting. These tenure transfers form one dimension of gentrification or changing social composition of areas of rented housing. In the late stage, homeownership has also become less exclusively housing for middle-class and affluent families. Household characteristics of homeowners have become more varied, partly as a product of the aging of the early homeowners and partly because of changing recruitment, with changes in access to subsidy and finance.

Differentiation in the sector has become more obvious in other ways. The relative uniformity in price, age, and quality no longer exists. While the ideology and imagery of the property-owning democracy and popular capitalism are more strongly associated with homeownership, the reality of instability—of fluctuations in house prices and interest rates and in debt encumbrance—is more apparent. The structure of subsidies for the homeownership market is generally regarded as regressive and inefficient (Hills, 1991). While some homeowners receive very substantial support, others, often with lower incomes and other resources, receive little or none. Differentiation in homeownership increasingly has involved problems of mobility (and labor mobility), mortgage arrears and repossessions, and repair and maintenance problems. Leakage of funds from housing to general consumption and realization of wealth have become more important. In addition to gentrification, homeownership has grown among nonfamily households, black households, female-headed households, and non-wage-earning households. Such households are concentrated in neighborhoods and price bands.

The late stage of development of homeownership has also seen a major rationalization and centralization of housing finance arrangements. Amalgamation and branching as features of building society finance have, with the Building Societies Act of 1986, developed into acquisition and development into insurance and estate agency and the provision of a wider range of financial services. The reorganization and changing role of housing organizations in this late phase have not been restricted to the private sector. State sponsorship and subsidy of homeownership have become important. Fiscal subsidies have been crucial to the development of the sector, but so have grants for improvements, special subsidies, and grants for low-cost homeownership and council house sales schemes and the general treatment of homeowners' housing costs by the social security system. The resilience of the sector and the capacity of building societies to postpone and adjust payments in periods of unemployment or other crises have been built upon the knowledge that state social security (income support) entitlements take into account mortgage interest repayments.

In the late phase of homeownership, the mass housing of its middle phase is now getting old, and its environment has changed with urban growth. The interwar suburbs, which were attached to rural and agricultural areas, have been engulfed by later urban development. Perhaps even more important, the owner-occupied sector has grown through transfer of properties from the rented sectors as well as through new building. The locations, ages, dwelling types, and conditions of transferred properties are mixed. Some 5.5 million of the 14 million dwellings in the owner-occupied sector were at some stage rented dwellings. Over 1.5 million of these are former council houses, with locations, ages, designs, and maintenance histories associated with whom they were built by and for. And the dwellings transferred from private renting have characteristics reflecting whom they were built by and for and when they were built. The nineteenth-century tunnel-back terrace house in an inner-city area and with a history of neglect of maintenance and repair by an absentee landlord is just as much part of the owner-occupied sector as the suburban semiattached dwelling built for the affluent middle classes between the wars. An increasingly aging and differentiated stock is as important an aspect of the transformation of homeownership as is its growth.

The cohort of homeowners in the middle phase when homeownership developed as a mass tenure appears to have been relatively young, white, white-collar families. But these younger households have grown old, and some older owners have low incomes. At the same time, access to owner occupation has widened and moved down the income and occupational ladder. Younger and single-person and childless couple households, the unemployed, and others on low permanent incomes are strongly represented among owner-occupiers. The number of homeowners on means-tested welfare benefit grew from 362,000 to 793,000 between 1967 and 1986. Redundancy and changes in economic circumstances have affected households in all tenures. Demographic changes, including the increase in the aged population, single-parent families, and female-headed households and the importance of divorce and separation have contributed to a changed profile. The changing availability of private renting has led to an increase in the use of homeownership by newly formed households and as starter housing. At the same time, those households with the least choice in the housing market—those unable to obtain council housing or unable to afford it—have increasingly looked to the bottom end of the house purchase market. Some households have become homeowners because of lack of choice and as a last resort—quite out of character with images of the tenure—and have very limited resources for maintenance or repair.

Major changes are also evident in the way homeownership has been financed and subsidized. Mortgage interest tax relief has unremarkable origins. The income tax system set up in 1803 allowed borrowers to repay the interest on any loans net of tax. In 1925–1926 the Conservative government allowed a special arrangement to be created whereby building societies received the interest on loans for house purchase without the deduction of the tax. The borrower was then allowed to set those interest charges against his or her income for tax purposes. This procedure was given legislative force in 1951 and consolidated in the Income Tax of 1952.

In 1963 the balancing factor in the equation—taxation on the imputed rental income of owning one's own dwelling (i.e., the extra income, or rent, one "earns" or "saves" by owning one's own dwelling)—was abolished. In 1969 tax relief on personal borrowing was limited to mortgages on residences and land in the United Kingdom. In 1974 the Labour government placed a ceiling on mortgage interest relief by specifying the maximum size of mortgage that could attract this subsidy—£25,000—and restricted this relief to the borrower's main residence. In 1983, the Conservatives raised this to £30,000. Rising house prices and high interest rates continued to increase the value of these reliefs, and the cost and distribution of them have been under increasing attack. In 1988 and 1991 amendments to tax relief arrangements reduced their scope, but they remain at the basic tax rate within a £30,000 limit per dwelling (rather than per purchaser).

The debate over tax relief has intensified as the amount of revenue forgone has risen. Initially, tax relief was relatively unimportant because most people did not pay income tax. However, as incomes have risen and the tax thresholds have been lowered, it has become increasingly significant. It has been estimated that in the late 1930s, tax relief amounted to £8 million to £10 million (Holmans, 1987), and this would have been out of a total taxation income (income tax and surtax) of £300 million to £400 million. The value of mortgage interest tax relief has risen sharply since the 1960s as house prices and interest rates have increased and the number of home purchasers has grown. It has also been affected by changes in tax rates. Holmans estimates that of the increase of £410 million in tax relief and option mortgage subsidy between 1973–1974 and 1975–1976, £140 million was the consequence of the basic rate of tax being raised from 30 percent to 35 percent. Changes in tax rates in the 1980s and increases in house prices have affected the rate of growth of this tax relief. In 1979–1980 Mortgage Interest Tax Relief (MITR) stood at £1,639 million; in 1989, at £6,900 million, out of a total taxation income of £47,692 million (income tax and surtax).

Holmans (1987) has commented "The structure of tax relief and exemptions just grew without being planned" (p. 465). This subsidy, along with the relief of taxation on capital gains, preferential tax treatment for lenders, improvement grants, and supplementary benefits payments to owners, is all part of a system that has done much to support the homeowner. While such arrangements are not peculiar to the United Kingdom, they do appear to be particularly generous.

These arrangements particularly encouraged homeownership among the affluent. However, this is not the whole story. Mobile and newly formed households looking for a home were more likely to become homeowners, while established households with no reason to move stayed in private renting (unless their landlord sold to them). So homeownership grew disproportionately among younger households in expanding suburban areas in more affluent regions. But at the same time, tenure transfers were a major source of growth, and these were often very high in depressed regions and inner-city areas. For example, some enterprises that provided housing for their employees and were faced with financial and trading problems sold properties to sitting tenants and others to relieve this situation. In such situations, homeownership grew not as a response to demand but as a result of decisions by absentee owners.

The pattern of supply-led growth in more recent years has been described for the flat-breakup market in London by Hamnett and Randolph (1988), and other examples can be given relating to the activities of private developers and the public sector, especially in relation to council house sales (Forrest and Murie, 1988). The growth of homeownership has been led variously by demand, supply, and policy elements. As the whole market has changed, individual households have adjusted preferences and aspirations and developed various strategies to cope with changing opportunities and constraints. Homeowners have not all become owners through the same routes or for the same rea-sons—nor are all nonowners frustrated would-be owners.

Prior to the 1960s then, tax expenditures on homeownership were neg-ligible and benefited only the relatively small proportion of the population paying tax. Payment of Schedule A tax on imputed rental income largely cancelled out the advantage. Council tenants benefited from exchequer and rate fund subsidies, although various devices, including rent policy and rent rebates, were used to restrict their growth. By 1985, however, the steady growth of tax relief had taken it to a level that both in total and per capita was greater than subsidy to council tenants. Many council tenants no longer benefit from any form of non-means-tested subsidy. But for owner-occupiers, both tax relief gains and gains from appreciating property values are ex-tremely uneven. Improvement grants and discounts on council houses sales have added to the financial opportunities available to homeowners and to the uneven pattern of benefit.

Finally, the control and management of homeownership have changed. Local authorities have largely ceased new lending for house purchase except in connection with the sale of council houses. New organizations have be-come involved in financing house purchase, and building societies, which have retained the bulk of the market share, have expanded, branched, amal-gamated, and reorganized to present a very different face. They have changed their methods of operation and, even in recent years, their policies in relation to lending and borrowing. Other parts of the owner-occupation industry have also developed. Builders have amalgamated and developed more spe-cific products for particular markets (from starter homes to sheltered units). Local authorities' role in the homeownership industry has shifted from lend-ing to sales of their own stocks and the development of special schemes. In some areas, local authority activity has contributed more to the growth of owner occupation than has private speculative activity.

The administration of improvement grants and development of local au-thority agency and other services for owner-occupiers mean that local au-thorities are involved in the resourcing and management of homeownership. Voluntary sector agency schemes such as Care and Repair and the Neigh-borhood Revitalization Service are also involved in this way—often consid-erably dependent on local authority support through grants. New financial arrangements to release the equity tied up in homeownership (for repair and maintenance or general consumption expenditure) represent ways of releasing house savings and dissaving in old age. They are important (al-though as yet minor) developments.

In all of these changes, local variation is considerable. In some localities, renting or even council renting is the dominant tenure; in others, there is little rented housing, and the market is a private one managed and organized by agencies involved in homeownership. National average figures give little indication of the variation between localities and the striking differences that result. In each of these and in other ways, the statistics of tenure change fail to indicate the full story of changes in tenure. And the failure to grasp some of this story is a problem in current policy debate in which it is too often implied that the main tenures are still what they used to be, or are relatively homogeneous.

MIXED FORTUNES

In spite of the changing nature of homeownership, there is a tendency to argue that homeowners as a group have common interests as homeowners. In addition, it has been argued that all homeowners benefit through wealth accumulation and that the greatest benefits often accrue to those on the lowest incomes. This key element of the euphoric, uniform presentation may also be linked with arguments about ontological security accruing to all owners through the fact of ownership. In Britain, these arguments have been pressed most uncompromisingly by Saunders, mainly based on limited survey evidence from 1986.

Saunders's (1990) views have been challenged in a number of ways. His analysis of wealth accumulation has been criticized in detail, and it is argued that absolute gains, which are the most relevant to questions of wealth accumulation, relate very closely to income and affordability issues (see, e.g., Forrest, Murie, and Williams, 1990; Murie, 1991). Poor homeowners gain least, and accumulation through homeownership reinforces other inequalities among homeowners. Even if the poor homeowner fares better than the tenant, this does not mean that homeowners have either a common experience or interest or interests that differ from tenants. Furthermore, homeowners at different stages in their housing history will be more or less concerned about interest rates, inflation, and levels of taxation and public expenditure. One stereotype would be that the heavily indebted owner in employment and with no savings favors low or negative real interest rates, while the outright owner on a pension with savings will least favor this situation. And there are other divisions among homeowners that can be argued to cast doubt on assumptions about common interests or gains.

In connection with these debates, arguments about ontological security remain at best unproved. Security in the home derives from a range of factors and is not an intrinsic, essential element of ownership. Nor is it automatically absent where ownership is absent. Public sector tenants and former tenants do not express dissatisfaction with council housing even where they prefer homeownership (see Forrest and Murie, 1990). What creates security and satisfaction is multifaceted and relates to various aspects of households' circumstances (including affluence, employment, health, and age) and various features of the house (including condition, size, and a range of issues associated with location).

In Britain there is a further dimension to these debates. Saunders's conclusions, for example, are based on a snapshot survey carried out when the housing market was particularly buoyant. In 1986 house prices were rising rapidly, especially in the South and East of England, and employment and incomes were rising. If Saunders's study were reproduced in 1990 or 1991, a very different picture would arise. House prices have fallen, and some of those who have to sell could fare a loss. For others, their property has declined in value. Saunders's rate-of-return analysis would produce very different results, and more of his respondents would refer to problems with mobility, sale, meeting mortgage payments, and other aspects of homeownership.

A boom in house prices commenced in 1986, spreading outward from the affluent Southeast and affected by rising employment and incomes, deregulation of financial institutions, general changes in taxation, and declining mortgage interest rates. The spectacular increase in house prices was fueled by the decision to restrict the £30,000 mortgage interest tax relief limit to the residence rather than the individual from August 1, 1986. This prevented joint purchasers' qualifying for tax reliefs in excess of £30,000, but sufficient warning of the policy change was given to enable purchases to be made to beat the withdrawal of multiple relief. The booming market was also visible in an increase in private sector housing starts: from 180,000 in 1986 to 216,000 in 1988.

But after August 1988, the private housing market faltered, and at the end of 1991, Britain was still in the longest sustained period of depressed housing market activity experienced in recent times. The number of house purchase transactions and house-building starts fell and has not recovered. Mortgage interest rates rose from around 9.5 percent in May 1988 (the lowest level for ten years) to a peak of 15.4 percent in 1990. This interest rate remained at 15.4 percent until October 1990 and fell in eight successive small steps to below 11 percent in 1992. The very high rates of interest had a devastating effect on the housing market, but what happened in the homeownership market is also widely believed to have triggered an inflationary spiral.

The consumer-led boom that had produced high inflation and resulted in a high interest rate policy and the slide into economic recession was widely attributed to the housing market. Nor did commentary refer purely to the impact of specific tax changes that had contributed to the volatility of the private housing market. There was reference to how far the system of housing finance and production in Britain was likely to produce surges and slumps, encourage credit-based consumption, increase the likelihood of credit-based inflation, and reduce the ability to bring such inflation under control. The homeownership success story was not being denied but had its problems and costs, and countries such as Germany that lagged in homeownership did not appear to suffer economic problems associated with the housing sector.

If the housing market had a role in the origins and stubbornness of inflationary problems, it was also the homeowner who was suffering the consequences of the higher interest rates. Building society interest rates on new mortgages rose to 15.4 percent in February 1990 and remained at that level—the highest on record—until October 1990, when they fell to 14.5 percent. The impact of these changes on individual owners varied especially because of the increased tendency for payments to be reviewed annually rather than to change with changes in the rate for new mortgages. For those (often higher-income households) who had taken out substantial mortgages in that period, payments were enormously greater than expected. Not surprisingly, mortgage arrears and repossessions increased. In the first half of 1990, 14,390 properties were taken into possession, 18,750 loans were more than twelve months in arrear at the end of the period, and 95,030 loans were more than six months in arrear. These were all higher figures than ever previously recorded. They related to a larger population of homeowners, and properties taken into possession represented 0.178 percent of loans. Nevertheless, it was an unsavory consequence of high interest rates and provided unhealthy preparation for the pressures arising from rising unemployment.

Increased arrears were not just a problem for the household involved but cost lenders money. For building societies, new capital adequacy regulations also required them to make a provision against all mortgages more than six months in arrears. Building societies became concerned about irresponsible lending and the continuing appearance of advertisements for mortgages and other loans where these gave insufficient information. At the same time, falling property values meant that some lenders felt obliged to reduce the size of the loan they had offered after the exchange of contracts. A declining market presented a variety of unfamiliar problems in homeownership. House prices continued to decline, and the number and value of mortgage advances in 1990 was lower than in 1989.

If inflated house prices and housing market activity had set off an inflationary spiral, the stagnant market had wider repercussions in 1990. Housebuilding activity was sharply cut back and resulted in falling profits, with builders going into receivership or coping with market problems by prolonging the building process and adopting various previously unnecessary marketing procedures to achieve sales. An estimated 30,000 newly built dwellings also remained unsold and would delay any recovery following falling interest rates. And by the time interest rates began to fall, the economic recession, redundancy, unemployment, and loss of earnings exacerbated the problems accumulated in the period of high interest rates.

The collapse of house building, especially in the Southeast, became an important component in the economic downturn. The finance and business pages of the press in 1990 and 1991 were littered with accounts of problems initially in the property sector, in buildings materials manufacturing and in the sales of consumer durables associated with new housing and moving house, and finally in estate agency and the insurance industry battered by claims under mortgage indemnity policies and among mortgage lenders.

There is a further policy-related dimension to this decline. Local authority and new town house-building programs had continued to fall—in line with government's policy intentions—and offered much less stability to house-building activity than in the past. Local authority completions in Great Britain in 1990 fell well below twenty thousand, compared with over one hundred thousand in 1980. The government's intention of the early 1980s to create the environment in which the private sector could prosper had created the environment in which a collapse of private sector activity had a more severe impact on the economy.

The problems in the housing market and the homeownership sector built up throughout 1991 and came to a head at Christmas. Unprecedented levels of repossessions were affecting lending institutions and companies that provided mortgage indemnity insurance. Repossessions contributed to a loss of confidence in the market, and an abnormally low level of transactions and falling house prices made it more difficult for households with mortgage arrears to clear their debts by selling and trading down. Rising concern with these problems generated a number of mortgage rescue schemes involving local authorities and housing associations in partnership with the private sector. Requests for government to make social security payments connected with mortgage tax relief direct to lenders also indicated lenders' concern. Finally, government ministers began to express concern.

The pace of activity was stepped up in 1992 with the prime minister's desire to announce a rescue package before the Christmas parliamentary recess. Lenders were given forty-eight hours to produce a satisfactory package. The package that emerged involved the commitment of some £750 million, mainly by building societies, to enable housing associations or others to purchase repossessed properties and relet them. The government's part of the package was initially only to allow direct payment of the £750 million of income support paid for mortgage interest. This was quickly followed by the suspension of stamp duty associated with house purchase. This last act was the first time in twelve years that a tax change had been announced outside the annual March budget.

The experience of the unprecedented depression in the homeownership market between 1988 and 1992 is likely to have some longer-term consequences. Banks and building societies are likely to be more cautious in the future, and there are implications for access and costs in homeownership. Movements of house prices are likely to be scrutinized by government and the Bank of England, and signs of rapid inflation are likely to draw in action to dampen progress. Borrowers are likely to find it more difficult to borrow unless they have a larger down payment than in the past. As lending is seen to be riskier than it was, borrowers will find they bear higher costs. How significant these factors will be and how serious the loss of confidence among homeowners in general or particular sections of homeowners is impossible to judge.

CONCLUSIONS

The picture of homeownership in Britain is one of diversity and change. The diversity of the sector has grown with its expansion, and the most recent phase had added to this. Homeownership is neither uniform nor static. In 1992 the majority of households own their own houses. This and the general restructuring of tenure have involved substantial changes in the way housing is produced and consumed; in the way it is financed, exchanged, managed, and controlled; and in housing costs and patterns of wealth, inequality, and saving. These changes have occurred alongside demographic changes affecting the numbers of households of different types and alongside growing social polarization and uneven economic development. Evidence from in-depth interviews and housing histories of individuals provides different but complementary perspectives on change. Different generations of households have had different experiences of housing because of when and where they have sought housing. Family size has declined and overcrowding fallen; slum clearance, improvements, and new investment have changed amenity provision and dwelling condition; and private landlordism has declined and other tenures grown. Households' frameworks of reference and experience have changed (Forrest and Murie, 1987, 1988). The early experience of the generation of households entering homeownership at the beginning of the century is generally very different from that of new entrants to the market today. Within any age cohort, important variations in housing experience relate particularly to income, employment, and bargaining power in the housing market, but, irrespective of this and irrespective of tenure status, the experience of housing has changed. Homeownership is not what it was.

Discussions of the interests generated by homeownership refer to a set of historically specific circumstances rather than to necessary attributes of the tenure. These circumstances include consistent promotion by the state, house prices that have risen faster than the rate of inflation and resulted in better returns than yielded by other investments, and mortgage interest rates that have often been lower than inflation rates. Changes in any of these factors and the increased volatility and instability of the market affect attitudes to the tenure. Homeownership has grown most among affluent sections of the population, in an environment of full employment, and supported by an expanding welfare state. As it moves downmarket in a period of greater inequality and declining welfare provision, homeowners are likely to have a much more mixed experience, and their views and interests will be affected by this. Furthermore, homeowners in retirement may find the costs of maintenance and repair a problem, and equity release schemes change the value of their asset holding. The quality of housing that homeowners are in and the rate of accumulation involved also reflect income and wealth and status in work, and the extent to which housing tenure differences crosscut occupational class differences should be tempered by a recognition of differentiation within homeownership.

The changing nature of homeownership in Britain was highlighted by a series of events in the early 1990s that generated newspaper headlines about problems in a tenure previously regarded as a source of security and success. The responses to these events by financial institutions and government will change homeownership further. There is likely to be considerable care to prevent a repeat of the boom-slump experience of the late 1980s. This, as well as the costs of mortgage indemnity insurance and greater caution over providing loans in riskier parts of the market, are likely to have a differential impact. Access will become more difficult, and costs will become higher for some groups to a greater degree than for others. Mature, mass homeownership is increasingly differentiated and is likely to become even less uniform.

Homeownership in Britain today is a diverse and fragmented tenure deriving from and generating a diversity of experiences. The differentiation within homeownership has increased as the tenure has grown and extended to different groups of people and types of property and as the organization and financing of the tenure have changed. It is not possible to read off the differences generated by housing processes from tenure alone. And many of the differences associated with tenure are the consequences of changes in other spheres that come together to produce particular associations with housing market sectors. The implication is that it is increasingly important to identify routes into, experience of, and segments or stratification within homeownership.

Without some attempts to distinguish between parts of homeownership, analyses of housing and social change are likely to have less and less purchase. For example, as homeownership continues to grow and to change, the differences between the nature and experience of homeownership of those employed in certain sectors of the economy and of those with less bargaining power deriving from occupational income and wealth status will diverge. Differences in material circumstances and interests will be significant, and analyses in which homeownership or other tenures are treated as single and undifferentiated categories will misrepresent what homeownership is.

REFERENCES

Ball, M. 1983. *Housing Policy and Economic Power*. Methuen: Andover, Hants.
Barlow, J., and S. Duncan. 1988. "The Use and Abuse of Housing Tenure." *Housing Studies* 3:219–231.

Boddy, M. 1980. *The Building Societies*. London: Macmillan.

Craig, P. 1986. "The House That Jerry Built? Building Societies, the State, and the Politics of Owner Occupation." *Housing Studies* 1(1):87–108.

Forrest, R., and A. Murie. 1987. "The Affluent Homeowner: Labor Market Position and the Shaping of Housing Histories." *Sociological Review* 35:370–403.

———. 1988. *Selling the Welfare State*. London: Routledge.

———. 1990. "A Dissatisfied State? Consumer Preferences and Council Housing in Britain." *Urban Studies* 27(5):617–635.

Forrest, R., A. Murie, and P. Williams. 1990. *Homeownership: Fragmentation and Differentiation*. London: Unwin Hyman.

Hamnett, C., and B. Randolph. 1988. *Cities, Housing and Profits*. London: Hutchinson.

Hills, J. 1991. "From Right-to-Buy to Rent-to-Mortgage: Privatization of Council Housing since 1979." Discussion paper WSP/61. London: Centre for Economics and Related Disciplines, London School of Economics.

Holmans, A. E. 1987. *Housing Policy in Britain*. London: Croom Helm.

Merrett, S. 1982. *Owner Occupation in Britain*. Andover: Routledge and Kegan Paul.

Murie, A. 1975. *The Sale of Council Houses*. Birmingham: Centre for Urban and Regional Studies, University of Birmingham.

———. 1991. "Divisions of Homeownership: Housing Tenure and Social Change." *Environment and Planning* 23:349–370.

Saunders, P. 1990. *A Nation of Homeowners*. London: Unwin Hyman.

5

Homeownership and the Sale of Public-Sector Housing in Great Britain

NICHOLAS J. WILLIAMS

The main housing policy objective of the Thatcher government elected in 1979 was a significant expansion of homeownership. In quantitative terms, the policies adopted were an undoubted success. In 1979 there were 11.3 million owner-occupied dwellings in the United Kingdom, or about 55 percent of the total stock. By 1990, this had risen to 15.8 million dwellings, accounting for 68 percent of the stock. The most effective mechanism adopted to achieve this expansion was the sale of public sector dwellings; such sales provided over 1.5 million of the increase in owner-occupied dwellings of 4.5 million between 1979 and 1990.

An evaluation of the policy of selling council houses to tenants should not, however, consider only the number sold. There have been losers as well as gainers from the sales, and the policy has to be placed in the wider context of housing and general social and economic change. The sale of council houses was part of a broader policy of privatization that had as much to do with ideological objectives and financial requirements as with housing issues per se. Sales were also seen by the Conservative party as a vote winner that would be most effective in those areas where the Labour party was strongest—the council estates. Losers and gainers from the policy in housing terms have been determined more by accident than conscious governmental choice.

THE LEGISLATION AND THE SCALE OF PURCHASES

The sale of public sector dwellings did not begin with the Thatcher government elected in 1979. Previous governments, both Labour and Conservative, had permitted local authorities to sell dwellings to sitting tenants under certain circumstances, but only the 1970–1974 Conservative government under Edward Heath had actively encouraged sales (sales rose to peak of 45,000 in 1972). The number of sales before 1979 was therefore low, amounting to fewer than 250,000, and was always in any one year fewer than the number of public sector dwellings built to rent (Murie, 1975). The 1980 Housing Act introduced by the Thatcher government dramatically altered the situation and instigated a period of rapid change in the British housing system, of which large-scale sales of council houses was arguably the most important element. The 1979 Conservative election manifesto promised to give public sector tenants a statutory right to buy their dwelling under very favorable terms. Notwithstanding the electoral significance of the policy, the impact of the Conservative victory on the British housing system and the general housing debate was profound.

The success of the policy in terms of the number of dwellings sold can be traced to the granting of a statutory right to buy for most public sector tenants (thus removing local authorities' discretion as to whether to sell, although there is some evidence that in the early years of the right to buy (RTB), some Labour-controlled councils did slow the rate of sales; see Hoggart, 1985) and the favorable terms on which tenants could purchase. Almost all public sector tenants of three years' standing were given the right to buy their dwelling (the exceptions were largely those living in dwellings specially built or adapted for the elderly and the disabled). Furthermore, there was minimum discount of 33 percent off the market price. This discount increased by 1 percent for each year of tenancy up to a maximum of 50 percent after seventeen years. Tenants had a right to a 100 percent mortgage from the local authority (subject to financial safeguards) and could resell after five years without repaying any of the discount. The secretary of state was given draconian powers to force local authorities to sell should they refuse or use bureaucratic means to slow the rate of sales. In addition, local authorities were given the option of selling on their own terms as under the previous discretionary arrangements, subject to the secretary of state's approval.

The legislation's impact was immediate. Figure 5.1 shows the number of sales in Great Britain from 1979 to 1990. Sales rose rapidly, reaching a peak of over 220,000 in 1982. This indicates a significant amount of pent-up demand for owner occupation that was released by the 1980 legislation. It is not clear, however, how many purchasers would have bought anyway in the private sector and how many were tempted into owner occupation by the attractive terms.

Sales fell after 1982, and the government introduced further legislation to boost purchases. The Housing and Building Control Act 1984 tightened up the 1980 Act right-to-buy (RTB) provisions. Most significant, the residency qualification for purchase was reduced from three to two years, with a minimum discount of 32 percent and the maximum discount increased from 50 to 60 percent. There were also extensions of the RTB to tenants of leasehold properties, tenants of county councils as well as district councils, and more tenants of properties built for the disabled. It is estimated that these changes increased the number of eligible tenants by over 250,000 (see Forrest and Murie, 1988). The Housing and Planning Act 1986 was not primarily concerned with the RTB but rather with a more general privatization of public sector housing, permitting sales of blocks of dwellings to private developers for onward sale to owner-occupiers and also the transfer of dwellings to private landlords. These measures contributed to the expansion of owner occupation and the decline of the public rented sector, but not on the scale of sales to sitting tenants. (Glendinning, Allen, and Young, 1989; Hills, 1991; Usher, 1987, 1988.) The act did, however, make it more attractive for tenants of apartments to buy. The overwhelming majority of the dwellings sold up to 1986 had been houses rather than apartments, and in order to boost the sales of the latter, the minimum discount for apartments was increased to 44 percent, the discount increasing thereafter by 2 percent per annum up to a maximum of 70 percent after 15 years.

Figure 5.1 indicates that total sales fell to a minimum of 104,000 in 1986 and then rose strongly up to 1989. Sales of apartments increased significantly but still made up less than 25 percent of all sales (table 5.1); the rising number of sales can be attributed more to the provisions of the 1984 act and other factors than to the 1986 legislation making the purchase of apartments more attractive. Sales fell sharply in 1990 to 135,000, mainly as a result of recession in the British economy and high interest rates (mortgage interest payments are subsidized in Britain, but those who had stretched their resources to become owner-occupiers were hit hard by sustained high interest rates, repayments that were possible at 10 percent became impossible at 12 percent). Total sales between 1979 and 1990 were over 1.5 million, or almost 20 percent of the total public sector stock in 1980. This significantly changed the balance of tenures. Public renting fell from 30 percent to less than 24 percent, and owner occupation rose to 68 percent.

THE PATTERN OF SALES

Sales to sitting public sector tenants thus made a significant quantitative impact on the growth of owner occupation in Britain. The pattern of sales is as significant as their total number, however, particularly with respect to the type of dwellings sold, their geographical location at the regional and local scales, and the type of tenant who purchased. The pattern of sales has not been random, and this has had important effects on the housing system in general and the public rented sector in particular.

Moreover, the gainers and losers from sales form distinct groups, and an important question arises as to whether sales have contributed overall to an increase in housing welfare and a more efficient housing system. Most tenants who have bought have benefitted considerably; households that have no

Figure 5.1
Sales of Public Sector Dwellings in Great Britain

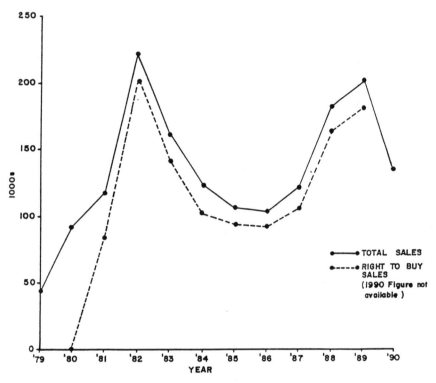

Source : Housing and Construction Statistics 1979 - 90. London : HMSO

choice but to rent, however, have found their housing opportunities considerably reduced. Sales alone have not had these results. Other factors, such as the level of construction of rented accommodation, rent levels, and general trends in the housing market, must also be considered. Before discussing the consequences of sales, however, the evidence relating to the pattern of sales will be presented.

Large-scale construction of council houses in Britain began in 1919 and has continued at varying rates up to the present, although at historically low levels since 1979. The level of subsidy has varied over time, as has the type of dwelling constructed. The 1960s, for instance, were dominated by the building of high-rise apartment blocks. Public sector housing thus varies considerably in terms of dwelling type and quality and also in terms of the general residential environment. Generally, semidetached and terraced single-family properties are more popular than apartments, and some estates are more popular and have markedly different socioeconomic profiles.

The physical quality of the dwellings and the environment tends to be

Table 5.1
Sales of Public Sector Dwellings, 1986–1990

ENGLAND					
YEAR	HOUSES		APARTMENTS		TOTAL
	NUMBER	PERCENT	NUMBER	PERCENT	
1986	77,872	90.1	7,738	9.9	85,610
1987	86,202	88.8	10,868	11.2	97,070
1988	117,987	82.8	24,550	17.2	142,537
1989	119,766	80.2	29,582	19.8	149,348
1990	71,985	75.0	24,016	25.0	96,001
WALES					
YEAR	HOUSES		APARTMENTS		TOTAL
	NUMBER	PERCENT	NUMBER	PERCENT	
1986	5,406	97.7	127	2.3	5,533
1987	5,587	97.7	133	2.3	5,720
1988	9,111	94.4	539	5.6	9,650
1989	11,792	92.1	1,013	7.9	12,805
1990	5,652	88.0	773	12.0	6,425
Source: Housing and Construction Statistics 1987-1990 Department of Environment, London: HMSO					

correlated with the characteristics of the tenants, with the poorer and socially disadvantaged tenants living in the worst housing on the worst estates (Gray, 1976; Taylor, 1979; Twine and Williams, 1983). Although not all apartments are unpopular with tenants and not all single-family dwellings are built of good quality on popular estates, the division between houses and apartments is a useful shorthand for the quality and desirability of public sector housing.

The pattern of sales reflects this, with the majority of sales to sitting tenants being of houses. Apartments have been purchased significantly less than expected given their share of the public sector stock as a whole. Foulis (1985) reveals that over the period 1979 to 1983, almost 87 percent of sales of sitting tenants in Scotland were of houses rather than apartments, although the latter constituted 50 percent of the stock. It was noted that the 1986 Housing and Planning Act aimed to increase the numbers of apartments sold by making the terms of purchase more attractive.

Table 5.1 shows sales in England and Wales for 1986 to 1990 split into houses and apartments. Sales of apartments as a proportion of all sales did indeed increase after 1986 (although less so in Wales), but the vast majority were still single-family dwellings. One long-term consequence of sales will therefore be to change the composition of the remaining stock, with the proportion of apartments increasing and the proportion of single-family dwellings decreasing. In the absence of new building to replace those dwellings sold, prospective tenants will face a restricted choice and less chance of obtaining one of the more popular single-family properties.

More detailed analyses at local levels (Forrest and Murie 1984a, 1984b; Sewel, Twine, and Williams, 1984) have confirmed that sales have been disproportionately in the more popular estates, and that on the estates with poor-quality dwellings and concentrations of deprived tenants, sales have been virtually nil. The picture is emerging of a public sector that is being denuded of its best-quality and most popular stock and that is becoming spatially segregated within urban areas. It has also been observed that sales have been higher as a percentage of stock in rural than in urban areas (Forrest and Murie, 1984b; Foulis, 1985; Williams and Sewel, 1987) and that there have been significant regional variations within the United Kingdom (Dunn, Forrest, and Murie 1987).

The pattern of sales among tenants has also been nonrandom. It might be expected that more affluent tenants would show a greater propensity to purchase than those on low incomes, even given the low discounted price of many dwellings. Furthermore, since the discount increases with length of tenancy, younger tenants might be expected to show a lesser propensity to buy.

Table 5.2 summarizes the findings of a nationwide survey in England conducted in 1985–1986 and reported by Kerr (1988). The data clearly show that purchasers have higher average incomes and are more likely to be in professional, managerial, or skilled manual occupations than nonpurchasing tenants. They are also more likely to be in the 35 to 54 age group and to be in large adult households with no dependent children. Purchasers are underrepresented among the young and elderly age groups. Kerr also found that over 70 percent of purchasing tenants were in full-time employment, as against less than 30 percent of nonpurchasing tenants.

There have now been several studies, both local and national, of the characteristics of sitting tenant purchasers and nonpurchasers, and they are in agreement with Kerr's findings (Forrest and Murie, 1984b; Foulis, 1985; Lynn 1991; Williams, Sewel, and Twine, 1988). The public sector is thus not only losing properties selectively through sales but also tenants. Households that remain tenants are increasingly the old, the young, the unemployed, single parents, and those in low-paid employment. Moreover, there is a correlation between the characteristics of the housing and the tenants. This means that the public sector is losing those estates with the highest-

Table 5.2
Characteristics of Purchasers and Nonpurchasers of Council Dwellings, England

Characteristic	Non-purchasers	Purchasers
AGE - HOUSEHOLD HEAD		
16-24	6	0
25-34	15	11
35-44	13	26
45-54	12	27
55-64	21	23
65+	32	12
HOUSEHOLD TYPE		
One adult	27	5
Small family	48	43
Large family	10	12
Large adult	15	40
GROSS HOUSEHOLD WEEKLY INCOME		
Under 100	69	20
100-149	15	18
150-199	8	24
200+	7	39
SOCIO-ECONOMIC GROUP		
Prof./Managerial	5	11
Other white collar	15	11
Skilled manual	43	55
Semi-skilled	25	18
Unskilled	8	3
Source: Kerr (1988)		

quality dwellings and the most affluent tenants; what remains is increasingly poor quality, unpopular, and dominated in numerical terms by the most disadvantaged groups in society. There is also a tendency for ethnic minorities to become concentrated in the poorer estates, although this has not occurred to the same extent as in the United States (Henderson and Karn, 1984; Robinson, 1980).

THE CONSEQUENCES OF SALES

The consequences of public sector sales cannot be considered in isolation from profound changes in the entire housing system since 1979. Council house sales are only a part, although an important part, of the process. The pervasive element of government policy since 1979, at least rhetorically, has been to drive back the frontiers of the state and allow markets more scope in the allocation of resources. In housing, this has meant an attempt to move from collectivized to individualistic forms of provision and consumption (although levels of subsidy may actually increase as a consequence because of the generous tax breaks allowed to owner-occupiers; see Forrest and Murie, 1986).

The sale of public sector housing, to both tenants and developers, is part of this shift, with the objective of increasing levels of owner occupation. There have also been attempts to shift the provision and management of rented housing from the public to the private and quasi-private sectors. Local authorities have effectively been prevented from building new properties to rent through financial controls exercised by central government. The government has been explicit about its view that local authorities should not be providers or managers of rented housing. It is against this background that the effects of the sale of council dwellings must be evaluated.

The loss of properties and tenants from the public sector through sales has been selective. This would have little significance if the properties sold were being replaced, but levels of new public sector construction have been low since 1979, and since 1980 sales have exceeded new dwellings completed. In consequence, the public sector has been decreasing in size, as well as declining in quality and containing an increasing proportion of disadvantaged households. This has led to the thesis that the public sector is becoming "residualized" as a low-quality safety net for the poorest members of society along the lines of public housing in the United States.

Residualization is a complex concept that has generated considerable debate (Clapham and Maclennan, 1983; Forrest and Murie, 1983, 1990a; Malpas, 1983; Williams, Sewel, and Twine, 1986a). We can say, however, with some degree of certainty, that the housing opportunities of those households who need, or prefer, to rent have been reduced because the private and quasi-private sector (the latter being the housing associations) have not been able to provide new property to rent on the scale required, or indeed achieved by local authorities in the past. The size and quality of the rented stock has decreased significantly since 1979, and the sale of council houses has played a part in this process.

Moreover, this process of tenurial polarization whereby the poorest households are being concentrated in rented accommodation is also increasing spatial polarization of different social groups, since the lowest-quality and least popular public rented stock, where sales are least or nil, tends to be physically isolated. Sociospatial segregation in British cities is thus increasing, with an increasing ghettoization of the poorest groups in a shrinking public sector (Forrest and Murie, 1990a; Sewel, Twine, and Williams, 1984; Williams, Sewel, and Twine, 1986a). The exact extent to which this has occurred on a national scale will be revealed by analysis of the 1991 census.

Moreover, the sale of council houses has contributed greatly to the expansion of ownership. Many purchasers may have bought in the private sector had the opportunity to buy their council house not arisen, but many would not, given that the discount enabled them to purchase a property the equivalent of which in the private sector may have been unaffordable. The sale of council houses has thus been highly effective in spreading homeownership down the income scale. Moreover, over 85 percent of sitting tenant purchasers are over 35 years old and probably would have remained as tenants if the opportunity to buy their dwelling had not arisen. Most are first-time buyers who are on the whole older than first-time buyers in the private sector (Kerr, 1988) and have been tempted into owner occupation by the very attractive terms offered. In addition, local authority rents have risen steeply since 1979 as part of the government's strategy to shift housing subsidies from buildings to individuals, and this has increased the relative attractiveness of buying. Ironically, the shift of tenants from public renting to owner occupation through the right to buy may have the net effect of increasing subsidies because of the generous tax breaks for owner-occupiers and the withdrawal of subsidies from the public rented sector.

RESALES OF THE DWELLINGS BOUGHT BY TENANTS

A longer-term consequence of sales is that the available private sector stock will be augmented when the purchasing tenants die or resell. This raises the general question of what role these dwellings play in the housing market and the more particular question of whether they will continue to offer a low-cost route into homeownership and expand the limits of owner occupation. Evidence is now available from England relating to voluntary sales in the 1960s (Forrest and Murie, 1990b) and from Scotland relating to the period since 1980 and the right to buy legislation (Williams and Twine, 1991).

Although the dwellings bought by tenants are generally good quality and on the more desirable estates, the fact that they are on predominantly publicly owned rented estates is likely to make their market price lower than dwellings of equivalent size and quality in the private sector. They may thus continue to offer a lower-cost route into owner occupation and also widen the choice for current owners who may desire a larger dwelling but cannot afford to buy in the mainstream private sector.

The evidence from the studies by Forrest and Murie and by Williams and Twine confirms this. Table 5.3 shows the responses of a sample of households who had bought public sector dwellings on resale from sitting tenant purchasers to questions about their route into owner occupation. The data are taken from the Scottish study by Twine and Williams. About a quarter of the sample said that buying the resold dwelling was their only route into owner occupation, and 64 percent said they could have bought in the mainstream private sector. Furthermore, almost 75 percent said they would be living in mainstream owner-occupied property if they had not bought the resold dwelling. These figures suggest that the resold dwellings are enabling about a quarter of the purchasers to gain access to owner occupation that they would otherwise not have and are widening choice within owner occupation for the remainder. The dwellings thus continue to offer a low-cost route to owner occupation at resale, but this role is considerably diminished compared to the sale to the sitting tenant purchaser with a generous discount off the market price. After resale, the dwellings have a more significant role in widening choice within the market.

The evidence also indicates that the new buyers of resold properties are younger than the households from whom they have bought but not different socioeconomically (table 5.4). Comparison of tables 5.2 and 5.4, however, does indicate that they are different from nonpurchasing tenants, being more likely to be in nonmanual or skilled manual occupations. This has important implications for neighborhood change in the long term, when allied with the trends toward residualization of the public sector stock. The better-quality and more popular estates, as more and more dwellings are bought by sitting tenants and subsequently resold, will become inaccessible to households preferring or needing to rent. These latter are generally the poorest households and over time will be concentrated to an increasing degree in a physically isolated and poor-quality rented sector. The better-quality estates, as they are gradually transferred by tenant purchase into the private sector, will become increasingly occupied by young, skilled, manual and nonmanual households. Dwellings originally built to provide good-quality housing for needy households will over time serve a totally different function and will be allocated to more affluent households under the influence of market forces.

The evidence from Scotland, and England, shows that the sitting tenant purchasers who resell make considerable capital gains on the resale of their dwelling. Table 5.5 shows the data for Scotland. Over the period 1980 to

Table 5.3
Alternatives to Resale Purchase

If you had not bought this dwelling, was there an alternative route to owner occupation for you?		
	n	%
Yes - Right to Buy	42	9.3
Yes - Mainstream owner occupation	290	64.0
No	105	23.5
Don't know	16	3.5
If you had not bought this dwelling, what sort of home do you think you would be living in now ?		
Owner occupied		
Purchased other ex-public sector	63	13.9
Purchased mainstream private	334	73.7
Renting		
Public	37	8.2
Private	3	0.7
Living with family/friends	10	2.2
Don't know	6	1.3
Source: Williams and Twine 1991		

1989, the average capital gain made was over £17,000. Some of this leaked from the housing system as equity withdrawal, but most was reinvested in housing as households traded up by moving to a bigger dwelling in the private sector. Those tenants lucky enough to have been allocated one of the better dwellings in the public rented sector were thus given a further advantage in the housing system when they resold their dwelling. The discount they received on purchase of their rented dwelling contributed significantly to their capital gain on resale, which in turn enabled them to escape from areas of predominantly public rented accommodation and purchase a higher-value property. Indeed, for most such households, purchase of their current property would have been impossible without the boost of the capital gain made on their formerly rented dwelling.

Table 5.4
Characteristics of Original and New Purchasers of Public Sector Dwellings,
Scotland

Characteristic	Sitting tenant purchasers who have resold	Purchasers of resold dwellings
AGE OF HOUSEHOLD HEAD		
18-25	0	10
25-34	9	49
35-44	56	28
45-54	24	6
55-64	9	6
65+	2	0
HOUSEHOLD TYPE		
One adult	4	4
Small family	53	72
Large family	10	13
Large adult	33	10
SOCIO-ECONOMIC GROUP		
Professional/ managerial	22	16
Other white collar	19	27
Skilled manual	44	43
Semi-skilled manual	13	11
Unskilled manual	2	1
Note: all data relate to date of resale Source: Williams and Twine 1991		

Table 5.5
Financial Experience of Sitting Tenant Purchasers Who Resold, Scotland

(1) Purchase price of rented dwelling	11,185
(2) Resale price of rented dwelling	28,321
(3) Purchase price of next property	40,498
(4) Capital gain (2)-(1)	17,006
(5) Deposit paid on next property	12,740
(6) Equity withdrawal (4)-(5)	4,571
Source: Williams and Twine 1991	

FUTURE SALES PROSPECTS

The sharp downturn in sales to sitting tenants in 1990 has been noted; most of this can be attributed to the recession in the British economy and the slack state of the housing market in general. Irrespective of the housing market, the government in the past has taken action to boost sales when they have declined, and the current period is no exception. The most important factors in deterring tenants from purchase have been shown to be income and dissatisfaction with their current dwelling (Kerr, 1988; Lynn, 1991). Both of these factors have been addressed by the government in the form of new programs to facilitate movement of tenants into owner occupation as part of more general policy to extend owner occupation down the income scale.

For tenants with incomes too low to afford mortgage repayments even under the generous discount terms of the RTB, the rent-to-mortgage scheme has been introduced in Scotland and in selected areas in England on a pilot basis. Under this scheme, tenants buy only part of the equity of the property and pay rent on the remainder. They may increase their equity share if their financial situation improves. The response has been small, since the program is not open to tenants claiming housing benefit (that is, the poorest tenants), and those who can afford to buy under the RTB scheme will do so since more generous discounts are available. Only tenants whose income falls between these two groups will consider rent to mortgage as a rational alternative to renting. As far as tenants living in dwellings they do not like are concerned, there may be more scope for encouraging them into owner occupation since they will not all suffer from income constraints. Local authorities, and indeed housing associations, can now offer tenants "portable" discounts. That is, if they wish to buy a dwelling other than their current rented dwelling, they can take the discount with them to offset the price of the property they do wish to buy. It is too early to state whether this will be effective.

On a longer-term basis, the scope for further sales to sitting tenants must be considered limited. Over 60 percent of public sector tenants in Britain claim housing benefit—that is, their income is insufficient to pay the subsidized rent. They thus have little potential for homeownership. Furthermore, the RTB may ironically be destroying scope for future sales by its very success in the period from 1980 to 1991. It is the best dwellings and the more affluent tenants who are disappearing from the public sector. In the absence of a public sector construction program, the number of potential sales is thus diminishing rapidly. The very success of the RTB in expanding homeownership down the income scale has been possible only because for a large part of this century Britain has had a vigorous public sector building policy, providing high-quality dwellings at subsidized rents. The RTB under present circumstances can thus be considered as a boost to owner occupation that will not be repeated. Further expansion of homeownership will have to look to different mechanisms.

CONCLUSIONS

Sales of public sector dwellings have had a profound influence on the British housing system. They have been the primary policy instrument in the significant expansion of homeownership that has occurred since 1979 and have been particularly effective in extending owner occupation down the income scale. Purchasing tenants have undoubtedly benefited from being allowed to buy good-quality dwellings at discounted prices, and those who have subsequently resold on the open market have made significant capital gains.

There have also been losers, however, and a balanced assessment of the policy must take these into account. The most obvious losers have been those households that for reasons of low income cannot attain homeownership and for which public sector renting is the only realistic avenue into acceptable housing. They have seen their housing choice dramatically reduced as the public sector has shrunk in size and deteriorated in quality. Moreover, since it is the wealthier tenants who have purchased, the sales have been highly regressive in terms of the redistribution of housing chances and conditions. To a large extent, this redistribution between households has been random and unintended.

It is true that the sale of public sector dwellings in itself has not been the cause of this redistribution of housing opportunities. If there had been a continuing program of public sector building or the government's attempts to expand housing association and private sector building for rent had been a success, thus replacing those dwellings sold, then sales would not have had an adverse effect on the housing chances of those needing to rent.

Moreover, as Murie (1989) has pointed out, local authorities were not allowed by the government to reinvest the proceeds of the sale of their dwellings into housing but instead were forced to use a proportion to write off debt. The remainder was retained by the treasury and used by the government to finance cuts in taxation. Sales in themselves therefore cannot be considered good or bad. The context within which sales occur is all important, and the period from 1979 to 1990 was one in which sales contributed to a deterioration in the housing opportunities of the poorest households.

The popularity of sales has tempted some commentators to conclude that deeply held preferences for owner occupation and aversion to public sector renting have been revealed by the RTB (Saunders 1990; Saunders and, Harris 1987). This argument overemphasizes the importance of tenure, and as Forrest and Murie (1990c) point out, ignores the highly favorable terms on offer to sitting tenants. Moreover, it is only because the public sector had provided dwellings that tenants wished to buy that purchase was chosen. The general conclusion that can be drawn from the experience of public sector sales since 1979 is that, once again, British housing policy has failed to integrate policies across the different housing sectors and has failed to address fundamental issues. Subsidies are unrelated to income and, in the case of owner occupation, inflationary. Moreover, households' true preferences between renting and owning are obscured because of the unequal subsidy treatment of the tenures. Sales to sitting tenants are not inherently good or bad, but over the period 1979 to 1990, they had negative consequences. They represented an additional subsidy to a selected group of homeowning households and further distorted the housing market by increasing the advantages of owning over renting. Within a broader and integrated package of policies designed to tackle the fundamental problems of the British housing system, it is conceivable that the sale of public sector dwellings to sitting tenants could play a valuable and rational role. The experience of the 1980s has, unfortunately, been different.

REFERENCES

Clapham, David, and Duncan Maclennan. 1983. "Residualisation of public housing: A non-issue." *Housing Review* 32:9–10.

Dunn, Richard, Ray Forrest, and Alan Murie. 1987. "The geography of council house sales in England." *Urban Studies* 24:47–59.

Forrest, Ray, and Alan Murie. 1983. "Residualization and council housing: Aspects of the changing social relations of housing tenure." *Journal of Social Policy* 12:453–468.

———. 1984a. "Right to Buy? Issues of Need, Equity and Polarisation in the Sale of Council Houses." Working Paper 39. Bristol: School for Advanced Urban Studies, University of Bristol.

———. 1984b. "Monitoring the Right to Buy 1980–1982." Working Paper 40. Bristol: School for Advanced Urban Studies, University of Bristol.

————. 1986. "Marginalisation and subsidised individualism." *International Journal of Urban and Regional Research* 10:46–65.

————. 1988. *Selling the Welfare State: The Privatisation of Public Housing*. London: Routledge.

————. 1990a. "Residualisation and Council Housing: A Statistical Update." Working Paper 91. Bristol: School for Advanced Urban Studies, University of Bristol.

————. 1990b. *Moving the Housing Market*. Aldershot: Avebury.

————. 1990c. "A dissatisfied state? Consumer preferences and council housing in Britain." *Urban Studies* 27:617–635.

Foulis, Michael B. 1985. *Council House Sales in Scotland*. Edinburgh: HMSO.

Glendinning, Richard, Patrick Allen, and Helen Young. 1989. *The Sale of Local Authority Housing to the Private Sector*. London: HMSO.

Gray, Fred. 1976. "Selection and allocation in council housing." *Transactions*, Institute of British Geographers 1:34–46.

Henderson, John, and Valerie Karn. 1984. "Race, class and the allocation of public housing in Britain." *Urban Studies* 21:115–128.

Hills, John. 1991. "From Right-to-Buy to Rent-to-Mortgage: Privatisation of Council Housing Since 1979." Discussion Paper WSP/61. London: Centre for Economics and Related Disciplines, London School of Economics.

Hoggart, Keith. 1985. "Political party control and the sale of local authority dwellings 1974–1983." *Environment and Planning* C3:463–474.

Kerr, Marion. 1988. *The Right to Buy: A National Survey of Tenants and Buyers of Council Houses*. London: HMSO.

Lynn, Peter. 1991. *The Right to Buy: A National Follow-up Survey of Tenants of Council Homes in England*. London: HMSO.

Malpas, Peter. 1983. "Residualisation and the restructuring of housing tenure." *Housing Review* 32:44–45.

Murie, Alan. 1975. "The Sale of Council Houses." Occasional Paper 35. Birmingham: Centre for Urban and Regional Studies, University of Birmingham.

————. 1989. "Lost Opportunities? Council House Sales and Housing Policy in Britain 1979–1989." Working Paper 80. Bristol: School for Advanced Urban Studies, University of Bristol.

Robinson, V. 1980. "Asians and council housing." *Urban Studies* 17:323–331.

Saunders, Peter. 1990. *A Nation of Home Owners*. London: Unwin Hyman.

Saunders, Peter, and Chris Harris. 1987. "Biting the nipple? Consumers, preferences and state welfare." Paper presented at Sixth Urban Change and Conflict Conference, University of Kent September 20–23.

Sewel, John B., Fred E. Twine, and Nicholas J. Williams. 1984. "The sale of council houses—some empirical evidence." *Urban Studies* 21:439–450.

Taylor, Peter. 1979. "Difficult to let estates." *Environment and Planning* 11:1305–1320.

Twine, Fred E., and Nicholas J. Williams. 1983. "Social segregation in public sector housing." *Transactions*, Institute of British Geographers 8:253–266.

Usher, David. 1987. "Housing Privatisation: The Sale of Council Estates." Working Paper 67. Bristol: School for Advanced Urban Studies, University of Bristol.

————. 1988. "Council Estate Sales: Studies of Local Experiences and Future Prospects." Working Paper 74. Bristol: School for Advanced Urban Studies, University of Bristol.

Williams, Nicholas J., and John B. Sewel. 1987. "Council House Sales in the Rural Environment." In Brian MacGregor and Mark Shucksmith, *Rural Housing in Scotland*. Aberdeen: Aberdeen University Press.

Williams, Nicholas J., John B. Sewel, and Fred E. Twine. 1986a. "Council house sales and residualisation." *Journal of Social Policy* 15:273–292.

———. 1986b. "Council house allocation and tenant incomes." *Area* 18:131–140.

———. 1988. "Council house sales: An analysis of the factors associated with purchase and the implications for the future of public sector housing." *Tijdschrift voor Economische en Sociale Geografie* 24:47–59.

Williams, Nicholas J., and Fred E. Twine. 1991. "Access, Choice and the Role of Public Sector Resales in the Housing Market. "Scottish Homes Research Report No. 18. Edinburgh.

6

Converting Multifamily Housing to Cooperatives: A Tale of Two Cities

WILLIAM M. ROHE AND MICHAEL A. STEGMAN

Interest in homeownership opportunities for low-income people has grown in recent years, with both the Reagan and Bush administrations pushing for the expansion of homeownership for public housing tenants (Rohe and Stegman, 1992a). According to Jack Kemp (1991), the main architect of these initiatives as secretary of housing and urban development, "Homeownership is the classic American pathway out of poverty. Mr. Lincoln's Homestead Act of 1862, which gave poor people 160 acres of government land, free and clear, if they agreed to live on it and improve it, is the most successful antipoverty program in American history. Now, through HOPE—Homeownership and Opportunity for People Everywhere—President Bush and I have begun to unleash the power of homesteading in our inner cities."

Although many approaches to providing homeownership to public housing tenants and other low-income people exist, the Reagan and Bush administrations emphasized the sale of existing public housing units. Bush's HOPE 1 initiative, for example, provides planning and implementation grants to public housing authorities (PHAs) interested in transferring public housing to existing tenants and other low-income households. For fiscal year (FY) 1992, $161 million was authorized. The FY 1993 budget of the Department of Housing and Urban Development (HUD) calls for HOPE 1 to be funded at $450 million.

HISTORY OF PUBLIC HOUSING HOMEOWNERSHIP PROGRAMS

Experience in transferring public housing units to tenants is limited in the United States. Privatization of public housing dates back to 1974 when

Congress added Section 5(h) to the Housing Act. This gave HUD authority to approve the sale of public housing units to tenants (not whole projects to resident organizations, as HOPE 1 permits) at prices determined by the local PHA, while the federal government continued to pay all outstanding debt on the units. Formal regulations governing sales under Section 5(h), however, were not developed until late 1991. Until then, HUD approved or denied requests on a case-by-case basis. From 1974 to 1984, only 540 units were sold to tenants, almost all of them scattered-site, single-family units (Koch, 1985).

In 1984, the Reagan administration proposed the Public Housing Home-ownership Demonstration (PHHD) to expand sales. Congress approved the PHHD but limited the number of units sold to two thousand. HUD then invited PHAs to submit proposals. They were given considerable flexibility in program design, including selecting which units to sell, how to price them, and the terms of the sales. HUD did, however, specify four criteria for all demonstration programs: (1) all properties had to be in good condition prior to sale, (2) there could be no involuntary displacement of sitting tenants, (3) prepurchase counseling had to be provided, and (4) there had to be a means of guarding against windfall profits for at least five years after the units were transferred U.S. (HUD, 1984).

HUD received thirty-six applications and selected seventeen to partici-pate. Together they proposed selling 1,315 units to tenants. Of the seventeen demonstration programs, twelve proposed the fee-simple sale of units. These PHAs wanted to sell their single-family units, which typically made up a very small proportion of their units, since they were expensive to maintain. An additional PHA proposed the sale of a multifamily development originally built for homeownership under the Turnkey III program as condominiums (Rohe and Stegman, 1992b). The remaining four PHAs (in Denver; Nashville, Tennessee; Paterson, New Jersey; and St. Thomas, Virgin Islands) proposed selling multifamily units, originally built as rental public housing, to tenant cooperatives.

Four years after the demonstration began, only 320 units had been trans-ferred. The reasons for this poor performance were a lack of sustained com-mitment by the sponsoring PHAs, difficulty in finding tenants who had both the means and the desire to buy their units, and problems with relocating tenants who did not want to participate (Rohe and Stegman, 1992b).

Impatient with the small number of sales under the PHHD, Jack Kemp in 1986 introduced a bill, patterned after the British council housing sales program, that would give public housing tenants the right to buy their units. (Kemp was a congressman in 1986.) The purchase price of the units was to be set at 25 percent of market value, and the local PHAs would be required to provide financing at an interest rate 30 percent below prevailing conven-tional rates. This bill, however, was defeated in Congress.

The following year, several congressional Democrats proposed an additional sales program that was adopted as Section 21 of the U.S. Housing Act. It authorized HUD to approve the transfer of entire developments to qualified resident management corporations (RMCs), which could then sell individual units to the tenants. The RMCs had to be approved by existing resident organizations or by a majority of the residents, have elected boards of directors, and have voting members who were residents of the project. They were also required to have there years of successful management experience before they could assume title to the units.

Unlike Section 5(h), the Section 21 program required that each unit sold be replaced, to ensure that the program would not result in a net loss in the supply of low-rent public housing. The definition of replacement housing included the development of a new unit, the rehabilitation of a vacant unit, or the acquisition of a privately owned unit. Some have argued that this replacement created a barrier to privatization by substantially raising program costs (Colwell and Mahue, 1991).

The act also imposed resale restrictions on the RMCs and the tenant purchasers. The RMC can sell units only back to the PHA or to tenants. Tenants can sell their units only to the RMC, the PHA, or another low-income family. Moreover, the amount the family receives upon resale is limited to its equity contribution, plus the value of any improvements and a portion of the unit's appreciated value equal to its equity contribution. The first Section 21 sale occurred in September 1990 when 132 units of the 464-unit Kenilworth-Parkside development in Washington, D.C., were sold to the RMC for one dollar. The number of future sales under this act is uncertain since it has been replaced by the HOPE program.

The most recent public housing privatization effort, HOPE 1, emerged as one of the main provisions of the National Affordable Housing Act of 1990. Unlike Section 21, HOPE 1 does not require properties to be transferred to a RMC with three years of successful management experience. Rather, it allows PHAs flexibility in methods of transferring units to tenants. Possibly the most significant aspect of HOPE 1 is the provision of funds both to plan and carry out a public housing sales program. The act authorizes planning grants of up to $200,000 and implementation grants of unspecified amounts to cover the costs of counseling and training, relocation expenses, property rehabilitation, administration, and economic development activities designed to increase the incomes of tenant purchasers. It also requires a 25 percent matching contribution from the sponsoring local authorities, although this can be met with cash contribution, administrative expenses, tax forgiveness, or infrastructure improvements.

HOPE requires one-for-one replacement, as in the Section 21 program. The major difference is that HOPE 1 allows five-year housing vouchers to be counted as replacement units. HOPE 1 also requires that in sales of multifamily housing, at least 50 percent of the units must be transferred. The idea behind this stipulation is that no cooperative or condominium can be viable without participation by a majority of residents.

HOPE 1 has less strict recapture provisions than did Section 21. If properties are sold within six years of purchase, the sellers are paid their contribution of equity, the value of any improvements, and a share of the appreciated value proportionate to equity contributed. On properties sold between six and twenty years, recapture is limited to the original discount from market value. The act does not require buyers to sell their units back to the PHA or RMC but gives participating PHAs the option of including resale restrictions in their sale agreements. The act authorizes up to $448 million for HOPE 1. Over Bush administration protests, however, Congress appropriated only $161 million for the program during fiscal year 1992.

CAN PUBLIC HOUSING BE SUCCESSFULLY CONVERTED TO COOPERATIVES?

In spite of limited experience, there are strong opinions on the desirability and feasibility of converting multifamily public housing to cooperatives. Proponents suggest that they offer less expensive and more secure housing (Zimmer, 1977). Cooperatives are also seen as a means of instilling community pride, a sense of empowerment, and greater satisfaction among the residents (Birchall, 1988; Franklin, 1981; Peterman and Young, 1991). According to Franklin (1981), "Many feel that the most important aspect of the cooperative concept is the high level of democracy and community spirit that develops; members take pride in their property and join together to make needed repairs and protect their buildings." Cooperators also have the same tax advantages as fee-simple owners and, depending on the cooperatives' bylaws, may accrue some equity.

Others, however, question the financial feasibility of cooperatives composed entirely of low-income, former public housing residents. According to Kunze (1981), "Just as public housing was never designed to serve the very low-income, public housing cooperatives are even less likely [to do so]." Incomes of tenants may be too low to cover costs, even if units are transferred to the cooperative at greatly discounted prices. Moreover, Peterman and Young (1991) have questioned the interest of public housing residents in cooperative ownership. They argue that "low-income households were often less interested in empowerment than in obtaining adequate shelter and therefore frequently showed little enthusiasm for the extra work and the risks associated with being a co-op member."

A STUDY OF TWO PUBLIC HOUSING COOPERATIVES

Given these different opinions and the likely expansion of public housing homeownership programs under HOPE 1, it is important to learn from the limited experience we do have in selling public housing to the tenants. This chapter analyzes two projects involving conversion of multifamily public housing to cooperatives: the New Edition Cooperative in Nashville, Tennessee, and the Upper Lawrence Cooperative in Denver, Colorado. Both were created under the PHHD. They were chosen for several reasons. First, they were the only two ownership cooperatives to take title to properties during the four-year PHHD. The conversion programs in both Paterson and the Virgin Islands stalled because of conflicts over the relocation of nonparticipating households and other problems (Rohe and Stegman, 1990). Denver did create a second cooperative during the demonstration period, but it was a rental and as such not a true homeownership program. Second, the Nashville cooperative has been relatively successful, while the Denver cooperative has been markedly less so. A comparison of these two experiences should help identify factors leading to successful public housing homeownership programs.

The description and evaluation of the two cooperatives is based on data collected through several methods. First, two visits were conducted at each of the sites: one in 1987, before transfer, and one in 1989, after the units had been transferred. During each visit, we conducted interviews with local program directors and their staffs, PHA board members and/or tenant council representatives, consultants providing technical assistance, and members of the interim or fully operational cooperative boards. Second, key documents were collected, such as initial applications, correspondence, progress reports, program publicity, contracts with technical assistance providers, and minutes of meetings.

Third, home interviews were conducted with cooperators and with relocatees in the summer of 1989. These focused on the cooperators' demographic characteristics; satisfaction with the unit, the neighborhood, and the performance of the cooperative board; cooperative fee payment experience; and the perceived impacts of becoming a cooperative member. Finally, we conducted periodic telephone interviews with key PHA staff members, management agents, and cooperative board members. The most recent interviews were conducted in February 1992. (Program characteristics are summarized in table 6.1.)

THE DENVER AND NASHVILLE CONVERSION PROGRAMS

Upper Lawrence Cooperative, Denver

The Curtis Park project in Denver was one of the most physically and socially distressed developments owned by the Denver Housing Authority (DHA). Built in 1954, it contained 448 units covering seven square blocks. Each block contained ten to twelve buildings, each containing five to eight

Table 6.1
Characteristics of Conversion Programs

PROGRAM CHARACTERISTICS	UPPER LAWRENCE DENVER	NEW EDITION NASHVILLE
Number of Units Transferred	44	85
Type of Units Transferred	Town house	Apartment, Duplex, Triplex
Number of sites	1	3
Rehabilitation needed	Extensive	None to moderate
Selection of cooperators	From other public housing and off waiting lists.	Tenants of units selected for sale and other public housing tenants.
Basis for sale price	Cost of rehabilitation	Cost of rehabilitation
Provisions for non-participants	All sitting tenants relocated	Offered Section 8 certificates to move or to rent from coop
Financing	State Division of Housing and HFA; DHA and the National Cooperative Bank	National Cooperative Bank and MDHA
Provisions for maintenance after sale	Maintenance fund established and warranty offered on plumbing and sewer lines.	Maintenance fund established.

townhouse units, for a total of sixty-four units per block. Forty-four of those units (eleven units per block) faced the surrounding streets, and the remaining twenty took up the interior of each block.

Since the units had never been modernized, extensive renovations were required before they could be transferred. To accomplish this, all existing residents were relocated. Although involuntary relocation violated PHHD guidelines, the DHA argued that the relocation was planned before application to the program. Furthermore, the DHA argued, none of the relocation was involuntary because the tenants were offered more desirable housing alternatives. In a survey of thirty-four of those relocated, however, 64.7 percent described their relocation as involuntary.

After tenants were relocated, the interior buildings of the block were razed to reduce density and to allow for small individual rear yards, playground space for young children, community open space for all residents, and controlled-access parking. This reduced the number of units to be included in the cooperative from sixty-four to forty-four. Renovations included all new plumbing, electrical systems, and heating systems; new kitchen cabinets, fixtures, and appliances; new windows; new bathroom fixtures; the replacement of flat roofs with sloped ones; all new playground equipment; and many other improvements. In addition, small fences were erected to help foster a sense of ownership and territoriality. These repairs cost approximately $22,000 per unit, not counting engineering and design, which were accomplished with DHA staff.

The DHA set an income limit of $12,000 to join the Upper Lawrence Cooperative. This was based on the amount needed to pay carrying costs and still keep the total housing expense-to-gross income ratio under 30 percent. The maximum income was the same as for public housing eligibility: 50 percent of the median for the area. All public housing households with incomes above the cutoff were notified by letter, and the program was also publicized in the authority's newsletter. Interested parties were encouraged to attend a series of meetings to discuss the program. The DHA originally hoped to keep monthly cooperative charges to around $250 per month, but initial charges were $329 per month.

The DHA set the sale price of the buildings to the co-op at $935,200, based on the renovation costs it incurred. Permanent financing for the sale came from the Colorado Housing Finance Agency (including a $100,000 grant and a $200,000 loan) and the National Cooperative Bank ($600,000). To secure the bank loan, the housing authority had to agree to indemnify the co-op against defaults on individual shares. This means that if a co-op member leaves or is forced to leave, the DHA is responsible for share payments until a new cooperator is found, as long as the unit is transferred to the DHA in broom-ready condition. If the current owner leaves without the co-op's knowing and the unit is not in salable condition, the co-op is responsible for arrears until the unit is ready for a new occupant. The remaining $35,200 came from $800 equity contribution required of each cooperator. For buyers who lacked the $800 in cash for the down payment, the Denver Families Housing Corporation, a local nonprofit agency, provided financing of up to $600, to be repaid over five years.

An initial group of twenty-six households moved into the renovated units in October 1986. They received group and individual training from DHA staff, who had been recently trained by staff from the National Federation of Housing Counselors (NFCH) on topics such as what a co-op is, how it is governed, how to put together a budget, and how to manage a cooperative. Since this was one of the first co-ops in Denver, there was a lack of local expertise in cooperative management. The sale of units to the cooperative was closed in May 1987. The remaining cooperators moved in later and did not receive the initial training.

New Edition Cooperative, Nashville

The demonstration program in Nashville was designed by the MDHA to sell three multifamily developments totaling eighty-five units: a forty-eight units, two-story apartment complex; a nineteen-unit duplex and triplex development; and an eighteen-unit duplex development. The three are several miles apart, but all are in the central city area of Nashville. The original proposal called for the apartment complex and the eighteen-unit duplex to be sold as two separate cooperatives, with the remaining development to be sold as condominiums. After program approval, however, the tenants decided they would rather be part of one larger, scattered-site cooperative, and the MDHA agreed to this change.

These three developments were chosen because they were attractive and in relatively good condition compared to other public housing. The eighteen-unit duplex development was new and had not yet been occupied. The other two had been built within the past ten years and required improvements such as roof repairs and improved drainage. The total cost of improvements was approximately $625,000. Unlike the Denver Public Housing Authority, the MDHA abided by the prohibition against involuntary relocation. Thus, it was crucial that a large percentage of the current tenants agreed to participate. Those who did not want to participate or who had very low incomes would either have to stay and rent from the co-op or be enticed to move. The MDHA set a 60 percent minimum participation rate for the project to move forward.

Marketing was done through distribution of brochures, home visits by MDHA staff, and meetings held in each development. MDHA staff visited each household to explain the program. A newsletter was also sent to residents, reviewing progress and announcing upcoming meetings.

Not all residents were offered membership. A screening process was created to identify prospective cooperators. It included review of information on employment stability, rent-paying histories, and maintenance requests on units. Recommendations were also sought from project managers, and the tenant's motivation to participate was assessed in an interview. No income limit was established for individual participation. Rather, a minimum group average was established. The original proposal was for each co-op member to pay rent based on 30 percent of income. Thus, the MDHA wanted to ensure that the average income for all participants was at least $10,000, the amount needed to cover carrying cost and maintain a reserve maintenance fund.

Based on the appraised value of the properties, the MDHA set a sale price of $1,825,000. To make conversion feasible, however, it offered the cooperative a $1 million silent second mortgage to be forgiven over the first five years of ownership. MDHA had hoped to receive from a third-party mortgage the remaining $825,000, the approximate out-of-pocket cost of conversion. This included the costs of making the necessary improvements before sale, administering the program, and establishing a maintenance reserve fund. They anticipated that the cooperative could secure financing for $800,000. The remaining $25,000 was to come from an escrow account containing payments to tenants for maintenance activities undertaken during the preconversion period.

Obtaining financing for the sale was more difficult than expected. After extended negotiations, the National Cooperative Bank (NCB) agreed to provide financing but only for $550,000. This led the MDHA to offer the cooperative a silent third mortgage for the remaining $250,000. This silent third will be forgiven at a rate of one-fifteenth per year if the cooperative adheres to a recognition agreement signed by both parties. That agreement, among other things, stipulates that the cooperative operate as a limited-equity cooperative.

After almost three years of planning, the eighty-five units were transferred on June 26, 1989. At that time, seventy units were occupied by members of the cooperative. Of the remaining units, seven were occupied by continuing renters who had received Section 8 certificates from the MDHA, and eight were vacant. As tenants moved out during the planning stages, their units had been intentionally left vacant so the co-op board could select new members after the properties were transferred to the cooperative.

Characteristics of the Cooperators

The comparison of the characteristics of cooperators in Denver and Nashville in table 6.2 shows that both groups have a high percentage of households with at least one full-time employee. Moreover, both groups have average household incomes of over $14,000 per year. It is interesting to compare these figures to a recent study of the characteristics of all public housing residents. Only 24 percent of all public housing households have at least one full-time wage earner, and the average income was $6,539 (NAHRO, 1990). Thus, it is clear the cooperators are well above average in income and the proportion who have full-time employment.

Households in Denver were more likely to include a married couple and were larger than those in Nashville; they were also less likely to have any member with a high school degree. The age of household heads and number of years in public housing are roughly similar. Finally, as might be expected, Hispanics made up a larger percentage of households in Denver.

Success of the Conversions

The success of these two cooperatives can be measured in several ways. Survival is the most basic measure of success. Beyond this, turnover and delinquency rates are important indicators of its health, since they are di-

Table 6.2
Characteristics of Cooperators

CHARACTERISTICS	UPPER LAWRENCE DENVER	NEW EDITION NASHVILLE
Percent Households with Full Time Employee	87.5	86.5
Average Household Income	$ 14,596	$ 14,008
Percent Married Households	40.6	20.9
Average Household Size	3.4	2.4
Average Age of Household Head	39	40
Average Years in Public Housing	5.7	6.4
Education		
No high school degree	31.3	19.4
High school graduate	34.4	52.2
Some college	31.3	23.9
College graduate	3.1	4.5
Race		
White	3.1	7.5
African American	56.2	92.5
Hispanic	37.5	0.0
Other	3.1	0.0

rectly related to its financial stability. Finally, given that a main goal of conversion programs is to improve the quality of life of public housing tenants, cooperator satisfaction with dwelling units, neighborhoods, and co-op boards are important.

Both cooperatives have survived—the Upper Lawrence Cooperative in Denver for five years and the New Edition Cooperative in Nashville for three years. The Upper Lawrence Cooperative, however, has been plagued by many problems since its inception and has required continual assistance from the DHA to remain viable. In contrast, the New Edition Cooperative has had fewer and less severe problems. It has required more minor assistance from the housing authority.

Upper Lawrence has experienced high turnover and delinquency rates. When DHA staff and the management agent were interviewed in mid–1989, there were seven vacancies (a 16 percent rate), and at least twelve of the original forty-four cooperators had left. Many were said to have moved out in the middle of the night without notice. Moreover, a survey conducted at that time found that one-third of the remaining cooperators were delinquent on their share payments.

Telephone interviews with DHA officials and the co-op's management agent in early 1990 revealed eleven vacancies (a 25 percent vacancy rate), and twenty-three of thirty-three households were behind more than one-half-month's rent. Similar interviews in early 1992 were a little more encouraging. They indicated three vacancies (a 7 percent rate) and eight households more than thirty days delinquent. At this time, only nineteen of the original cooperators remained. It appears that if the housing authority had not agreed to pay the monthly charges on vacant units, the cooperative would have failed.

The New Edition Cooperative has experienced vacancy and delinquency problems but not nearly as severe as those at Upper Lawrence. In a survey of cooperators in mid–1989, only one was in arrears, and there had been no turnover. At that time, however, the co-op was only several months old, so it is not a fair comparison with the Upper Lawrence Cooperative.

Interviews with housing authority staff and the management agent conducted in early 1992 indicate that ten of the original cooperators have left. Rather than disappearing without notice as in Denver, however, orderly transfers occurred. Six left to purchase their own homes, and two left because they needed larger units. Of the remaining two, one was evicted for failure to pay fees and the other for behavioral problems. The management agent reported that eight to nine households were delinquent in an average month, but most paid by the end of the month in which charges are due. The combination of vacancies and late payments has strained the co-op's budget and caused it to pay late fees on several mortgage payments, yet it has not yet had to dip into reserve funds.

Based on survey data collected in 1989, cooperators in Nashville were considerably more satisfied with their units, neighborhoods, and early performance of the cooperative board than were their counterparts in Denver. Table 6.3 shows that satisfaction levels in Denver are substantially lower than those in Nashville. Satisfaction with the performance of the co-op board was also much lower in Denver than in Nashville.

When asked if they had regrets about buying, 65.6 percent of the members of the Upper Lawrence Cooperative said they did, while only 23.8 percent of New Edition members said so. About half the cooperators in Denver felt that the cooperative had a positive impact on their lives; almost three-quarters of those in Nashville felt that way. Moreover, almost 10 percent of those in Denver felt that joining the cooperative had actually had a negative impact on their lives—and this does not include those who had already left at the time of the survey. These data provide strong support for the relative success of the New Edition Cooperative compared to Upper Lawrence. What

Table 6.3
Levels of Satisfaction among Cooperators

VARIABLE	UPPER LAWRENCE DENVER	NEW EDITION NASHVILLE
SATISFACTION WITH HOUSE		
Very Satisfied	15.6	28.8
Satisfied	21.9	48.5
Neutral	25.0	16.7
Dissatisfied	21.9	6.1
Very Dissatisfied	15.6	0.0
N	32	66
SATISFACTION WITH NEIGHBORHOOD		
Very Satisfied	15.6	9.0
Satisfied	37.5	59.7
Neutral	9.4	19.4
Dissatisfied	25.0	10.4
Very Dissatisfied	12.5	1.5
N	32	67
SATISFACTION WITH COOP BOARD PERFORMANCE		
Very Satisfied	0.0	9.1
Satisfied	12.9	65.1
Neutral	19.4	18.2
Dissatisfied	45.2	4.6
Very Dissatisfied	22.6	0.0
N	31	66
REGRETS ABOUT PURCHASING		
Yes	65.6	23.8
No	34.4	76.1
N	32	67
OVERALL IMPACT OF OWNING ON LIFE		
Positive	51.6	73.1
Negative	9.7	0.0
No impact	38.7	26.9
N	31	67
ASSESSMENT OF COOP FEES		
More than expected	65.6	31.3
About what expected	31.3	50.8
Less than expected	3.1	17.9
N	32	67

accounts for this difference in success? A more detailed look at differences in the design and implementation of these cooperatives should shed light on this question.

FACTORS IN THE SUCCESS OF THE COOPERATIVES

The variation in the success of the two programs can largely be explained by differences in the motives for undertaking the projects, the degree of tenant involvement in project design, choice of units to be sold, quality of repairs, and training.

Motives for Undertaking the Project

The Denver project was part of a larger effort to revitalize the problem-ridden Curtis Park development and the surrounding neighborhood. The transfer of portions of the rental housing development to cooperatives was intended to increase homeownership and ultimately increase the level of resident concern for upkeep and safety. Moreover, DHA officials believed the conversion program "significantly affected HUD approval for the demolition of buildings in the adjacent blocks of public housing, and the availability of funds to modernize the remaining housing stock." Thus, the main motivation in Denver was to improve Curtis Park and its neighborhood rather than improve the quality of life of the public housing residents.

The motivation for the cooperative in Nashville was quite different. It was to find ways for public housing residents to become homeowners. They were particularly interested in working out an effective homeownership counseling program. Prior experience with the Turnkey III program had convinced officials that effective counseling was the key to a successful program. Thus, the program staff in Nashville was more interested in improving the lives of residents than it was in improving the neighborhoods or solving difficult management problems. This difference in motivation affected program characteristics, such as the degree of resident involvement and the selection of cooperators, which in turn influenced program effectiveness.

Resident Involvement

The extent of resident involvement in designing the program was markedly different in the two programs. In Denver, involvement was limited to a survey of the design changes residents would like to see made to their units. The survey was conducted by an architect hired to recommend building improvements before sale. The original group of cooperators had no involvement in the development of the cooperative bylaws, occupancy agreement, and other management documents. These were drafted by the staff or by consultants and were simply presented to the cooperators when they moved in. In an interview after the co-op was formed, the management agent bemoaned the lack of resident involvement in developing these documents. "The sense of being a community," she said, "is really a spiritual rather than a financial thing." Denver cooperators never had a chance to form a community before they assumed management responsibility. Moreover, many did not understand the responsibilities involved.

In Nashville, many of the eventual cooperators were involved in the design of the program from the beginning. Before the original proposal was sent to HUD, MDHA held two meetings with the residents to explain the program and to have them vote on whether to participate. Moreover, once the proposal was approved, residents were instrumental in making two important changes. First, the original proposal called for two separate cooperatives and one condominium. During an early training workshop, the residents decided they would rather have one scattered-site cooperative. Second, the MDHA had proposed basing share prices and monthly charges on current incomes rather than on unit size. This would mean that higher-income tenants would pay more than lower-income tenants for identical units. In discussing this plan, residents decided it would be better to base sale prices on unit size and elderly status: those occupying units containing more bedrooms should have to pay more, but the elderly should receive a discount. The MDHA agreed to both recommendations.

Prospective cooperators in Nashville were also given a chance to participate in the maintenance of their units well before taking title. The MDHA offered prospective members the opportunity to save money toward the cooperative subscription fee by performing routine maintenance work. An earned credit account was established for each prospect, and the MDHA then deposited $20 per month in each account for services provided.

Possibly more important than the program changes attributable to tenant participation was the process of arriving at these recommendations. During many meetings, the prospective cooperators learned to take charge of their destinies and to work together. Moreover, leaders emerged from these meetings and were subsequently elected to the interim co-op board. Clearly, the extensive tenant involvement in the process increased resident commitment to its success.

Choice of Units to Be Sold

The choice of units sold in each program also helps to explain the relative levels of program success. One of the biggest differences in the units selected in Denver and in Nashville is in the desirability of the surrounding neighborhoods. The fact that cooperators in Denver were much more dissatisfied with their neighborhoods compared to those in Nashville is not surprising since the buildings selected in Denver were a small part of a troubled development located in a troubled neighborhood. Rather than the cooperative pulling the neighborhood up, the neighborhood may be pulling the cooperative down. Many cooperators had moved from what they considered better areas and were unwilling to stay in Curtis Park.

The units selected in Nashville were clearly in better neighborhoods. They had a mix of incomes, and satisfaction with the areas was much higher. Higher satisfaction levels, in turn, led to increased commitment to making the cooperative a success.

Extent and Quality of Repairs

The condition of the units transferred was an issue in both programs. Again, Denver's problems were more severe. In spite of extensive renovations made by the DHA, cooperators complained of defective workmanship and design problems such as the lack of gutters, which caused rain to run down the front of the buildings and leak into the units. This and other conflicts with the DHA led the co-op to retain legal counsel to assist it in negotiations with the housing authority. After several months of contentious negotiation, the DHA and the co-op signed a memorandum of understanding in which the housing authority agreed to complete an itemized schedule of repairs at its own expense in return for the board's agreement not to file legal action.

In Nashville, the MDHA hired architects to inspect the units to be sold and to prepare a list of needed improvements. These lists were then presented to tenants, who were given a chance to suggest others. Due to higher-than-expected costs, a number of agreed-upon repairs were eliminated. After closing, however, the MDHA assisted the cooperative in making some of these repairs by providing a 3 percent loan from its Community Development Block Grant (CDBG) funds. Still under discussion are the repairs of roof and gutter problems affecting several of the units. The cooperative contends that the MDHA is responsible for the repairs, but the MDHA contends they are not covered in the warranty it offered the cooperative.

Cooperative Board and Member Training

The length and depth of the training offered to cooperators differed dramatically in the two programs. Moreover, there were important differences in the approaches to this training. In Denver a "train the trainers" model was adopted. This involved a contract with the National Federation of Housing Counselors (NFHC) and two local firms to train a core group of DHA staff members, who would then train the cooperators.

This model did not work well. When it came to such basics as being able to explain financing arrangements, how co-op sales prices were determined, the nature of individual cooperators' responsibilities, and other important topics, the housing authority personnel often did not know much more than the families they were supposed to train. Moreover, training began less than six months before the buildings were transferred—insufficient time to prepare low-income residents to manage a housing cooperative. A year after the transfer, the minutes of a DHA meeting contain the following comment: "Although Doris [the co-op president] stated that she attended all the training seminars provided by the Authority, she feels totally unprepared for the task of managing a co-op, being a board member or president."

Another problem in Denver is that not every buyer received training. The co-op members arrived in two groups. The first group of approximately twenty-six residents received training before they moved in. A second group of approximately eighteen residents moved in after the training sessions had been held. According to the co-ops' annual report, "The lack of training bore a relation to subsequent delinquencies and ultimate evictions."

The experience in Nashville was quite different. Realizing their own lack of experience, the MDHA sought assistance from the Cooperative Housing Foundation (CHF), which has sponsored or provided technical assistance to over forty cooperatives since it was established in 1952. The CHF agreed to provide samples of legal documents needed, assist in the formation of the cooperative, train the tenants on co-op management, and conduct special training sessions for board members. The bulk of CHF's activities revolved around a series of weekend workshops for tenants designed, according to the CHF trainer, "to build a sense of community for the residents . . . to improve the residents' knowledge, and develop the necessary leadership, community building and personal skills; then make certain that those skills were applied over and over again until they become habit."

The training was done well in advance of the transfer. In fact, the interim cooperative board was in operation for more than a year before the units were transferred. During this time, they received additional training by attending the meetings of national cooperative organizations.

CONCLUSIONS

The experiences in Denver and Nashville suggest that public housing developments can be converted into cooperatives, although they are likely to require continuing assistance from the sponsoring PHAs. Both cooperatives have survived for more than three years, but Upper Lawrence would likely have failed if it were not for the continuing financial support of the DHA. In looking at vacancy and delinquency data, as well as self-reported satisfaction levels, it is clear that the Nashville cooperative has been more successful than its Denver counterpart. This is at least partially a function of differences in motives for undertaking conversion, the level of resident involvement, the selection and rehabilitation of the units, and the quality and duration of the training provided to participants.

The experiences in Denver and Nashville suggest that the time, effort, and expense of carrying out conversion programs is extensive. Such programs require hours of staff time to select units, assess rehabilitation needs, manage the rehabilitation process, set eligibility requirements, screen applicants, arrange appropriate financing, market the units to tenants, do the necessary legal work, train the tenants, and other tasks. Moreover, the staff time and legal work required will be costly for the sponsoring PHAs. In Nashville the conversion cost the MDHA over $500,000. We were unable to calculate the full costs to the DHA, but they were clearly large.

Housing authorities need to be realistic about both the effort and expense. The new HOPE 1 program provides partial funding for activities associated with the transfer of units to tenants; however, the sponsoring housing authorities have to provide a 25 percent match. This may still be a substantial amount.

The sponsoring PHAs should be prepared for continued assistance to the co-ops well after their units are transferred. In both examples, the authorities have provided this ongoing support. In Denver, continuing involvement is required under the terms of the financing agreement, and, given the problems experienced, it has been extensive. In Nashville, the authority has no contractual obligation but feels a moral obligation to the co-op and its residents. Thus, PHAs should not see the transfer of units to cooperatives as an easy way of ridding themselves of unwanted developments. Rather, they need to make a genuine long-term commitment to any co-ops they create.

Clearly, one of the main differences between the Denver and the Nashville programs was the commitment of the cooperators. Many of the original cooperators in Denver simply left when problems arose, while cooperators in Nashville stayed and worked to correct the problems. Several factors seem to have contributed to the higher level of commitment in Nashville. First, most of the cooperators in Nashville had lived in the developments before they were transferred. This meant they were already familiar with the neighborhood and with at least some of their neighbors. In contrast, almost all the cooperators in Denver had moved in from other areas and lacked such familiarity.

Second, the training sessions held in Nashville before transfer helped to strengthen community in the development. The cooperators spent many hours discussing the provisions of subscription agreements, bylaws, and house rules. This led to common understandings of what was expected from each. In Denver, the cooperators did not have this opportunity to modify the governing documents to suit their own needs.

A well-designed training program managed by experienced staff also seems crucial to the success of conversion programs. In Nashville, the authority brought in experienced trainers to handle topics with which they were unfamiliar. They also offered training well before the tenants took title. By the time the cooperative took control, the board members felt confident in their duties and responsibilities. In Denver, the training period was shorter, it did not involve all the cooperators, and it was conducted mainly by housing authority staff who had recently been trained themselves.

The experiences in Denver and Nashville suggest that the sponsoring PHAs should select units in desirable neighborhoods and make sure they are in good shape before transfer. Residents should not be encouraged to buy into an area that has little chance of improving. The main objective should be improving the quality of life of the residents, not improving conditions in a problem-ridden area. Since the condition of the units transferred in both cities was a major source of conflict, it would be wise for HUD to require independent certification that units are in good condition before a transfer. The participating PHAs should also offer warranties on the major mechanical systems and building components of the units transferred to address problems that may have been overlooked in the repair process. Substantial reserve accounts should be established to fund unanticipated repairs and other unanticipated expenses or revenue shortfalls. Initially these funds could be capitalized out of sales proceeds.

Our evaluation leads to several general conclusions about the sale of multifamily housing developments to cooperatives composed of former public housing tenants. The characteristics of the cooperators in both Nashville and Denver suggest that ownership is limited to higher-income residents of public housing. The mean incomes of both sets of cooperators were well above that of all public housing residents. Even so, many cooperators had difficulty keeping up with their payments. Thus, the potential for converting public housing to cooperatives appears limited unless continuing subsidies are provided to the participants. Section 8 certificates could be provided to some, yet this would be a major additional cost, and it may undermine the sense of self-sufficiency that these programs are trying to instill in the cooperators.

The relatively high income level of the cooperators also indicates that a major expansion of public housing sales, as envisioned under HOPE 1, is likely to remove higher-income working households, thereby further concentrating very poor, nonworking households in public housing. This may. have a negative impact not only on the remaining public housing households but also on the financial position of public housing authorities.

The costs associated with transferring units to tenants raise the larger issue of whether the benefits of conversion programs are worth the cost. A careful cost-benefit analysis is needed to compare the relative advantages of public housing homeownership programs with other approaches to providing low-income families with homeownership opportunities. It may, for example, be more cost-effective to provide such opportunities outside the public housing stock. This approach would have the added advantage of increasing the total number of affordable units. The departure of buyers from existing public housing units would also free up units for poorer families on the waiting lists.

REFERENCES

Birchall, J. 1988. *Building Communities the Cooperative Way*. London: Routledge and Kegan Paul.

Colwell, P., and M. Mahue. 1991. "Privatization of Public Housing in the U.S." *ORER READER* (Winter) (Office of Real Estate Research at the University of Illinois at Urbana-Champaign).

Franklin, S. 1981. "Housing Cooperatives: A Viable Means of Home Ownership for Low-Income Families." *Journal of Housing* 38, 7:392–398.

Kemp, J. 1991. " 'HOPE': Winning the New War on Poverty." *Stone Soup* (Winter 1991).

Koch, J. 1985. Statement before the Subcommittee on Employment and Housing, U.S. House of Representatives, July 9.

Kunze, C. 1981. "Public Housing Cooperatives Reduce Dependence on Operating Subsidies, Modernization Funding." *Journal of Housing* 38, 9:489–493.

National Association of Housing and Redevelopment Officials (NAHRO). 1990. *The Many Faces of Public Housing*. Washington, D.C.

Peterman, W., and M. A. Young. 1991. "Alternatives to Conventional Public Housing Management." Technical Report No. 1–91. Chicago: Voorhees Center for Neighborhood and Community Improvement, University of Illinois at Chicago.

Rohe, W., and M. Stegman, 1990. *Public Housing Homeownership Assessment*. 2 vols. Washington, D.C.: U.S. Department of Housing and Urban Development.

———. 1992a. *Privatizing Public Housing in Britain and the United States*. Chapel Hill, N.C.: Department of City and Regional Planning, University of North Carolina.

———. 1992b. "Public Housing Homeownership: Will It Work and for Whom?" *Journal of the American Planning Association* 58, 2 (Spring):144–157.

U.S. Department of Housing and Urban Development. 1984. "Public Housing Homeownership Demonstration." *Federal Register*, October 25, pp. 43028–34.

Zimmer, J. 1977. *From Rental to Cooperative: Improving Low and Moderate Income Housing*. Beverly Hills, Calif.: Sage Publications.

Part 3

Alternative Forms of
Housing Control

7

Resident Management and Other Approaches to Tenant Control of Public Housing

WILLIAM PETERMAN

Upbeat television and newspaper reports, along with near-evangelical rhet-oric emanating from the Department of Housing and Urban Development (HUD) and its secretary, Jack Kemp, give the impression that resident management is the cure for ailing public housing in the United States. The claim is that residents can manage their developments better than local housing authorities, and that if they are empowered through resident man-agement, they can pull themselves out of poverty. Homeownership, it is said, is the natural end result of resident management, and thus it becomes a way for public housing tenants to obtain one piece of the American dream, a "home of their own."

But is all this true? What does the evidence, if any, actually show? Is resident management good public housing policy, and, if so, is it applicable in all situations? Should it be the only public housing policy or even a key policy? Is ownership a logical outcome of resident management, or are man-agement and ownership distinct issues?

Critics of HUD's resident management program argue it is too much to expect it to correct all public housing problems, including physical decay and numerous social and economic ills. Good management, they argue, whether by residents or by housing professionals, can do little to change conditions without significant additional resources. But the administration's support of resident management does not seem to carry with it the promise of increased funding.

In the Housing Act of 1949, the federal government committed itself to a "decent home and suitable living environment for every American family." In this chapter I explore whether resident management offers a means of fulfilling this commitment.

A BRIEF HISTORY OF RESIDENT MANAGEMENT IN U.S. PUBLIC HOUSING

Resident management, originally called tenant management, was a response to the decline of public housing, which began in the 1960s. It initially arose in two cities, Boston and St. Louis, in what can be described as acts of desperation. Tenants were forced to assume control of their developments in order to keep from losing them.

In Boston, residents at Bromley-Heath, an eleven-hundred-unit development consisting of town houses and high-rise buildings, first became organized in the mid–1960s, working to improve health services, taking over operation of social services in the community, forming a crime patrol, and developing a drug center (Hailey, 1984). In 1969, the resident organization proposed taking over management of the development. This was accomplished on January 1, 1971. Bromley-Heath recently observed its twentieth anniversary as a tenant-managed development, the oldest in the United States.

In St. Louis, tenant management was an outgrowth of the settlement of a successful 1969 rent strike that resulted in the collapse and reorganization of the St. Louis Housing Authority. Two tenant management corporations were formed in 1973, two more in 1974, and management of a fifth development was given to a nonprofit neighborhood organization in anticipation of conversion to tenant management. Funds to initiate tenant management were provided by the Ford Foundation (Wendel, 1975).

The Ford Foundation's involvement in St. Louis led to joint sponsorship, with HUD, of a National Tenant Management Demonstration Program. Involving seven public housing sites in six cities—Jersey City, Louisville, New Haven, New Orleans, Oklahoma City, and Rochester—the program operated between 1976 and 1979. It was not as successful as its sponsors had hoped. In a book-length evaluation, the Manpower Demonstration Research Corporation (1981) noted that while tenant management seemed to have worked as well at most sites, as had previous housing authority management, several objective measures, such as rent collections, vacancy rates, and speed of response to maintenance requests, showed no improvement. Resident satisfaction with their tenant managers, however, was higher than it had been with housing authority managers.

Manpower also found that tenant management had been costly. Expenditures were from 13 to 62 percent above conventional management costs, due primarily to training, employment, and technical assistance. There were, nevertheless, benefits from the increased expenditures: employment for some tenants, a sense of personal development among participating tenants, and greater overall satisfaction with management among all tenants. Noting the additional costs, along with varying attitudes of housing authorities about tenant management and the rapid turnover rate of housing authority directors, Manpower suggested it was unlikely that tenant management would be universally successful and recommended against expanding the demonstration program.

Although this program was discontinued, several program sites initially remained under tenant control, but by the mid–1980s only one was still tenant managed (Monti, 1989). Also, of the five St. Louis sites, three had returned to housing authority management. It appeared that this was an idea whose time had come and gone.

Tenant management soon gained a new set of champions, a new name (resident management), and a new lease on life. Conservative policymakers and politicians became attracted to resident management, seeing its "self-help" focus as a way both to instill responsibility among public housing residents and to reduce, or perhaps eliminate, federal involvement in housing. Taking the lead in promoting it was the National Center for Neighborhood Enterprise (NCNE), a Washington, D.C., think tank, headed by a conservative black Republican, Robert Woodson.

Assisted by a sizable grant from the Amoco Foundation, NCNE set out to promote resident management by working with several fledgling resident management groups and attempting to promote the idea nationally. A CBS television "60 Minutes" segment highlighting the redevelopment of St. Louis's Cochran Gardens and featuring its dynamic leader, Bertha Gilkey, brought resident management to the attention of the American public. The development of resident management at Kenilworth-Parkside in Washington, D.C., led by another dynamic individual, Kimi Gray, seemed to provide evidence that resident management was what was needed to revitalize public housing.

Conservatives added a feature to resident management, ownership, that had not previously been part of it. In a 1984 report, subtitled, "From Tenant to Resident to Homeowner," NCNE argued that "many residents of public housing . . . believe that once they have made the commitment to turn their developments around . . . they, more than anyone else, deserve and have the right to maintain and own their homes in those developments" (NCNE, 1984).

Conservatives also suggested that resident management could work better than conventional management at no greater cost and that ownership, once implemented, carried with it the possibility of eliminating most, if not all, federal support. They conveniently ignored the findings from the National Demonstration Program that tenant management had been found more expensive and the fact that successful efforts had been supported by considerable federal dollars. The revitalization of Cochran Gardens in St. Louis, for example, had been accomplished as part of a federal Urban Development Action Grant (UDAG) for the revitalization of downtown St. Louis.

NCNE was instrumental in getting a resident management provision included in the federal Housing and Community Development Act of 1987.

This created a formal procedure for establishing resident management corporations and provided up to $100,000 for the development and training of new resident corporations. Implementation of the act coincided with the arrival of the Bush administration. Jack Kemp, the new HUD secretary and a strong proponent of resident management, created a Resident Initiatives program to coordinate resident management efforts and appointed an NCNE staffer to direct it.

With HUD's encouragement, local authorities began exploring the establishment of resident-managed developments, and resident groups, taking notice of successes elsewhere, began seeking resident management status. By the end of the decade, resident management groups were springing up all over the country. In Chicago, for example, seven different developments had resident management organizations, although only one, LeClaire Courts, was actually managing its development.

Passage of the National Affordable Housing Act of 1990 put the final piece of the administration's resident management policy in place. Title IV of the act, Homeownership and Opportunity for People Everywhere Programs (HOPE), establishes procedures and authorizes funding for selling public housing to qualified resident management groups. Thus, as the decade proceeds, we can expect to see several developments transferred to private ownership through the resident management process.

RESIDENT MANAGEMENT: AN EXPLANATION

Successful resident management corporations (RMCs) are a delicate balance between community-based advocacy organizations and professional businesses.[1] They must have the support of the residents and work to build the social and economic character of the community. But at the same time they must collect rents, keep the grounds clean, and discipline misbehaving tenants. If these two roles are not properly balanced, RMCs can stumble and ultimately fail.

Structurally an RMC is a nonprofit corporation that contracts with a housing authority to manage a development. All tenants are members, with the right to participate, but the core of an RMC is its officers and board of directors. The board hires a director of the corporation, and many boards also take part in hiring and monitoring staff. Staff are usually hired from the tenant population, but nothing precludes the hiring of a professional manager and staff or even the subcontracting of management services.

There are two types of RMCs: shared management and independent management. Although outwardly similar, they are based on differing underlying assumptions (Peterman and Young, 1991). These assumptions are important in determining the nature and scope of an RMC's activities.

Shared management can be described as liberal reform in which resident participation is encouraged. It usually occurs when a housing authority supports the concept of resident management. The RMCs created during the National Demonstration Program were of this type, as are most of the RMCs formed under the current HUD Resident Initiatives program.

In shared management, a housing authority assists in forming the RMC and training its board and staff. The contract negotiated between the authority and RMC identifies which management tasks the RMC will assume and which will be left to the housing authority. Typically the RMC elects to do tenant screening and recertification, counseling, discipline, and on-site maintenance. The authority retains most central functions, especially budgeting, purchasing, major maintenance, and renovation. In effect this is a dual-management model, which can continue indefinitely. However, most shared management RMCs hope eventually to take over full management of their developments.

Shared management can be effective in revitalizing distressed public housing (Rigby, 1989), but it may result in only a modest transfer of power to residents. When an authority does not want to give up power, it may be little more than a ploy to cede unpleasant responsibilities to tenants, while the authority retains actual control.

Independent management is rooted in traditional community organizing, and its goal is to empower residents through taking full control. It commonly arises when relationships between a housing authority and its residents are hostile, usually due to the authority's inadequate management. Most of the better-known RMCs—Boston's Bromley-Heath, St. Louis's Cochran Gardens, Washington's Kenilworth-Parkside, and Chicago's LeClaire Courts— approached resident management from the independent perspective.

Independent RMCs receive most of their training and financial resources from outside the housing authority. The quality of training and other technical assistance and the ability to raise funds is critical to both an RMC's independent status and its success. Legal assistance is of key importance, particularly during the period when an RMC negotiates its contract with an authority. An RMC will attempt to negotiate maximum control over operation of the development, including budget authority. Since any housing authority may be unwilling to transfer all responsibilities to an RMC at once, it may take several years and contracts before an RMC gains full control.

Dual management also frequently occurs with independent management, but instead of being viewed as a period of shared management, it is seen as a time of transition during which responsibility is gradually shifted to the RMC. Independent RMCs are likely to be stronger, better trained, and more focused than their shared management counterparts, but they often find themselves in a precarious position due to their hostile relationship with the housing authority and dependence on outside support. They may also find it difficult to make the transition from a community organization that is used to fighting with the housing authority to a management firm that must cooperate with it. Developing resident groups may have little choice as to whether to seek shared or independent management. Where a housing authority opposes increased resident involvement, independence may be the only route open, and where the authority promotes resident management, it may be difficult or even impossible to avoid the shared approach.

A comprehensive evaluation of the success rate of RMCs has never been done, but it appears that at best it is no more than 50 percent. Although the Bromley-Heath Tenant Management Corporation recently celebrated its twentieth anniversary, only two of the original five RMCs formed in St. Louis survive, and only one National Demonstration site is still resident managed. Of seven RMCs in Chicago, only one is managing a development.

Community organization, technical assistance, and financial resources seem critical to at least the initial success of an RMC (Peterman, 1989). The difficulty in procuring these essential items limits the development of RMCs, despite the interest of many tenant groups and housing authorities in the idea. Thus, it seems unlikely that the idea will become widely adopted.

Monti (1989) has studied eleven resident-managed public housing sites and identified four conditions basic to the success of RMCs:

1. Adequate and continuing resources must be available for operating subsidies, modernization, and technical assistance.
2. The desire for resident management must be demand driven, arising from the grass roots. It cannot be legislated into existence by bureaucrats, no matter how well intentioned.
3. The relationship between residents and the local authority must be neither too friendly nor too confrontational. An atmosphere of creative tension appears most appropriate.
4. Residents must build and maintain strong and direct ties with community institutions other than the housing authority.[2]

The first condition suggests, consistent with Manpower Demonstration Research Corporation's finding, that successful resident management is costly, but it also identifies a need for the housing to be in a condition such that it can be successfully managed. Condition 2 points out that it is residents, not the authority or anyone else, who must want resident management. Condition 3 suggests that the type of relationship between an RMC and its authority is critical, and condition 4, which is perhaps a corollary of condition 3, stresses the importance of an RMC's broadening its base of support.

The role of resident organizing in forming and maintaining an RMC needs clarification. RMCs are both community organizations and businesses. The creative tension mentioned in Monti's point 3 reflects this dual character. An RMC unable to move beyond its initial organizing phase and to work cooperatively with its housing authority puts itself in a precarious position because, feeling threatened, the authority will probably seek to regain the power it has given up. On the other hand, an RMC that deemphasizes its role as community organizer may lose tenant support and be seen as little more than an agent of the housing authority. RMCs, in this sense, are similar to other community-based organizations attempting to balance organizing and development activities (Giloth, 1988).

OTHER MANAGEMENT OPTIONS

Although resident management is very popular, it is not the only option for residents who are seeking something other than conventional housing authority management. Two other approaches—increased resident participation and community based management—should be considered.

Most public housing sites have resident councils whose role is to advise management on issues relating to operation and improvement. These councils are a result of tenant activism in the 1960s and a direct outgrowth of a rent strike among tenants in St. Louis (Kunze, 1981). They are often poorly trained, seen as window dressing by tenants and housing authorities alike, and thus have not been very effective.

The resident council mechanism could, however, be used by residents to gain significant influence in the governance of their development. A strong and knowledgeable council, elected by an active and organized tenant population, could, no doubt, accomplish nearly as much as an RMC without becoming involved in routine management. Because of its official link to the housing authority, it is unlikely that a resident council could ever become as fully independent as can an RMC.

Community housing development corporations (CDCs) are another option. CDCs have become a major source of new and renovated low-income housing in the United States, and at least one housing expert (Connerly, 1986) has suggested they be considered for constructing and operating public housing. Connerly argues they are appropriate because of their ability to direct benefits to households in greatest need, to act with a sensitivity arising from knowledge of the community, to instill pride and confidence, to give low-income people both expertise and control, and to provide jobs for the poor.

CDC management of public housing seems particularly appropriate where there is tenant concern for improvements but little interest in taking on management responsibility. In Chicago, one CDC, the Housing Resource Center (HRC), currently manages forty-five scattered-site Chicago Housing Authority buildings. HRC promotes resident involvement in management through councils and committees but has noticed that resident interest has declined as their quality of management has improved.

OWNERSHIP OPTIONS

Proponents of resident ownership of public housing rarely are specific as to what they mean by ownership. While some units may be converted to condominiums, it is likely that most conversions will be to cooperatives. Procedures for establishing a public housing cooperative are contained in the Housing and Community Development Act of 1987. These identify resident management as an interim step between conventional public housing and private cooperative ownership. Once RMCs demonstrate their ability to manage a development, they can, if they so choose, initiate conversions. They are responsible for determining the price of a cooperative share, the rate at which a share would be allowed to rise, the monthly co-op charges (rent), and whether the RMC would manage the cooperative or would contract with a management firm for services.

The concept of limited equity is usually promoted as the way to ensure that a cooperative developed for low-income households remains that way. In limited equity situations, the price of the cooperative share is controlled and usually allowed to rise only a small amount over time. While this helps to keep the housing affordable, it eliminates a major benefit of ownership: the ability to build equity. Thus, residents of the cooperative may gain few advantages not obtainable through resident management alone. In fact, they could be at a disadvantage should conversion to a cooperative be accompanied by loss of federal subsidies and other forms of support.

Mutual housing is an alternative model that may be more appropriate for application to public housing. Although little known in the United States, there are millions of mutual housing units worldwide. Over 4.4 million were constructed in West Germany alone between 1949 and 1971 (Barnes, 1982). Recently the Neighborhood Reinvestment Corporation (NRC) has been actively promoting the mutual housing concept in the United States.

A mutual housing association (MHA) is a corporation whose members are residents, along with other individuals and organizations. The MHA owns all the property, and residents lease their individual units (Goetze, 1985). The lease gives resident households the right to remain in their unit indefinitely, to will their unit to a qualifying relative, and to decorate it to suit individual tastes. As an umbrella corporation, an MHA adds a degree of stability to housing that can be missing with a cooperative. NRC emphasizes that in order to keep mutual housing affordable, it is necessary to obtain construction or renovation financing in the form of grants rather than loans. This eliminates, or at least significantly reduces, indebtedness, freeing the mutual housing from ongoing subsidies. Resident members primarily pay operating costs.

Bratt (1990, 1991) recently evaluated NRC's mutual housing program, concentrating on the Baltimore Mutual Housing Association, which at the time consisted of forty-nine units of new construction and another forty-eight units under development. She found the MHA model suitable for providing low-income housing but critically dependent on up-front capital financing and concluded, with respect to residents, that "there is strong evidence that psychological empowerment has occurred and there is a high level of satisfaction with the physical environment" (Bratt, 1990:xi).

The evidence suggests that mutual housing could be workable for public housing families. Although residents are not true owners, they have many rights normally associated with ownership. Moreover, the MHA provides a more stable structure than a cooperative. However, even if developments were to be transferred at no cost to an MHA and renovation grants obtained, operating subsidies may still be needed due to the very low incomes of most public housing households.

PUBLIC POLICY, RESIDENT MANAGEMENT, AND RESIDENT OWNERSHIP

Among the many questions that might be asked about resident management and ownership of public housing, three seem critical. Do they work? Do they offer real benefits to tenants? Are they good public policy?

The failure rate of RMCs is high, and conditions for success are strict. As many as 50 percent of all RMCs formed before the recent revival of the concept no longer exist. At least during its infancy, an RMC is a fragile entity needing considerable nurturing, including good technical support, a workable relationship with the housing authority, supporting allies, and money. Getting out of the way and letting tenants take charge by no means ensures success.

The evidence also indicates that homeownership programs may not be as successful as their supporters hope. Rohe and Stegman (1990) recently evaluated HUD's Public Housing Homeownership Demonstration initiated in 1985. In this program, scheduled for thirty-six months, seventeen housing authorities proposed selling 1,315 units to tenants. After fifty months, only 320 units had been transferred, although the authors speculate that as many as 50 percent of the proposed units may eventually be sold. Some 10 to 15 percent of the home buyers had experienced late payments or more serious delinquencies within the first eighteen months of closing on their homes, and some 30 percent felt mortgage payments were causing a strain on their budgets. These rates seem quite high, especially since this was a demonstration program and it is likely that both good buildings and good tenants were selected for involvement.

In the Homeownership Demonstration, the number of units transferred to private ownership per housing authority was small. The formation of public housing cooperatives through resident management will involve many more units and families. Without some form of operating subsidy, many of these families will have difficulty in making monthly-charge payments, and this could cause a severe financial strain on many of the new cooperatives.

Kenilworth-Parkside was one of the first developments proposed for sale and conversion. In reviewing the proposed sale, the U.S. General Accounting Office (GAO, 1989) raised three concerns: there had been no study to determine the financial feasibility of existing families' purchasing units or cooperative shares, it was unclear whether the RMC would be able to raise money to make necessary physical improvements, and the issue of how residents would be protected in the case of financial mismanagement by the RMC had not been considered.

Resident management, with or without ownership, may not work in all circumstances, but there is no reason to reject it totally. Many residents and developments are better off because of it, and there is nothing to suggest that it cannot be successful at other developments under the right conditions.

Proponents of resident management talk of its empowering effect on residents. The term *empowerment*, however, is frequently undefined, and there is a tendency to confuse community empowerment and personal growth. Social activists stress the relationship between resident management and the growth of community, while conservatives stress its relationship to personal growth.

Studies by Monti (1989) and Peterman and Young (1991) find that successful resident management develops out of a process of community empowerment through resident organization. Nearly all enduring RMCs were preceded by a long period of community organizing during which residents slowly took over control of their developments. Creating an RMC does not result in community empowerment, but an empowered community can create an RMC. Programs and policies that encourage the formation of RMCs in order to create community growth and development are therefore misguided.

RMCs do result in personal growth for some residents, particularly those directly involved. However, there appears to be little about the function of management that suggests it is the only or even the best vehicle for promoting the personal development of large numbers of public housing residents. Some RMCs have programs that promote personal growth, but these are not related to management and have grown out of the process of community organization rather than the RMC itself.

Some community activists believe the current emphasis on resident management is causing public housing residents to become confused and to associate the goals of community and personal growth exclusively with managing a development. They suggest that housing authorities and policymakers are using resident management as a means of diverting attention from the serious state of public housing and from their responsibilities to provide decent housing for the poor. Some professional housing managers also believe the emphasis on resident management is misplaced. Housing management, they contend, is a technical task best left to professionals. In their estimation, residents would be better off if they focused their energies on personal growth issues or on important community issues such as education, crime prevention, and programs for young people.

Resident satisfaction should be the bottom line of any program to improve the quality of public housing, argues Stanley Horn (personal communication), who as director of the Clarence Darrow Center played a major role in developing resident management at Chicago's LeClaire Courts. While supportive of resident management, Horn contends that residents should be less concerned with who is doing the management than with how good it is. To be sure, in some circumstances good management may be obtained only when residents assume some or all management responsibility. But the bottom line should always be whether management results in a livable, healthy community.

Low-income-housing expert Rachel Bratt (personal communication) suggests that when housing authorities turn developments over to residents, they in effect abrogate their responsibilities as landlords. Private sector tenants do not expect to shoulder the responsibility of managing their developments, and even in cooperatives, where residents make policy decisions, management firms usually carry out the day-to-day management tasks. Bratt (1990) believes that resident management could easily become a kind of second-class tenantry or a form of "lemon socialism," where residents are given the management because housing authorities are no longer able to do the job.

We are left with a mixed conclusion. Resident management does work and is sometimes both appropriate and necessary. But when it works, it is almost always part of a larger process of community empowerment and development. It cannot be legislated into being, nor should it be viewed as an automatic replacement for all conventional public housing management. As resident organizations arise within public housing, resident management should be a strategy available to them. For the most part, however, management will remain the responsibility of housing authorities, and thus it is important that public policy not deal exclusively with resident management but instead look to multiple strategies for maintaining and revitalizing public housing.

There is strong disagreement over the appropriateness of federal efforts promoting resident management and ownership, as evidenced by a recent heated debate in the *Journal of Housing* between Missouri congressman William Clay (1990) and HUD secretary Jack Kemp (1991). Critics of the administration's program (e.g., Silver, McDonald, and Ortiz, 1985; Sultmeier, 1987) contend it unfairly raises residents' expectations by promising middle-class status through homeownership. The real intent of the program, they contend, is not improving housing opportunities for the poor but the creation of a way for the federal government to get out of the public housing business.

The administration and its supporters respond that there has been too much government intrusion into the lives of public housing residents and that resident management and ownership are ways to remove the heavy hand of government intervention (Caprara and Alexander, 1989). They argue that government policies and regulations created intolerable conditions in public housing and disincentives for people to seek personal development. While they do not believe government should abandon the poor, they feel that both community and personal improvements will come about only when the government steps aside and returns rights and responsibilities to the people.

The perspectives on resident management thus are widely divergent. Progressive housing activists are wary of it, feeling it sidetracks residents from real issues of control, and they believe that ownership is a cruel hoax being played on unsuspecting tenants. Liberals tend to support it because of its promise of community empowerment but are skeptical of any link to ownership. Conservatives support both resident management and ownership because to them empowerment is not complete without ownership.

Could a policy be fashioned that would reconcile these perspectives and at the same time benefit a maximum number of public housing families? Since there are several alternative management schemes, it would appear that a flexible policy allowing residents to choose the alternative most suitable to their needs would be desirable. Thus, some developments would remain authority managed, others resident managed, and yet others would be converted to ownership.

HUD's rhetoric supports such a flexible policy, but it is unlikely that its rhetoric will match reality. The codification of resident management in the 1987 and 1990 federal housing acts and implementing regulations and the rush by housing authorities and residents to jump on the resident management bandwagon suggest that flexibility will be discarded in favor of expediency. In the past two years, I have attended several workshops where residents from high-rise big-city developments, alongside residents from garden-style small-town developments, are given identical information about how to do resident management despite obvious differences in problems and opportunities. Although residents are told they can be flexible, they are rarely given the opportunity to explore the kind of management that would be most appropriate for their situation.

The biggest unresolved issue is whether resident management and ownership should be linked. Poverty is the common characteristic of public housing families, and data suggest that only a few families will be able to purchase their units without both up-front and ongoing subsidies. Rohe and Stegman's findings (1990) with respect to public housing homeownership should be sobering to those who believe successful resident ownership can become widespread.

If, as is likely, limited equity cooperatives become the common form of conversion, then the actual benefits of ownership may be far fewer than residents are being led to believe. Ownership without operating subsidies will result in most public housing families' paying more for their housing, and the limited equity restriction will keep them from the major economic benefit of ownership, the profit occurring at time of sale. Thus, although there may be real psychological benefits to being an owner, it is unlikely that ownership will provide any concrete mechanism to allow a family to move up and out of poverty.

The vehicle that will be used to convert public housing to homeownership is the HOPE program (Title IV) of the National Affordable Housing Act of 1990. HOPE authorizes funding for planning and implementation grants to help develop and carry out public housing ownership. HUD can provide HOPE funds up to and through the purchase of the units but cannot provide further subsidies from any sources. For families not wishing to become owners, replacement housing is to be available in the form of new public housing, rehabilitated vacant public housing units, five-year Section 8 certificates or vouchers, or comparable state or local programs. While HUD argues that this is a one-to-one replacement, only the new public housing option actually adds a unit for the unit lost to ownership.

This potential for loss of low-income housing units resulting from ownership is a troubling policy issue. Since vacant units, certificates, and vouchers can be counted as replacement housing, the real number of public and subsidized units is most certain to drop as developments are converted. A 1986 survey of public housing in eight major U.S. cities found nearly seventy-eight thousand families on waiting lists—approximately 70 percent of the capacity in these eight cities (Davis, 1986). There is unquestionably a need for more, rather than less, housing. A policy whose net effect is to reduce the number of units seems unwise.

Opposition to selling public housing to qualified resident groups would largely disappear if HUD were to articulate a real policy of one-to-one replacement and seek funds sufficient to carry it out. Where housing authorities are failing to provide adequate management and where residents have organized to improve their environments, they should have the opportunity to manage and own, provided it is feasible. New units that would be constructed as older units were sold to tenants would most likely be scattered-site housing or at least designed with greater sensitivity so that the nation's public housing stock could be improved rather than diminished. HUD's failure to fashion a real replacement policy gives credibility to critics who claim HUD is no longer interested in providing housing for the poor and is using resident management as a way to eliminate as much public housing as possible.

A BRIEF SUMMATION

Resident management is a practical response to the failure of a housing authority to manage properly, but it must develop out of community organization. It is, however, only one of several management options residents should consider. Ownership does not directly follow resident management, and its advisability is questionable. HUD's ownership policies seem misdirected and are likely to decrease rather than increase housing opportunities for poor families.

NOTES

1. The material in this section is largely drawn from my experiences in working between 1983 and 1988 with a developing resident management corporation at LeClaire Courts in Chicago and from a two-year study from 1989 to 1991 of alternatives to conventional public housing management supported by the John D. and Catherine T. MacArthur Foundation.

2. These four conditions represent a slight modification of those in Monti's article. The current form arose from discussions among Monti, Charles Connerly, Rachel Bratt, and me in January 1990 (Peterman and Young, 1991).

REFERENCES

Barnes, K. 1982. "Housing Associations: European Ideas, American Applications." *Journal of Housing* 39: 10–13.
Bratt, R. G. 1990. *Neighborhood Reinvestment Corporation-Sponsored Mutual Housing Associations: Experiences in Baltimore and New York.* Washington, D.C.: Neighborhood Reinvestment Corporation.
———. "Mutual Housing: Community-based Empowerment." *Journal of Housing* 48: 173–180.
Caprara, D., and B. Alexander. 1989. *Empowering Residents of Public Housing: A Resource Guide for Resident Management.* Washington, D.C.: National Center for Neighborhood Enterprise.
Clay, W. L. 1990. "Don't Sell Public Housing." *Journal of Housing* 47: 189–194.
Connerly, C. E. 1986. "What Should Be Done with the Public Housing Program?" *Journal of the American Planning Association* 52: 142–155.
Davis, M. 1986. *Public Housing Today.* Washington, D.C.: Council of Large Public Housing Authorities.
Giloth, R. 1988. "Community Economic Development: Strategies and Practices of the 1980s." *Economic Development Quarterly* 2: 345–350.
Goetze, R. 1985. *The Mutual Housing Association: An American Demonstration of a Proven European Concept.* Washington, D.C.: Neighborhood Reinvestment Corporation.
Hailey, M. 1984. "Bromley-Heath Tenant Management Corporation." In *The Grass Is Greener in Public Housing: From Tenant to Resident to Homeowner,* 29–37. Washington, D.C.: National Center for Neighborhood Enterprise.
Kemp, J. 1991. "A Homeownership Challenge." *Journal of Housing* 48: 7–9.
Kolodny, R. 1981. "Self-Help Can Be an Effective Tool in Housing the Urban Poor." *Journal of Housing* 38: 35–142.
Kunze, C. 1981. "Public Housing Cooperatives Reduce Dependence on Operating Subsidies, Modernization Funding." *Journal of Housing* 38, 9:489–493.

Manpower Demonstration Research Corporation. 1981. *Tenant Management: Findings from a Three Year Experiment in Public Housing*. Cambridge, Mass.: Ballinger.

Monti, D. J. 1989. "The Organizational Strengths and Weaknesses of Resident-Managed Public Housing Sites in the United States." *Journal of Urban Affairs* 11: 39–52.

National Center for Neighborhood Enterprise. 1984. *The Grass Is Greener in Public Housing: From Tenant to Resident to Homeowner*. Report on Resident Management of Public Housing, submitted to U.S. Department of Housing and Urban Development, Washington, D.C.

Peterman, W. 1989. "Options to Conventional Public Housing Management." *Journal of Urban Affairs* 11: 53–68.

Peterman, W., and M. A. Young. 1991. "Alternatives to Conventional Public Housing Management." Technical Note No. 1–91. Chicago: Voorhees Center for Neighborhood and Community Improvement, University of Illinois.

Rigby, R. J. 1989. "Revitalizing Distressed Public Housing: A Management Case." Address given at National Association of Housing (NAHRO), Canadian Housing Renewal Association (CHRA), Institute of Housing (IOH) international conference, University of Illinois, Urban-Champaign.

Rohe, William, and Michael Stegman. 1990. *Public Housing Homeownership Assessment*. Washington, D.C.: U.S. Department of Housing and Urban Development.

Silver, H., J. McDonald, and R. J. Ortiz. 1985. "Selling Public Housing: The Methods and Motivations." *Journal of Housing* 42: 213–228.

Sultmeier, D. 1987. "Buying In, Buying Out: The Future of Public Housing." *Shelterforce* 10, no. 1: 12–14.

U.S. General Accounting Office. 1989. *Public Housing: Planned Kenilworth-Parkside Sale Raises Issues for Future Transactions*. Washington, D.C.: U.S. Government Printing Office.

Wendel, G. D. 1975. *Tenant Management Corporations in Saint Louis Public Housing: The Status after Two Years*. St. Louis, Mo.: Center for Urban Programs, St. Louis University.

8

People in Control: A Comparison of Residents in Two U.S. Housing Developments

DANIEL J. MONTI

The United States, unlike European countries, has little experience with alternatives to conventionally managed public housing sites for its less-well-off citizens. A few sites in different cities have been managed by their residents to varying degrees and lengths of time. The Housing and Community Development Act of 1987 promised to increase the number of these sites substantially by providing operating subsidies and political legitimacy to resident groups that want to run their sites. The Bush administration seemed committed to encouraging such groups to purchase their sites. These possibilities notwithstanding, not much is known about how well resident management works or how well the people who live in these places fare (Meehan, 1979; Hexter, 1986; NCNE, 1984; Rigby, 1982; MDRC, 1981; Kolodny, 1983).

This chapter presents a preliminary analysis of survey data based on interviews conducted at two public housing sites during the summer of 1987. One site has been managed by a resident council for more than fifteen years after waging a rent strike against the local housing authority. The second entered into resident management at the end of the 1980s. Its rise was less contentious but no less determined. A comparison of the residents from these two sites offers some insights into who these people are and their views on a range of issues that bear on resident management. As assessment of these views can provide those responsible for running resident management corporations (RMCs) or monitoring their progress with valuable insights into what they can expect to find before and after an RMC is put in place.

THE RMC TENANT SURVEY

Fewer than two dozen public housing sites in the United States probably have had some degree of resident management since the early 1970s. Only five sites have had it longer than four years. Most sites have lost their RMC contracts. People at a few sites are working toward building a RMC or have recently succeeded in that effort. The record of success for RMCs is fairly thin. Nevertheless, resident management is a politically attractive reform because of its few apparent successes and the inability of local housing authorities to carry out a difficult mandate.

Given the interest in resident management, it is appropriate and useful to consider how the people living at such sites view their situation. To this end, I conducted a survey at two public housing sites participating in a demonstration project underwritten by the Amoco Foundation. The project was carried out by a minority development of new RMCs. I evaluated the progress of these sites during the first year of the project.

The survey was conducted at the Carr Square public housing development in St. Louis and the LeClaire Courts public housing site in Chicago. Both consist of townhouse apartments spread among a number of buildings no more than two stories tall. Carr Square was completed in 1942 and has 658 apartments spread among fifty-three buildings just north and west of downtown St. Louis. It has approximately 1,225 residents and has received no substantial rehabilitation work. It has been under resident management since the mid–1970s. The LeClaire Courts site was built in two stages. The first part was completed in 1950 and has 316 apartments spread among fifty-five buildings. The second section was completed in 1954 and has 299 units spread among forty-nine buildings. The site has approximately 2,600 residents and has received some rehabilitation work. It became managed by its residents in the late 1980s.

Approximately a hundred households were interviewed at each site. Just over 15 percent of the households at Carr Square were interviewed (N = 99). About 16 percent of the households at LeClaire Courts were interviewed (N = 102). Buildings at each site have varying numbers of apartments. A stratified sampling procedure was employed in order to guarantee that apartments in smaller (or larger) buildings were not selected disproportionately. The interviewers were college students who lived on the site. They were trained along with at least one member of the resident council who monitored their work but did not attend the interview sessions. The head of each household was interviewed, and the respondent's anonymity was carefully guarded. Respondents were free not to answer any question with which they were uncomfortable. The option was not exercised often, but it tended to be used most in relation to more personal items such as their income.

The survey items dealt with a range of subjects: personal characteristics (e.g., income), their neighborhood (e.g., availability of a grocery store, neighborhood problems (e.g., crime), site management (e.g., helpfulness of the manager), personal problems (e.g., children's schooling), problems with the apartment (e.g., poor plumbing), and their involvement in community affairs (e.g., knowledge of RMC officers). People were asked if problems they perceived had been growing worse and what, if anything, had been done to deal with the problems in question.

The answers provided a good overview of conditions on and off the site. More important, perhaps, they could be compared with the answers of people at a site that was on the verge of being awarded an RMC contract. That both sites were relatively comparable in structure (i.e., both have low-rise buildings) was important. Equally important was the fact that both had relatively good leadership and strong resident councils. This not only distinguished them from many former and present RMC sites, but it also made comparisons between Carr Square and LeClaire Courts more legitimate (Monti, 1989a, 1989b).

RESULTS FROM PREVIOUS RESIDENT SURVEYS

The only previous survey of people living in resident-managed public housing sites was conducted at six places during the 1970s. The Manpower Demonstration Research Corporation helped to establish RMCs at those sites and evaluated their progress over a three-year period. Surveyed were 181 people randomly selected from the six sites and 395 residents from eighteen control sites (MDRC, 1981). Interviews were completed in 1976 and 1979.

Residents at the RMC sites seemed pleased with their new situation. They were satisfied with the condition of their units, maintenance work, and safety at the site and believed that the RMC was both more vigilant and stricter than the local housing authority. Finally, about one-third of the people in RMC sites found themselves involved in affairs at the site, while only 15 percent of the people at the control sites defined themselves in this way.

People may have been happy that fellow residents were in charge of the site, and they may have been more actively involved in life at the site, yet they had only a modest understanding of what the RMC's responsibilities were. They also were not impressed with the RMC's ability to respond to complaints or perform regular management chores and were not certain how much better the RMC was than the old tenant council of the local housing authority manager.

These negative reviews were not quite so severe, MDRC analysts noted, at the better RMC sites. Furthermore, one can see how it would take longer to make a difference in the way the site was run than in the way residents behaved. Resident leaders often complain that they have more responsibilities than they have authority or resources. Such a situation would make it difficult for RMC leaders to have much of an impact on how well the buildings are maintained or look. Nevertheless, the perception that RMCs may not perform much better than conventional public housing authority managers cannot be ignored and must be kept in mind when reviewing the survey results presented here.

THE RESIDENTS AT RMC SITES

The demographic profile of public housing residents in the United States today is fairly well known. The households usually are black or Hispanic, led by an unmarried adult with several children, poor, and have few options on where to live. Originally conceived as temporary housing for the working poor, public housing has become the housing of last resort for a large number of people with few skills and little money. The people of Carr Square and LeClaire Courts resemble the typical public housing resident population in some ways, but they differ in some ways too.

The households are overwhelmingly black (Carr Square, 95 percent; LeClaire Courts, 94 percent). They are not led by married couples (90 percent at both sites are divorced, separated, or have some other living arrangement). Many have numerous children (38 percent in Carr Square and 68 percent in LeClaire Courts have two or more children). They tend to be poor (60 percent in Carr Square and 41 percent in LeClaire Courts have no adults employed on a full-time basis; only 46 percent in Carr Square and 14 percent in LeClaire Courts have one or more adults employed on a part-time basis; 59 percent or more at both sites do not have checking or savings accounts with at least $100; 74 percent in Carr Square and 82 percent in LeClaire Courts have one or more adults receiving some kind of public assistance; a majority own no car and use no credit cards). The jobs they hold do not provide much income (59 percent of Carr Square households and 55 percent of LeClaire Courts households report earned income of less than $10,000). Public assistance is reported to provide comparable amounts of money to more households (79 percent in Carr Square and 68 percent in LeClaire Courts). They report paying low rents (67 percent in Carr Square and 54 percent in LeClaire Courts say they pay less than $200 each month). In these ways, at least, the resident populations at Carr Square and LeClaire Courts would seem to have much in common with most other people in public housing.

A minority of the residents, at times a quite substantial minority, do not fit the typical profile for public housing tenants. Many households have no children or only one child (61 percent in Carr Square and 31 percent in LeClaire Courts). There also appear to be many households with two or more adults between the ages of 21 and 50 (21 percent in Carr Square and 39 percent in LeClaire Courts) and one or more adults older than 50 (59 percent in Carr Square and 43 percent in LeClaire Courts). There is a fairly good mix of juveniles, adults, and older people at these sites. One might have expected more households with many children and fewer households with only one adult or older person.

A good portion of the households have at least one adult who has a full-time job (34 percent in Carr Square and 29 percent in LeClaire Courts). Over 30 percent of the households in LeClaire Courts and 6 percent in Carr Square have two or more adults so employed. While many households do not earn much money, most are able to pay their bills on a regular basis (70 percent in Carr Square, 51 percent in LeClaire Courts). There also is a segment of the population that receives no public assistance (26 percent in Carr Square, 18 percent in LeClaire Courts), has savings in excess of $100 (18 percent in Carr Square, 35 percent in LeClaire Courts), and has a checking account with more than $100 in it (17 percent in Carr Square, 13 percent in LeClaire Courts), owns an automobile (approximately 40 percent at both sites), uses credit cards (13 percent in Carr Square, 17 percent in LeClaire Courts), and has household members attending or graduating from a four-year college or university (29 percent in Carr Square and 17 percent in LeClaire Courts). A good share report obtaining a better job or raises in salary over the past two years (32 percent in Carr Square and 21 percent in LeClaire Courts). Even more people perceive their household's financial situation improving during the same period of time (57 percent in Carr Square and 45 percent in LeClaire Courts).

These two sites are able to attract or hold working people and people who receive no public assistance. Although these people may be a minority at the site, they represent an important element in the population that many RMC leaders say was lost to public housing sites after 1960. It is a segment of the population that RMC leaders would like to grow because it provides them with a broader range of residents and often more stable families.

Stability is something that a RMC needs in order to solidify the community and develop a pool of potential leaders and helpers. The clearest sign that these sites possess some stability is in the tenure of residents. The established RMC site, Carr Square, has many households with long tenure (42 percent with more than ten years in residence). The prospective RMC site, LeClaire Courts, has 80 percent of its households having lived there for more than ten years. However, it is likely that Carr Square lost many more. It is an older site, more worn, and directly across the street from a new apartment complex that has drawn away many long-time residents. The irony is that RMC owns part of that development. Nevertheless, RMC leaders have worried about the erosion of their base of support and their inability to integrate the 38 percent of its population that has lived in Carr Square less than four years. This is a problem the LeClaire Courts site eventually will have to confront. Failure to acquire the cooperation of new residents will undermine the RMC's viability as a community organization and property manager.

THE RMC NEIGHBORHOOD

The RMC faces a difficult chore. Not only must it work with older, often rundown buildings, it also must deal with a neighborhood surrounding the site that has severe problems or few amenities. This is apparent in the case of Carr Square and LeClaire Courts. At the same time, people at these sites seem to think that conditions are improving. What cannot be revealed in these surveys is just how much the residents themselves have contributed to these improvements.

The neighborhoods surrounding Carr Square and LeClaire Courts do not provide everything the typical resident might have occasion to need or use. A majority of Carr Square residents claim that they have access to a grocery store, convenience shop, a bar or liquor store, a fast-food restaurant, a medical doctor, and a dentist. Auto or appliance repairmen, if they can be found, usually will come onto the site. The quality of the food they buy generally is good. It must be noted that a new grocery store only recently had opened in the neighborhood. Prior to that, residents had to travel a great distance to buy groceries.

The services readily available to LeClaire Courts residents are a bit different. Most people claim to have regular access to a Laundromat, pharmacy, and a nicer restaurant. Like their counterparts in St. Louis, they also have fast-food restaurants, a bar or liquor store, a dentist, and a doctor readily available. Twice as many claim to have auto and appliance repairmen in the area, as was the case for Carr Square (41 percent and 19 percent, respectively); but they have less success in having them come onto the site (50 percent versus 76 percent for Carr Square). They are far less satisfied with the quality of food they usually purchase in the area (36 percent versus 82 percent for Carr Square).

The number and quality of services available to LeClaire Courts residents will likely improve as the RMC becomes better established and businesspersons see the work it does. To a certain degree, both Carr Square and LeClaire Courts will benefit from the redevelopment going on around them. This process has advanced further in St. Louis, where approximately 70 percent of Carr Square residents note an influx of new people and shops in the area. Over half of LeClaire Courts residents noted these newcomers.

This represents progress, but residents are not certain how much progress they want. LeClaire Courts residents are generally eager to have more middle-class and white families move into the area. About half of those interviewed took that position. The same portion said that it did not want more black families moving into the neighborhood. The responses from Carr Square residents were less emphatic, probably because they have seen more middle-class and white families moving into their area. Although one-third of the Carr Square respondents wanted more of these people, over 40 percent were not certain that they did. The same portion was unsure about having more black families move in as well. The irony, of course, is that the community organizing undertaken by the RMCs makes their area a better place to live and more attractive to outsiders.

Over one-third of the Carr Square respondents thought their neighborhood was a good place to live. Another 43 percent thought it was at least part of the time. Nearly 57 percent of the LeClaire Courts respondents said that their neighborhood was good, and nearly 17 percent said it was so at least part of the time. These are curious findings inasmuch as Carr Square residents generally view their neighborhood as a safe place to live.

Evidence for this last point came from a series of questions about neighborhood crime and safety. A majority of residents from both sites walk freely through the neighborhood almost any time they like (57 percent), but more LeClaire Courts residents than Carr Square residents did not feel that way (31 percent versus 23 percent). More Carr Square residents also believed that their property was safe when they were out of their apartment (56 percent versus 45 percent for LeClaire Courts). Many more LeClaire Courts residents thought that their property was not safe (44 percent versus 14 percent for Carr Square). On the other hand, more LeClaire Courts residents thought it safe to allow children to play outside unattended (52 percent versus 36 percent for Carr Square). More Carr Square residents than LeClaire Courts residents thought it was not wise to do this (32 percent versus 27 percent).

Only 35 percent of Carr Square residents in 1987 knew area people who had a problem with drugs. Nearly half thought the problem had been worse two years earlier. More LeClaire Court residents knew people with a drug problem (54 percent), and 64 percent thought drug use was a bigger problem today than two years ago. One-third of the respondents from both sites knew someone who had been robbed or assaulted recently. Yet 36 percent of the LeClaire Courts respondents thought such crimes had increased, while only 11 percent of Carr Square people thought this. Only 5 percent of Carr Square's people had known of a rape occurring recently. Nearly 20 percent of LeClaire Court's people knew someone who had been raped, but as many people thought this problem was worse two years earlier. Only 12 percent of Carr Square's people knew someone who carried weapons for protection, while 45 percent of LeClaire Court's people did. Again, however, the latter saw improvements occurring. Over 28 percent thought more people carried weapons two years ago. Carr Square residents were evenly split on the question of vandalism. Over 46 percent saw it as a problem (52 percent), but half also thought that vandalism had been worse two years earlier. Only 22 percent of Carr Square's people said that.

Police department records indicate that reported crimes dropped dramatically in the area around Carr Square over 1971–1983, a time when residents were organizing themselves and people were moving out of the area. Crime at the LeClaire Courts site dropped a bit between 1984 and

1985 but remained fairly steady through 1987. Whatever impact the LeClaire Courts RMC can have on criminal behavior has not yet become apparent. One suspects that less criminal behavior will be evident and people will feel more secure two years from now if the RMC works well.

SITE MANAGEMENT

In a survey conducted during the late 1970s, people expressed satisfaction with RMCs but were uncertain how much better residents were at managing the property. RMC leaders seemed stricter, but they did not necessarily change how the site looked. This might be attributable to the inexperience of RMC leaders or the absence of resources, but the perception that RMCs may do no better than the housing authority would not help the RMC in the long run. That many have ceased to operate supports this conclusion.

It is clear from the survey that resident management can command much respect. The RMC at Carr Square was rated higher than the housing authority managers at LeClaire Courts in terms of its presence on the site. The manager was viewed as being available when needed (56 percent versus 17 percent for LeClaire Courts) and enforcing the lease (49 percent versus 24 percent for LeClaire Courts). The RMC manager also was perceived as knowing the tenants better (75 percent versus 16 percent at LeClaire Courts). In neither case, however, was the management staff generally viewed as being overbearing or harassing the residents.

Residents at LeClaire Courts were more likely to ask management staff for help (40 percent versus 25 for Carr Square), though residents at Carr Square had done so on occasion (25 percent versus 5 percent at LeClaire Courts). Over 50 percent of the LeClaire Courts respondents said that the resident council kept people informed at least part of the time. The better-established Carr Square RMC was so described by 83 percent of those surveyed.

Most people at both sites think that resident management is a good idea (67 percent at Carr Square, 59 percent at LeClaire Courts). There are sizable minorities at both sites, however, who are not certain (27 percent at Carr Square, 29 percent at LeClaire Courts). Furthermore, the enthusiasm for resident management does not carry over to several activities favored by many tenant leaders and some private interest groups.

Less than 33 percent of those surveyed at Carr Square in 1987 thought individual tenants should own their apartments. Less than 20 percent thought it would be a good idea for the RMC to own their site or organize businesses. As many people believed these are not good ideas. It is important to note that most of those surveyed at Carr Square had not reached a decision on the advisability of homeownership or resident-run businesses. Nevertheless, given the RMC leaders' enthusiasm for these activities, one might have expected more people to support such initiatives. Site leaders believed support would increase once the ideas were more widely discussed.

More people at LeClaire Courts were interested in owning their apartment (41 percent versus 31 percent at Carr Square), RMC ownership (36 percent versus 15 percent at Carr Square), and RMC-run businesses (46 percent versus 18 percent at Carr Square). Yet approximately one-third of those surveyed did not support such initiatives. Some were not certain where they stood on these matters, and opinions can change. If LeClaire Courts' leaders want these things, they will have to work hard to convince others. That so many people at Carr Square remain unconvinced about the advisability of tenant ownership and resident-run businesses indicates that it will be hard work indeed.

Public housing residents often have other, more pressing concerns, some of them of a personal nature and others relating to the condition of their apartment or building. More than 70 percent of those living at Carr Square do not go to the manager with specific personal problems. The percentage of people from LeClaire Courts who do not is only a bit smaller. At one time or another, though, between 9 and 21 percent of Carr Square's residents probably have approached the manager with a personal problem. The comparable statistic for people at LeClaire Courts is 29 to 43 percent, depending on the problem.

This is not so strange as it seems. People at a well-run RMC site are less likely to approach the manager, or the resident council for that matter, with personal problems. They have learned how to cope on their own, or they get help from someone who volunteers as a floor or lane captain. An informal system for resolving disputes or addressing personal hardships gradually emerges, and management staff have less need to serve as social workers. A site such as LeClaire Courts has not yet developed such a system. More people turn to the manager, in this case a housing authority official, for help. As resident management takes hold at LeClaire Courts, one can expect to find fewer people as a fairly reliable source of help when it is requested.

People at Carr Square were much more likely to bring problems with their apartment or building to the attention of management staff. Complaints about the condition of walls and floors were made at least occasionally by 39 percent of the people surveyed. Nearly 66 percent had complained about the plumbing. The percentage of people registering problems with their apartment's windows, electricity, and heating and cooling systems fell between these extremes. Only 13 percent had complained about dogs and rodents, but 56 percent had noted problems with garbage or insects.

Even more people at LeClaire Courts complained about the condition of their apartment. Half noted problems with the electrical, heating, or cooling systems. Nearly three-fourths of those surveyed had difficulty with their windows. The percentage of people noting other problems with their apartments fell between these extremes. Rodents or dogs had troubled over 35 percent of the LeClaire Courts people, and over 50 percent had complained about insects and garbage around the site.

It is important to keep several things in mind when evaluating these data. First, Carr Square's buildings are older and more worn out. Second, we have no idea how severe the problems being cited were. Third, we do not know if residents at Carr Square appreciated the difficulty RMC leaders had in securing assistance from the housing authority personnel when large problems arose. Finally, it is hard to say what combination of long- and short-term maintenance work would better satisfy residents. With these points in mind, one can assess more fairly the degree of satisfaction expressed by residents with the maintenance work that was done.

Nearly half of the Carr Square residents (45 percent) did not think that maintenance men or groundskeepers came quickly to handle reported problems. Just over 49 percent thought that workers did respond promptly at least part of the time. The people at LeClaire Courts, which still was under public housing authority management at the time of the survey, answered the question similarly.

Carr Square's maintenance and grounds crews may not have come as quickly as many people thought they should, but residents tended to be pleased with the work that was done. Only 23 percent thought that reported problems were not handled well. Nearly 70 percent of those responding found the work satisfactory part or most of the time. The people at LeClaire Courts generally were a bit less satisfied with the work their maintenance and grounds crews did. Given the condition of Carr Square's buildings, any comparison we make between work accomplished there and work done at LeClaire Courts probably understates the success of Carr Square's work crews.

Some indication that this is so can be seen in the way residents answered questions about their general satisfaction with life at their respective developments. Those at Carr Square generally were satisfied with the appearance of their apartment and building. Half said outright that the appearance was good; only one-third of the respondents thought otherwise. On the other hand, only 43 percent of the LeClaire Court's residents said the appearance of their apartment and building was good, and 39 percent did not approve of the appearance. When asked if the appearance was better than two years ago or in their previous apartment building, 40 percent of Carr Square residents disagreed that their place was looking better, but over 67 percent of LeClaire Courts' people disagreed.

Carr Square residents also were relatively satisfied with how quiet their building was (78 percent said it was not noisy) and how well behaved young people were (16 percent said that they were not well behaved). Well over half thought that at least some improvements had been observed on both counts recently. More LeClaire Courts residents found their buildings noisy at least part of the time (54 percent) and young people not well behaved (44 percent). A majority of LeClaire Courts residents also thought that their building was not becoming quieter (59 percent) or that young people were behaving better (52 percent).

An RMC must act as both a community and a property manager. A previous survey of people living at such sites indicated that RMCs had made some progress as a community organization. People were better informed and seemed satisfied with the leadership provided by their fellow residents. They were not so certain that the RMC actually responded better to specific complaints about maintenance at the site, however. Results from this survey indicate that people living at a RMC site may indeed notice a difference in the performance of certain management chores, and that difference is good. Whether the prospective leaders of LeClaire Courts' RMC can do well remains to be seen.

RESIDENT PARTICIPATION

Learning to run a public housing site successfully is not easy. It is the second skill resident leaders must master. The first is organizing their community. The leaders at Carr Square and LeClaire Courts have shown some ability to bring their fellow residents together and, in the former's case, to hold them together. In previous research on RMCs, this ability was taken for granted, or the presence of a few strong leaders was thought to be sufficient to keep almost everyone at the site behaving properly (MDRC, 1981). As I have argued elsewhere, this was a serious mistake (Monti, 1989a).

Carr Square is among the more successful RMC sites in the United States. The vast majority of its residents (69 percent) have no interest in leaving, yet a good share of them (17 percent) would prefer to live somewhere else, and another portion think about leaving at least part of the time (12 percent). To be sure, willing replacements could be found for these relatively dissatisfied people. Nevertheless, conditions at the site are not so good that everyone wants to stay. RMC leaders acknowledge that many families with employed people have left because their rents were tied to their income and the apartments needed basic repairs. The fact remains that people the RMC would rather keep have moved away. New residents are moving in who have no sense of the work that went into salvaging Carr Square and no immediate commitment to the community.

A comparatively small segment of Carr Square's resident population (12 percent) participates in the tenant organization on a regular basis. Another 15 percent participate intermittently. These people may know the site's leaders quite well. Some 16 percent said that they knew the organization's officers, and even more said they knew one or more people involved in the tenant organization and many people across the site. This enables RMC leaders to remain informed about what is occurring and to communicate with many residents when the need arises.

Another source of strength in Carr Square RMC is that nearly 60 percent of the residents have relatives living on the site. Almost as many people (57 percent) say that they visit their friends and relatives on the site. Clearly, many people are well integrated into the Carr Square community. They may not participate in the tenant organization, but they certainly have ways of making their influence felt and of being informed about current events.

It is equally apparent that a good-sized segment of Carr Square's population is not especially well integrated into the community. Most have no friends involved in the tenant organization (67 percent); over half say that they do not know the tenant organization's officers (55 percent); most important, perhaps, 34 percent have no relatives elsewhere on the site, and 28 percent say they do not visit whatever friends they have have at the site. This could make it difficult for leaders to renew or ignite many persons' commitment to Carr Square as a RMC site. This would prove true especially when new ventures such as beginning a business or purchasing the site were involved.

It could have an impact on routine affairs as well. Nearly 56 percent of the people surveyed from Carr Square thought the resident board regularly kept them informed, but almost the same portion (56.6 percent) say that they do not know what the tenant organization usually is doing. This may be less a contradiction than it appears. The resident council or RMC board may, and likely does, make decisions or consider alternative approaches to different problems without consulting many people. That is part of what leaders do. An equally important part of leading a community organization, particularly one that owes its existence to a popular uprising by its members, is keeping communication channels with one's followers not only open but filled with information. A majority of Carr Square's households say that does not happen routinely.

There is a tension built into an RMC. It must work like an efficient business even as it nurtures its communal roots. Based on firsthand observations of a number of RMCs and previous studies, it seems fair to say that most RMCs find this difficult, and the failed ones could not do it at all. A relatively successful RMC such as Carr Square's has learned to balance these seemingly contradictory demands better than most others, but it probably has not done as well as it could or should.

Evidence of this is seen in answers to several questions about residents' satisfaction with the decisions made by the resident council, which also serves as the board of directors for the RMC. Only 20 percent said they agreed with most of what the tenant organization does. (Another 39 percent could agree with its actions at least some of the time.) Just over 39 percent said they never had disagreed strongly with something the tenant organization did. On the other hand, some 41 percent said they had disagreed strongly with the organization at least once, and 20 percent said that they did not agree with most of what the tenant organization does. (It should be noted that about 20 percent of the respondents answered neither of these questions.

Only the questions dealing with money earned or received from public assistance had a higher nonresponse rate. A number of people were reluctant to address what to them apparently was a sensitive matter.)

It is hard to reconcile these findings with the fact that most residents never tried to make the tenant organization do something (77 percent), filed a complaint against someone in their building (92 percent), or passed word to the tenant organization of someone breaking a rule (92 percent). People are not quite so upset at times with the tenant organization as some of their answers implied, do not think it would do much good to try changing its positions on one or another matter, or make a distinction between their everyday life on the site and some of the bigger questions addressed by the tenant organization. The evidence seems to support this last explanation.

Most people say that living at Carr Square is good and the RMC usually manages the site well. While there are problems with their apartments and sometimes with their neighbors, people do not seem to hold the RMC responsible for these shortcomings. Those who move do so because they can find a better apartment, sometimes for less money than they pay at Carr Square. Whatever attraction the community has, and it is not insubstantial, does not seem sufficient to hold these residents. Most people seem relatively satisfied at Carr Square, however.

A complement to this fact is that most people find no need to involve themselves in many big and not-so-big issues confronted by site leaders. Hardly anyone, for instance, knows about plans to start resident-run businesses (98 percent), and no one said he or she was involved in planning such businesses, yet the resident council is making such plans.

This arrangement may work well enough with routine affairs at the site. It likely will not work when important issues such as the RMC's ownership of the site finally are raised. It is on those occasions that the tension between the RMC as a property manager and community organizer will be played out in a more public way.

Carr Square's RMC is experienced and relatively successful. Some of the findings and potential problems alluded to reflect that fact. The resident council at LeClaire Courts was inexperienced in the late 1980s and had not yet had an opportunity to manage its site. It had not yet needed to work out a solution to the problem of balancing the roles of community organizer and property manager. Instead, it had been concentrating more on drawing its community together. The survey results bear out these points and hint at what is gained and lost when an RMC becomes better established.

Less than half of LeClaire Courts' households (40 percent) say that they do not want to leave. Over half would prefer to live somewhere else (32 percent) or sometimes think about leaving (19 percent). Inasmuch as 80 percent of those surveyed had lived there for more than eight years, it means that dissatisfaction with the site probably is rooted in hard experience. Yet it is this very fact, when coupled with a solid minority who do not want to leave, that provides the basis for organizing the community and establishing an RMC.

Nearly one-third of the respondents participate in the tenant organization, and another 26 percent do so intermittently. That is more than twice the percentage of people from Carr Square who said they participated at least sometimes in the tenant organization. Some 28 percent said that they had friends in the tenant organization, versus 16 percent at Carr Square. Nearly half (45 percent) said they know the group's officers, and even more said they knew one or more people involved with the organization (79 percent). The comparable statistics for Carr Square were lower. At LeClaire Courts, a majority of the residents said they are involved with the tenant organization and are in contact with nearly everyone around the site. The LeClaire Courts resident council at this point in its career is doing a good job of mobilizing the people at the site. It is doing a better job than the Carr Square group for at least two reasons. First, it is still establishing its presence at the site and developing a base of support. Second, it has yet to be challenged and occupied by management problems.

The LeClaire Courts groups probably will have to work harder in the future to maintain that base of support. Only 35 percent of the residents reported that they had relatives living somewhere on the site, and less than half (46 percent) said that they visit friends and relatives on the site. The comparable statistics for Carr Square were higher. Furthermore, a good portion of LeClaire Courts' people said they did not know the tenant organization's officers (34 percent), and nearly half (47 percent) have friends who are active in the tenant organization. Since the resident council has done a credible job of making early contact with most residents, the group needs to maintain its high profile. Otherwise, it will be hard to overcome some of the barriers to renewing or igniting commitment to the group that are built into the site's social structure.

There is evidence that this problem already has surfaced. Only one-third of the LeClaire Courts people surveyed (32 percent) said that they knew what the resident council usually was doing. Another 30 percent said that was true only part of the time. While these percentages are higher than the ones for Carr Square, it still means that fully one-third of the LeClaire Courts residents usually do know what the resident council was doing. A new resident management organization has to make a special effort to build good channels of communication with its constituents and to keep them well informed. Otherwise, it will have difficulty running the site once problems arise.

The LeClaire Courts resident council has not yet succeeded in convincing most people that its positions are correct. Only 26 percent agree with most of what the tenant organization does. (Another 28 percent could agree with its actions at least some of the time.) Nearly half (48 percent) had disagreed strongly with the organization at least once, and 23 percent usually did not agree with the group. These statistics are similar to those found at Carr Square.

These similarities notwithstanding, LeClaire Courts' residents are more actively engaged in identifying problems and solutions at the site. Almost two-thirds had tried to make the resident council do something, and a good portion of them (24 percent) had succeeded. Some 26 percent had filed a complaint against a neighbor, and another 30 percent had passed word of someone breaking a rule. The statistics for Carr Square are substantially lower. (On the other hand, life at Carr Square is more stable today.)

This activism spills over into other areas. Many more people at LeClaire Courts, for example, knew about plans for resident-run businesses (16 percent) or are involved in making those plans (13 percent). Virtually no one at Carr Square could say that. Clearly, resident council efforts to promote activism have drawn people into discussions about little and big issues affecting their welfare. Much work will have to go into maintaining that degree of involvement, especially once the RMC gains full responsibility for the site. As the experience of Carr Square's RMC seems to indicate, this will be hard work indeed.

CONCLUSIONS

The results of this study tell us some interesting things about people who live in public housing run largely by the residents themselves. The federal government is committed to encouraging more public housing residents to do this, but we still do not know much about these sites and why they succeed or fail. This chapter begins to address these issues as well.

From a strictly academic standpoint, we find some qualified support for a theory about blacks' political participation that has nothing necessarily to do with public housing or resident management. In the so-called ethnic community theory, it is proposed that "race- and class-conscious blacks will engage in high levels of political action to achieve social changes for the black community" (Spain, 1987:6; Henig and Gale, 1987; Guterbock and London, 1983). Surveys of blacks outside public housing seem to support this line of reasoning. The effort to create RMCs offers obvious support for it inside public housing. So, too, does an initial inspection of the results from these surveys.

Only 34 percent of the Carr Square respondents and 40 percent of those from LeClaire Courts said that they belonged to a church in the area. On the other hand, approximately 70 percent of the respondents from both sites (68 percent at Carr Square, 71 percent at LeClaire Courts) said that they participate in a political organization or vote in most elections. Informed politicians from each city readily concur that political participation by people from these sites is high. Given the general record of political involvement of low-income minority people, these findings are impressive. What occurs at these sites in the way of tenant organizing is affecting other types of political activity off the site. The people at these sites intend to change their own situation and play a bigger part in the community around them.

This chapter reinforces several things indicated in previous studies. A good RMC likely will be viewed as doing more on the site and being stricter than the local housing authority. People also will say they generally have more knowledge of what occurs on the site because of information coming from the tenant organization. On the other hand, the results from this study differ in at least two important ways from those published previously. The residents at sites with an RMC or moving to create one may participate in local affairs at a fairly high rate; however, that degree of involvement may not be sustained over long periods of time. People and the tenant organization serving them may grow a bit complacent as they gain control over the site and make some improvements. The other noteworthy finding is the fact that a more experienced RMC can be viewed as performing relatively well, even under conditions that are less than ideal. People who were interviewed at other sites only a year or two after those places acquired RMCs were not at all certain that their fellow residents were carrying out routine management chores in a competent manner. The people at Carr Square live under a more experienced RMC and generally endorse its performance.

There were similarities as well as differences in the way people from Carr Square and LeClaire Courts answered questions. They will not be repeated here. I will point out only that the situation facing new and old RMCs is different and likely to be reflected in who lives there, how involved they are in the tenant organization, and how they view their situation. Although more people tend to view public housing as a more permanent place to live, there can be a substantial turnover in the resident population of these sites. New residents will not have had the experience of struggling to gain control over the site, nor will they be immediately integrated into the social network of those who do. This places a burden on some long-term residents who may have moved on to consider new and, in some ways, bigger challenges. The problem is that new ventures such as resident-run businesses or homeownership will require just as much organizational work and hand holding as did resident management, and maybe more. The residents of Carr Square and LeClaire Courts are neither well informed nor especially convinced about the merit of such ventures. Resident leaders and federal officials may like these things. It is by no means clear at this point that the people living at these sites share their enthusiasm.

There is an inherent tension between the RMC as a community organizer and as a property manager. People have just so much time and energy that they can give to something, and that includes an RMC. It appears that an experienced RMC cuts back on some of its more self-conscious attempts to organize people at the site as it wrestles with routine and not-so-routine management tasks. Yet this may create some serious problems for the RMC as it greets new residents and attempts to sponsor new ventures.

The primary strength and weakness of RMCs is that they are drawn simultaneously in two different directions. On the one hand, they are a communal group that works hard to keep its members behaving properly and together. On the other, they are a business organization overseeing a multimillion dollar real estate development. It is difficult enough to do one of these tasks well. There are few historical precedents for an organization forged in controversy and conflict accomplishing both (Tilly, 1988). The resident groups at Carr Square and LeClaire Courts have the chance and, perhaps, even the ability to do both, but it is unlikely that they will do so without a great deal of outside assistance for a long period of time.

Current government policy is predicted on the assumption that RMCs are capable of becoming self-sustaining enterprises more easily and sooner than the history of such organizations would indicate is possible. Furthermore, the Bush administration behaves in a manner that suggests that RMCs can be created or encouraged into existence by local housing authorities, foundations, and/or federal agencies. There is nothing in the history of resident management to indicate that this is feasible, and there is much evidence to indicate that such an approach is bound to fail. Certainly, the results of this survey show how uncertain public housing tenants are about resident management and ownership. Persons intent on promoting these reforms would be well advised to listen more intently to what resident groups are saying than to what they, as leaders, want to hear.

NOTE

The work reported in this chapter was conducted through the Institute for the Study of Economic Culture at Boston University. Funding for this work originated from the Amoco Foundation. The work was part of an evaluation of efforts undertaken by the National Center for Neighborhood Enterprise, Washington, D.C., to improve the effectiveness of resident management corporations.

REFERENCES

Guterbock, T., and London, B. 1983. "Race, Political Orientation, and Participation: An Empirical Test of Four Competing Theories." *American Sociological Review* 48: 439–453.

Henig, Jeffrey, and Gale, Dennis. 1987. "The Political Incorporation of Newcomers to Racially Changing Neighborhoods." *Urban Affairs Quarterly* 22, no. 3: 399–419.

Hexter, James. 1986. "Tenant Management: Can It Succeed as an Alternative to Traditional Management Strategies in Boston Public Housing." Master's thesis, Massachusetts Institute of Technology.

Kolodny, Robert. 1983. "What Happens When Tenants Manage Their Own Public Housing." Unpublished report. Washington, D.C.: Office of Policy Development, U.S. Department of Housing and Urban Development.

Manpower Demonstration Research Corporation. 1981. *Tenant Management: Findings from a Three-Year Experiment in Public Housing.* Cambridge: Ballinger Publishing Company.

Meehan, Eugene. 1979. *The Quality of Federal Policymaking: Programmed Failure in Public Housing.* Columbia: University of Missouri Press.

Monti, Daniel J. 1989a. "The Organizational Strengths and Weaknesses of Resident-Managed Public Housing Sites in the United States." *Journal of Urban Affairs* 2, no. 1: 459–469.

———. 1989b. "Economic Development in Low-Income Neighborhoods: The Case of Tenant-Managed Public Housing Sites in the United States." *Built Environment* 14, no. 3/4: 201–208.

National Center for Neighborhood Enterprise. 1984. *The Grass Is Greener in Public Housing: From Tenant to Resident to Homeowner.* Washington, D.C.: National Center for Neighborhood Enterprise.

Rigby, Robert. 1982. *The Residents as Resource: A Public Housing Management Demonstration in Jersey City.* Trenton: Bureau of Neighborhood Preservation, Department of Community Affairs.

Spain, Daphne. 1987. "Racial Differences in Housing, Neighborhoods, and Political Participation." *Urban Affairs Quarterly* 22, no. 3: 421–424.

Tilly, Charles. 1988. "Collective Violence in European Perspective." Working paper 56. New York: New School for Social Research.

9

The Role of Neighborhood-based Housing Nonprofits in the Ownership and Control of Housing in U.S. Cities

KEITH P. RASEY

In the past fifteen years, government officials and urban planners in the United States have increasingly viewed nonprofit organizations, including community development corporations (CDCs), as preferred providers of housing to low- and moderate-income and special-needs households. (In the United States, *CDC* is commonly used to designate nonprofit organizations primarily involved in housing and economic development, especially at the neighborhood or community level. Because of this, *CDC* and *housing nonprofit* are used interchangeably in this chapter to refer to modern nonprofit housing providers.) Nonprofits' housing products and services have been highly targeted based on income, and they have been responsive to neighborhood and community needs.

Common goals of CDCs have been to make decent housing more affordable and to increase community control over the housing inventory (Mayer, 1990: 366–368). Low- and moderate-income renters have been helped to become homeowners through publicly and privately subsidized grant and loan programs, lease-purchase agreements, pre- and post-purchase counseling, and affirmative action. Existing homeowners, including elderly households on fixed incomes, have been helped to meet higher housing expenses through low-cost maintenance agreements, home repair and weatherization grants, reduced-interest-rate loans, and housing counseling. Higher homeownership rates have, in turn, helped stabilize blocks and, in some cases, whole neighborhoods.

Nonprofits have also developed rental housing for low-income households with special needs, including the physically and mentally disabled. CDCs have provided temporary and transitional housing for the homeless and encouraged tenant participation in management and, in some cases, ownership of rental property.

Since their emergence in the 1960s, nonprofits have often launched initiatives exceeding the stated requirements of public and private funding sources. For example, nonprofits provided housing counseling to owners and renters before federal funding for counseling was made available.[1] Community-based nonprofits were also among the first to encourage tenant participation in management (Atlas and Dreier, 1986: 385).

THE EVOLUTION OF HOUSING NONPROFITS IN THE UNITED STATES

In many European countries, nonprofit organizations have played a major role in the provision of low- and moderate-income housing since the mid–1800s (Birch and Gardner, 1981: 409). In contrast, their role in the United States was limited prior to 1960. The only nonprofits to develop urban housing in the 1800s were a small number of philanthropic housing associations operating in eastern cities—New York, Boston, and Philadelphia (Lubove, 1962; Glaab and Brown, 1967; Friedman, 1968). In the absence of government subsidies, nonprofit providers sought to attract private capital through limited-dividend corporations, borrowed from the British experience (Birch and Gardner, 1981).[2]

In the United States, the limited-dividend model proved relatively unproductive. Private investors preferred the higher rates of return available from speculative real estate ventures (20 percent or more) compared to limited-dividend offerings of only 3 to 7 percent (Birch and Gardner, 1981: 405–406). Further, much of the development by limited-dividend sponsors was of middle-class rather than low-income housing (Glaab and Brown, 1967: 297–298).[3] The failure to target incomes effectively was due to the limited amount of interest forgone by investors (Birch and Gardner, 1981: 406) and the high architectural standards imposed by developers (Bowly, 1978; Glaab and Brown, 1967). The most successful nonprofit sponsors of housing prior to 1960 were cooperative associations. These first appeared in New York City in the 1920s, operating under state tax-exempt status (Sullivan, 1969: 25).

Only after the Great Depression brought about national recognition of a major urban crisis did the federal government become an active participant in housing.[4] The Roosevelt administration's main federal objectives were job creation and temporary relief, including housing, for the unemployed. The Public Works Administration (PWA), created in 1933, included two housing programs: the first, the forerunner of public housing, and the second, a loan program for limited-dividend sponsors of low-rent housing.[5] Most other federal housing initiatives from 1930 to 1948, including federal mortgage insurance and the creation of a secondary mortgage market, enhanced home purchase.

While nonprofits were mostly excluded from postdepression federal housing policy,[6] there were several initiatives designed to increase their use. Harland Bartholemew, an urban planner, proposed using neighborhood-based corporations as vehicles for redevelopment in 1937. Draft legislation authorizing such corporations, with the power of eminent domain, was prepared by Bartholemew and presented to the National Association of Real Estate Boards (NAREB), but it was rejected. A year later, NAREB itself proposed the creation of quasi-public rebuilding corporations, but no one in Congress would agree to sponsor the legislation. In 1943, NAREB persuaded New York senator Robert Wagner to introduce a neighborhood development bill. The proposal failed to clear committee (Gillette, 1983: 433–435).[7]

Without federal backing, most nonprofit housing built between 1930 and 1960 was through cooperatives sponsored by educational, religious, labor, and social services organizations or self-initiated by members. A primary motivation for a number of sponsors was interracial housing. Following passage of the Housing Act of 1949, at least one cooperative, the United Housing Foundation in New York City, was granted a write-down on land cost under Title I of the act (Grier and Grier, 1960).[8]

It was not until 1959, however, that major federal support for housing nonprofits emerged, when the Section 202 direct loan program for the elderly, the first program specifically designed for nonprofit sponsorship, was enacted. It featured low-interest financing of development costs, for a term of up to fifty years. Cooperatives were added as sponsors in 1961, and program authority was expanded in 1964 to include the physically disabled. In the first ten years, the Department of Housing and Urban Development (HUD) approved loans for 333 Section 202 projects containing more than 45,000 units for the elderly and disabled (U.S. Department of Housing and Urban Development, 1969: 14).

The Modern Neighborhood-based Housing Nonprofit

The modern neighborhood-based housing nonprofit was born out of the community organizing movement of the 1950s and early 1960s.[9] Federal support was ensured by antipoverty, economic development, and community development legislation in response to growing urban turmoil, fostered by high unemployment, underemployment, and growing racial segregation. More than a hundred riots erupted in U.S. cities between 1964 and 1968.

In 1964, Congress created the Office of Economic Opportunity (OEO) and the Community Action Program (CAP). Because CAP funds could be used to train poor people as organizers and leaders in their own communities (Perry, 1971: 59–60), many saw empowerment of the poor as the principal benefit of OEO (Marris and Rein, 1967). The Economic Development Administration (EDA) was created in 1965, providing funding for neighborhood-based economic development, including housing construction and rehabilitation. EDA viewed housing production by nonprofits as an economic stimulus that increased local employment (Blaustein and Faux, 1972: 110–111).

Because neighborhood-based nonprofits were linked to both antipoverty and economic development legislation, they received bipartisan support in Congress (Hampden-Turner, 1975: 129).[10] In 1967, OEO was authorized to provide Special Impact funds to neighborhood-based CDCs[11] to begin comprehensive neighborhood redevelopment. Many early CDCs were expansions of existing single-purpose organizations, reflecting general support for a more comprehensive multipurpose approach (Blaustein and Faux, 1972: 114–116).

Among the earliest CDCs were the Hough Development Corporation in Cleveland, Ohio, incorporated in 1967, and FIGHTON in Rochester, New York, launched in January 1968 (Perry, 1971: 60–61). A third, the Bedford-Stuyvesant Restoration Corporation, was organized in New York City in 1967 (Hampden-Turner, 1974: 128). OEO made its first grant to a CDC in 1968, and between 1968 and 1974, it allocated $68.5 million to twenty-three urban CDCs.[12] Another major funding source was the Ford Foundation (Garn, 1975: 561–562).

Citizen participation was a major theme in the evolution of neighborhood-based nonprofits, encouraged initially by grass-roots organizing efforts (what Rachel Bratt has described as "bottom-up" approaches to citizen involvement). At the other end of the spectrum, federal community development programs of the 1960s contained citizen participation requirements (Bratt's "top-down" initiatives). The latter was an attempt to shift citizen participation from the streets to the negotiating table (Bratt, 1989: 35–36).

A second theme in the rise of the neighborhood-based housing nonprofit was the transition in federal policy from the virtual disregard and/or discriminatory treatment of the central city to providing direct support to neighborhood organizations. Up to 1954, Federal Housing Administration (FHA) credit programs overtly discriminated on the basis of race, income, and location of housing (Bratt, 1989: 126–128). In 1954, new FHA insurance programs were added for residential construction and rehabilitation on urban renewal sites and to assist families displaced by federal actions. One of these, Section 221(d)(2) mandated a change in FHA underwriting criteria from "economic soundness" to "acceptable risk." While these changes represented a major policy shift, their implementation was substantially slowed by an entrenched FHA bureaucracy, private appraisers, and lending institutions closely allied with traditional FHA practices.

It was not until the mid–1960s that the new generation of nonprofits began to see their housing role bolstered. The 1965 rent supplement program

permitted lower-income targeting in federal rental housing programs (Taggart, 1970). During the Johnson administration, federal support for low- and
moderate-income housing grew dramatically. HUD achieved cabinet-level
status, ten-year national housing production goals were established, and
below-market interest rate programs for rental and ownership housing were
created. To meet the higher production levels, nonprofit sponsorship of
assisted housing was authorized by the Congress and supported by new
seed-money loans and technical assistance grants.

Between 1969 and 1973, federally assisted housing production, including
new construction and rehabilitation, approached 1.8 million units. While
the proportion attributable to nonprofits is unknown, it is likely that they
sponsored at least one-fourth of this federally subsidized production (roughly
450,000 units) and that the nonprofit share in urban areas was significantly
higher.[13]

A period of uncertainty followed. In January 1973, the Nixon administration announced a moratorium on community development and low- and
moderate-income housing programs (Hays, 1985: 133). After almost two years
of delay and debate, the main source of funds for CDCs remained with the
federal government, although the nature and scope of the support changed
substantially. In 1974, the Community Development Block Grant (CDBG)
program was created, consolidating seven HUD programs and giving local
governments more control over how the funds were to be spent. In the same
year, the Section 8 rental assistance program replaced earlier subsidy programs, shifting federal support from the supply side to the demand side.
Under the Carter administration, additional federal support for CDCs came
from two sources: the Neighborhood Self-Help Development (NSHD) program, created in 1977, which provided direct operating support to CDCs,
and the Urban Development Action Grant (UDAG) program, created in
1977, which supported large-scale neighborhood development projects, including housing.

The performance of housing nonprofits in the late 1960s and 1970s was
mixed. They were viewed favorably because of their commitment to neighborhoods and their sensitivity to resident needs. Most of them undertook
high-risk projects unacceptable to for-profit developers. Further, they were
viewed as empowering neighborhood residents by encouraging their participation as board members, employees, and volunteers (Roberts and Portnoy,
1990: 305–306). Yet in January 1980, fewer than a hundred neighborhood-
based housing nonprofits were operating in American cities (Peirce and
Steinbach, 1987: 23).

Early evaluations of nonprofit sponsors questioned their ability to perform.
For example, project failures in the Section 236 program were attributed to
the limited resources and inadequate experience of nonprofit sponsors, many
of which were churches and labor unions, not housing developers in terms
of "inclination or past performance" (Mayer, 1990: 374). Further, the tar-

geting by nonprofit sponsors of their projects to the neediest tenants increased the risk of project failures (U.S. GAO, 1978: 93–96).[14] However, not all problems of implementing assisted housing programs can be attributed to the shortcomings of nonprofits. In the Section 235 homeownership program, where nonprofits were much less active, there was widespread program abuse by for-profit developers and realtors (Shafer and Field, 1973: 468–471).

The Reagan administration's opposition to federal housing and community development programs came more swiftly than the Nixon moratorium. From the outset, Reagan proposed the elimination of housing production subsidies. While he was not completely successful, budget authority for HUD-assisted housing decreased from $26.7 billion in 1980 to $8.3 billion in 1988 (HUD budget documents, 1982–1990). In addition, some HUD grant programs intended for urban recipients, such as the NSHD and UDAG, were eliminated.[15] CDBG grants to cities remained the primary source of federal support for housing nonprofits.

The effect of the Reagan cuts was to test CDCs' survivability. Nonprofits wholly dependent on federal funding could disappear in its absence. In fact, most of the neighborhood-based housing nonprofits survived. New sources of revenue came from state and local governments, private foundations, other private sources (corporations, banks, and individuals), and operations. Nonprofits further enhanced revenue through such mechanisms as internal economies and leveraging. Nevertheless, some housing nonprofits were forced to shift their focus to activities permitting lower per-unit costs.

Three factors influenced CDC survival during the period. First, federal cutbacks in housing assistance, combined with the removal of real estate development tax incentives, led virtually all for-profit developers to withdraw from low- and moderate-income housing production. Nonprofits remained the predominant sponsors of such housing. As a consequence, elected and nonelected government officials grew more aware of the roles and contributions of CDCs.

Second, beginning in the 1960s, intermediaries were created at the local, state, and national levels to support CDC operations. They provided seed money and operating support, arranged construction and permanent financing, and provided technical assistance. At the national level, two foundations were established to support CDCs. In 1979, the Ford Foundation sponsored the Local Initiatives Support Corporation (LISC), primarily to solicit corporate and private foundation support for CDCs. Since then, LISC has raised over $460 million to sustain the economic development and housing activities of more than 750 CDCs.[16] Loans and equity investments arranged by LISC assisted in construction or renovation of 28,800 units. LISC has also supported CDC operations and human resources development (LISC, 1990).

In 1982, developer James Rouse created the Enterprise Foundation to promote neighborhood-based housing. Since then, $270 million in equity and permanent financing has been obtained from over 750 individuals, corporations, and foundations, supporting the construction and rehabilitation of over 14,500 housing units by CDCs. In 1990, a Community Services Department was set up to work with CDCs and local governments in linking housing development with appropriate social services to ensure resident self-sufficiency and increase neighborhood stability (Enterprise Foundation, 1990). Examples of local intermediaries include the Boston Housing Partnership and the Cleveland Housing Network. These developments significantly enhanced the capacity of the nonprofits, making possible larger-scale projects not feasible for a single nonprofit. Third, many states and localities became active supporters of CDCs. Local governments provided contributions of land, tax abatement for residential and commercial projects, and local allocations of CDBG funds. Many state legislatures authorized new housing programs to offset cuts in federal assistance. Tax-exempt bonds were also issued to provide lower interest rates. A smaller number created housing trust funds from appropriations and/or dedicated revenue sources (e.g., real estate transfer taxes).

By the mid–1980s, CDCs had reduced their dependence on federal programs. Their track records and a growing number of horizontal and vertical supports helped increase the number and magnitude of alternative funding sources. Further, many nonprofits increased operating revenues, including, for example, fees for service, rent collections, and sale of assets.

One side effect of lessened dependency on federal programs was increased diversity in the organization, mission, and role of CDCs. The modern CDC may be single purpose (e.g., housing only) or multiple purpose (e.g., housing, job training, commercial revitalization). Others operate as umbrella organizations, involved in program delivery and/or the provision of technical assistance to member organizations. In some cases, the nonprofit is directly controlled by neighborhood residents; in others, residents must rely on nonprofit officials, especially the executive director, to provide leadership consistent with their needs.

The number of CDCs currently active in the delivery of low-income housing is unknown. A survey of local governments conducted in 1990 found CDCs as active developers of housing in 95 percent of U.S. cities with populations of over one hundred thousand. The highest regional concentration of CDCs occurred in midwestern cities, where the average per city exceeded ten (Goetz, 1992: 424).

Authors of a 1991 national survey sponsored by the National Congress for Community Economic Development (NCCED) estimated that there were two thousand community-based nonprofit corporations engaged in housing production, commercial/industrial, and/or enterprise development. Emphasis in this survey was placed on nonprofits as producers—those that had "completed at least one development project; played an active role in financing or management of the development, or had direct involvement in the financing, creation or operation of a business" (NCCED, 1991: 2).

Production of low-income housing was reported by 88 percent of the respondents (approximately 1,750 nonprofit organizations). Of these, 421 had completed more than a hundred housing units by the end of 1990. Between 1988 and 1990, the total units produced by CDCs was estimated at eighty-seven thousand, with the annual completion rate increasing almost 40 percent over the period. If this growth continues, production by CDCs will approach fifty thousand units a year by 1993.

The work of neighborhood-based nonprofits typically extends beyond construction, rehabilitation, and general improvement of housing. According to the NCCED survey, over 75 percent of CDCs provided resident services (e.g., homeowner counseling), and 70 percent engaged in community advocacy and organizing activities. Another 60 percent provided community-building activities, such as child care services, anticrime campaigns, and job training and placement (NCCED, 1991: 3–7).

In the 1970s and 1980s, other nonprofit efforts accompanied the growth of neighborhood-based CDCs. One of them, Neighborhood Housing Services (NHS), originated as a neighborhood initiative in Pittsburgh in 1968. The model was later adopted by a joint HUD–Federal Home Loan Bank Board task force in the mid–1970s (Shafer and Ladd, 1981: 307–308). In 1978, the Neighborhood Reinvestment Corporation (NRC) was created to assist in the revitalization of transitional neighborhoods and to help residents upgrade their housing.[17] Locally, resident-based partnerships, including local government and business representation, form the basis for NHS programs and mutual housing associations (MHAs). The NRC provides grants, training, and technical assistance to local affiliates (NRC publications).

A revolving loan fund is the central NHS financing mechanism. Loans are tailored to individual needs and circumstances. At the national level, a private, nonprofit corporation, Neighborhood Housing Services of America (NHSA), operates as a secondary market for the local programs. The corporation purchases nonbankable loans and sells them (or secondary market notes backed by the mortgages) to large institutional investors, including insurance companies, church pension funds, and private foundations. Through the end of 1991, nearly $78 million in note purchase agreements had been sold in the NHS secondary market (NRC publications).

The NRC's mutual housing development program represents a step in the direction of "decommodifying" housing. Local MHAs are formed as private, nonprofit partnerships that develop, own, and manage new and existing housing. MHA membership consists mainly of the residents and potential residents. In return for a monthly housing charge covering maintenance, repairs, replacement reserves, property taxes, insurance, and other operating costs, residents are given a lifetime right of occupancy (as long as they comply with the occupancy agreement) and the right to nominate a family or household member as a successor. Cities where MHAs have been organized include New York; Baltimore, Maryland; Hartford, Connecticut; and Madison, Wisconsin (NRC publications).

EXPERIENCE IN THREE CITIES

U.S. cities with well-developed nonprofit housing organizations in the early 1990s included Baltimore, Boston, Chicago, Cincinnati, Cleveland, Denver, Hartford, Indianapolis, Kansas City, Los Angeles, Miami, Minneapolis, Newark, New York, Oakland, Philadelphia, Pittsburgh, Providence, St. Louis, San Francisco, Seattle, and Washington, D.C. (Vidal et al., 1989). The experiences of three of these cities—Cincinnati, Cleveland, and Pittsburgh—form the basis for examining the CDCs' contemporary role.

Variations in the evolution of these cities help to explain the roles of nonprofit housing organizations in each. For example, all three experienced major population declines after 1950. Between 1950 and 1990, Pittsburgh's population declined by 45.3 percent, Cleveland's by 42.4 percent, and Cincinnati's by 20.2 percent. In the 1980s, only Cincinnati experienced a population reduction of less than 10 percent. Other historical factors include the evolution of city planning and local housing policies and the role of the private sector in center city redevelopment.

Pittsburgh

Modern nonprofit housing activity in Pittsburgh predated the federal housing initiatives of the 1960s. In 1957, the Allegheny Council to Improve Our Neighborhood's Housing, or ACTION-Housing, a nonpartisan civic organization, was created to mobilize resources from local banks and corporations to finance new and rehabilitated housing within Allegheny County. Its formation followed a long tradition of public-private partnerships and bipartisan support for local development in Pittsburgh.[18]

Without federal support, ACTION-Housing's early programs were targeted primarily to moderate-income renters and home buyers. Initial funding included $350,000 in seed money from three separate Mellon family foundations and $1.5 million in below-market rate loans and grants from local banks and corporations. While production was constrained by the absence of federal subsidies, it was noted for its innovation as a housing provider. For example, a large-scale residential development (East Side Hills) depended on a waiver of existing land use and building codes to permit innovative design, production, and site layout. Further, an apartment project on the North Side sponsored by ACTION-Housing included racial occupancy quotas (Lubove, 1969: 146–151).

During the same period, the Urban Redevelopment Authority (URA) of Pittsburgh initiated a large number of urban renewal projects.[19] Only one of nineteen renewal sites was used for the construction of moderate-cost housing. To make way for downtown commercial redevelopment and the construction of high rise, luxury apartments, fifty-four hundred low-income families were displaced (Lubove, 1969: 122–130).

Neighborhood resistance to urban renewal grew in the mid–1960s. In 1966, residents of the Central North Side, supported by two neighborhood-based nonprofits, obtained a written agreement from Mayor Joseph Barr that the neighborhood would remain residential. In September 1967, the city designated Central North Side as a code enforcement area. Lacking federal support, neighborhood leaders were encouraged to take action on their own.

As a first step, neighborhood organizations obtained verbal commitments from local lending institutions to make conventional loans in the area. With the support of the mayor's office, a proposal for a loan fund for high-risk borrowers, mainly elderly, low-income minority, and poor credit risk residents, was submitted to the Sarah Mellon Saife Foundation for funding. The foundation awarded $125,000 to establish the fund, and ACTION-Housing was designated as its agent. Neighborhood groups returned to the banks and obtained operating and technical assistance for the fund. In 1968, the Central North Side Improvement Fund was established, soon renamed Neighborhood Housing Services, Inc. (Ahlbrandt and Brophy, 1975: 127–129).[20]

Other opposition to urban renewal led to the creation of community-based organizations in the Manchester and Oakland neighborhoods. Manchester was a North Side neighborhood that became home to black families displaced by the Lower Hill urban renewal project. Community and historic preservation activists worked together to fight housing demolition. The Manchester Citizens Corporations was created in the late 1960s out of a compromise between the URA and residents and later played a major planning and monitoring role in area redevelopment (Metzger, 1992: 4–5).

In the Oakland neighborhood, working-class residents opposed the expansion plans of the University of Pittsburgh. People's Oakland and Oakland Directions, Inc., a community planning organization, worked together to force a compromise with the university and city. In 1980 a new Oakland Plan was approved, and the Oakland Planning and Development Corporation (OPDC) was formed to revitalize older residential and commercial areas (Metzger, 1992: 4–5). OPDC and MCC represented a new wave of activist nonprofits. They received funding from city-controlled CDBG funds, local foundations, and the city's sale of tax-exempt mortgage revenue bonds (Metzger, 1992: 6).

By the early 1980s, five nonprofits were operating: OPDC, MCC, North Side Civic Development Council, East Liberty Development, Inc., and Homewood-Brushton Revitalization and Development Corporation. In 1983, the Pittsburgh Partnership for Neighborhood Development (PPND) was created by funding organizations to provide support to CDCs. Initial funding came from the Mellon Bank, Howard Heinz endowment, Ford Foundation, and the city. By 1990, PPND was providing core operating support to ten CDCs and two technical assistance agencies. PPND identified twenty-two different funding sources for member nonprofits: five local banks, six local and one national foundations, nine private corporations, and the city (PPND, 1990).[21]

Another major development in Pittsburgh occurred in the late 1980s. At the time, the Union National Bank was attempting a merger with a regional bank. The Pittsburgh Community Reinvestment Group (PCRG), organized in 1988 to represent low- and moderate-income neighborhoods, challenged the proposed merger, arguing that Union National Bank had virtually no record in inner-city lending. Through a series of protests and threats of public exposure, the PCRG successfully negotiated a five-year, $109 million neighborhood lending agreement with the bank (Metzger, 1992: 1, 11).

The agreement included $55 million in home mortgages and $6 million in home improvement loans spread over five years. In addition, $40 million was committed for real estate loans to for-profit and nonprofit developers in low- and moderate-income areas with no time limitation. The bank set aside $250,000 to write down the financing costs for real estate loans to nonprofits during the fist year of the program (Metzger, 1992: 17). Special features for home mortgages included an interest rate reduction of 50 basis points, a waiver of origination points, a 95 percent loan-to-value ratio with a mortgage insurance waiver, and more liberal debt-to-income limits.

Housing financed by the agreement included the North Side Civic Development Council's efforts to encourage employees of a large hospital located in the North Side neighborhood to purchase and occupy homes in North Side neighborhoods. As an additional incentive, the hospital's foundation provided a grant that reduced the home buyer's down payment from 5 to 2 1/2 percent (Metzger, 1992: 18–20).

The city's 1992 Comprehensive Housing Affordability Strategy (CHAS) reported that community-based nonprofits had sponsored twenty-one single-family housing developments involving 225 units between 1986 and 1991. These are separate from infill new construction or the rehabilitation of individual single-family homes in Pittsburgh.

Cincinnati

In 1950, Cincinnati was lauded in *Fortune Magazine* as one of the best-run and best-planned big cities in the United States (Futterman, 1961: 258–259). In the 1920s, reformers had broken the existing mayoral machine, replacing it with a city manager form of government. Ward politics gave way to an at-large nonpartisan ballot, with proportional representation of racial and ethnic minorities built in.[22] A framework for metropolitan planning was also adopted (Miller and Tucker, 1990: 91–92).

In the 1930s, Cincinnati became one of the first cities to seek federal Public Works Administration funds for downtown revitalization, slum clearance, and construction of public housing. The rebuilding strategy, endorsed by public and civic organizations including the City Planning Commission, Better Housing League, and neighborhood-based civic associations, called for large-scale, high-density public housing in slum clearance areas and on vacant land to house the displaced (Fairbanks, 1988: 105, 114–115).[23]

Metropolitan planning in the post–World War II years culminated in the Plan of 1948, which called for riverfront clearance and the development of a sports stadium, government office buildings, a museum, a park, and an upscale apartment complex. Additional downtown clearance was mandated for commuter and intermetropolitan highways. In an attempt to stem out-migration to the suburbs, neighborhood rehabilitation and conservation were incorporated in the plan (Miller and Tucker, 1990: 92).

During the 1950s, however, the impact of urban renewal threatened the viability of many center city neighborhoods, and opposition grew. Supported by the city's planning director, neighborhood-based community councils were formed to reflect resident interests. The first was the Avondale Community Council, created in 1956. While some councils resisted racial transition, others fought "blockbusting" to stabilize racial change and retain an interracial mix (Thomas, 1986: 28–29). In support of integration, a city-wide nonprofit organization, Housing Opportunities Made Equal (HOME), was organized (Miller and Tucker, 1990: 95).

According to Donald Lenz, a former CDC director in Cincinnati, the earliest nonprofits sponsored rental housing primarily under Section 202. The first neighborhood-based housing nonprofit was Mt. Auburn Good Housing. Other early nonprofits included the West End Development Corporation (WEDCO) and Over-the-Rhine Development Corporation. Most were founded by community councils that had added housing to their agendas in the 1960s. By the mid–1970s, nine CDCs were operating at the neighborhood level.

Cincinnati was selected as one of the first seven Neighborhood Housing Services cities (interview with Lenz). In 1979, the Neighborhood Development Corporation Association (NDCA) of Cincinnati was organized to provide technical assistance to CDC staffs. In 1983, a city-wide development corporation was created to facilitate public-purpose housing and economic development projects (interview with Donald Lenz). By 1990, there were twenty-five nonprofits active in housing production and housing services in the city (conversation with Barbara Milon, executive director of NCDA).

Cleveland

Like most other industrial cities in the Northeast and Midwest, Cleveland is undergoing major change. Unlike Pittsburgh and Cincinnati, Cleveland lacked a long-term planning focus after World War II. Its urban renewal grants were used almost exclusively for downtown redevelopment. The effect on older neighborhoods close to downtown was devastating. Slum clearance and highway construction (primarily intended to reduce commuting times for suburban residents) displaced thousands of residents (Swanstrom, 1985: 99).

Up to the 1970s, housing for the poor in Cleveland was left primarily to the Cuyahoga Metropolitan Housing Authority (CMHA). One of the first in the country, CMHA manages some twelve thousand units, virtually all located within the city of Cleveland. Workable alternatives to public housing were limited in the 1970s and 1980s in Ohio because of federal cutbacks and a state constitutional prohibition against financing family rental housing with tax-exempt mortgage revenue bonds.[24]

The earliest nonprofits to produce housing in Cleveland were located in the Hough neighborhood east of downtown, where the first of two race riots occurred in the mid–1960s. Hough had become home to blacks displaced by downtown urban renewal.[25] By the mid–1960s, the area had been transformed into what Swanstrom describes as a "pressurized ghetto of misery [ready to] explode." In July 1966, a week-long race riot began (Swanstrom, 1985: 100).[26]

The Hough Area Development Corporation (HADC) was organized by community leaders in 1967 to develop low- and moderate- income housing, including scattered-site housing for large families (Perry, 1987: 19). A second nonprofit, NOAH (Neighbors Organized for Action in Housing), was founded in 1968 by members of two neighborhood churches with the goal of "uplift[ing] the esteem of the human being and provide adequate housing" (NOAH, 1989).[27] A third, the Famicos Foundation, was organized by Sister Henrietta Gorris, C.S.A., in 1969, to help Hough residents with their basic living needs and to raise public consciousness about the extreme poverty in the neighborhood. Decent, affordable housing was seen as one of several keys to neighborhood restoration (Famicos, 1990).

By 1981, there were at least ten CDCs operating in Cleveland. Besides Famicos and HADC, there were Broadway Area Housing Coalition, Clark-Fulton-Denison United, COHAB, Collinwood Area Development Corporation, Glenville Development Corporation, Near-West Housing Corporation, Tremont West Development Corporation, and Union-Miles Development Corporation (Keating, 1990: 6). In 1981, the Cleveland Housing Network (CHN), a coalition of CDCs, was established to centralize financing, construction, and property management. CHN programs include a lease-purchase home rehabilitation program, originated by the Famicos Foundation. In 1989, the Homeward program, a variant of the lease-purchase program, was initiated to promote the transfer of single-family homeownership to low- and moderate-income households on a short-term basis (Keating, 1990: 5–7). The two programs have rehabilitated nearly a thousand units since 1981.

Other support for neighborhood housing in Cleveland comes from the city, the state of Ohio, and special-purpose organizations created to support CDCs. City support has ranged from the allocation of CDBG and other federal funds to CDCs to locally derived program initiatives. In support of homeownership, these have included below-market home purchase and home repair grant and loan programs and a recently added demolition policy aimed at removing abandoned housing from the inventory where rehabilitation or resale is not feasible. The state now provides seed money and operating support directly to CDCs.

Special-purpose organizations include Cleveland Housing Partnership, an informal coalition organized in 1986 by CHN, the Enterprise Foundation, and BP America to attract corporate investors and other financing. In 1988, the Cleveland Housing Partnership Equity Fund was organized with the added support of Cleveland Tomorrow, an association of Cleveland's major corporations and businesses. Finally, in 1991, Neighborhood Progress, Inc. was created by Cleveland Tomorrow to coordinate strategy for addressing the various needs of housing nonprofits.

As a measure of the growth of nonprofits in the 1980s, a 1991 directory of neighborhood-based organizations involved in neighborhood redevelopment in Cleveland indicated that forty-eight were active in housing. Of the total, thirty-six (75 percent) support ownership through new construction, rehabilitation, home repairs, weatherization, and paint programs and represent virtually all housing activity in such categories targeted to low- and moderate-income households. In addition to direct purchase, ownership options include cooperative and lease-purchase arrangements. Of eighteen other nonprofits involved in community development in the city but not neighborhood based, twelve (two-thirds) were active in housing (Cleveland State University, 1991).

A CDC SURVEY

To show the nature of contemporary nonprofits and their activities supporting low- and moderate-income owners and renters, thirty-five CDCs in Cincinnati, Cleveland, and Pittsburgh were surveyed in 1991. Nonprofits selected for the survey were housing providers and typically members of local funding, technical assistance, and/or networking intermediaries. Responses were received from twenty-four CDCs: ten from Cleveland, seven from Pittsburgh, and seven from Cincinnati. Their organizational characteristics, in the three cities and on a combined basis, are shown in table 9.1.

Organizational Characteristics

The average number of full- and part-time employees was nine. By comparison, the average number of members on CDC boards of directors was

Table 9.1
Characteristics of CDC Engaged in Housing in Three Cities, 1991

	COMBINED	CIN	CLE	PIT
1. Average number of employees	9	5	11	11
2. Average size of Board	14	12	13	18
3. Representation on Board (as % of total)	COMBINED	CIN	CLE	PIT
Community residents/clients	47%	39%	60%	41%
Community businesses	11	8	9	16
Other community-based organizations	10	12	3	16
Private donor organizations	1	1	2	0
Financial institutions or (non-donor)businesses	7	1	9	10
Housing/CD "experts"	11	19	12	5
Government officials	2	0	3	3
Other	10	19	4	9
[Community representation]	[69]	[60]	[72]	[73]
4. Geographical scope of operations	COMBINED	CIN	CLE	PIT
1 neighborhood or less	63%	71%	60%	57%
2 neighborhoods	8	0	10	14
3 or more neighborhoods	17	17	10	29
City-wide or larger	12	17	20	0
5. Average age (in years)	13	12	12	15
6. Factors most responsible in founding of CDC (as % of total)	COMBINED	CIN	CLE	PIT
Preexisting neighborhood or community organization	39%	29%	44%	43%
Ad hoc group	48	57	44	43
Local church(es)	35	43	33	29
Private foundations, banks, or corporations	13	0	22	14
Federal government	9	24	11	0
State government	4	0	11	0
Local government	22	14	22	29

fourteen, with the highest average in Pittsburgh (eighteen). While larger board size may reflect an organization's desire for significant community representation, the smaller staff sizes probably reflect the limited nature of available resources. Community representation on boards was high, averaging 69 percent across the three cities. In Cincinnati, board representation by housing and neighborhood development "experts" was higher than in either Cleveland or Pittsburgh.

In terms of geographical scope, fifteen of the twenty-four CDCs (63 percent) operated at or below the neighborhood level. Two CDCs identified their service areas as involving two neighborhoods, four others indicated at least three, two identified their areas as city-wide, and one identified its service area as the county.[28]

The average of the CDCs surveyed was thirteen years. The majority were organized between 1975 and 1980, with two founded prior to 1970 and four founded after 1980. Almost half were founded by an ad hoc group of neighborhood residents and/or businesspersons. Other important factors in the founding of the organization were a preexisting neighborhood or community organization (39 percent), a local church (or churches) (36 percent), the federal government (9 percent), state government (4 percent), local government (22 percent), and private foundations, corporations, or banks (13 percent).

Federal funding, the primary source of revenue for housing nonprofits formed in the 1960s and 1970s, was viewed as a major factor in the founding of only two (8 percent) of the nonprofits surveyed. Five (21 percent) reported local government funding as a major factor, and only one indicated state funding as a major factor.[29]

Housing and Neighborhood Conditions

Respondents were asked to characterize changes in the physical condition of the housing stock in their service areas between 1980 and 1990 (table 9.2). Forty-one percent reported that housing conditions had worsened. A smaller percentage (37) felt that the physical condition of housing had improved. Respondents from Cincinnati and Pittsburgh were less sanguine about improvements than their Cleveland counterparts. When asked about future conditions, between 1991 and 2000, over three-quarters (78 percent) believed housing conditions would improve, 9 percent thought housing conditions would worsen somewhat during the decade, but none believed conditions would worsen substantially.

Respondents were also asked about social and economic conditions in their service areas in 1980 and 1990. Half or more in each year characterized their areas as "very distressed"—among the most distressed in their cities. Another 26 percent in 1980 and 39 percent in 1990 viewed their areas as "moderately distressed."

Table 9.2
CDC Perceptions of Neighborhoods Served in Three Cities

1. Percent expressing an opinion regarding the physical condition of housing in neighborhood(s) served				
Between 1980 and 1990	**COMBINED**	**CIN**	**CLE**	**PIT**
Improved substantially	14%	14%	13%	14%
Improved somewhat	23	14	38	14
Stayed about the same	23	29	25	14
Worsened somewhat	18	29	13	14
Worsened substantially	23	14	13	43
Expectation: Next 10 years	**COMBINED**	**CIN**	**CLE**	**PIT**
Improved substantially	27%	29%	38%	14%
Improved somewhat	52	57	44	57
Stayed about the same	11	0	19	14
Worsened somewhat	9	14	0	14
Worsened substantially	0	0	0	0
2. Percent expressing an opinion regarding the degree of social and economic distress in neighborhood(s) served				
In 1980	**COMBINED**	**CIN**	**CLE**	**PIT**
Very distressed (among most distressed in city)	54%	64%	67%	43%
Moderately distressed (more distressed than most in city)	26	36	11	21
About the same (as other neighborhoods in city)	20	0	22	36
In 1990	**COMBINED**	**CIN**	**CLE**	**PIT**
Very distressed (among most distressed in city)	50%	50%	67%	29%
Moderately distressed (more distressed than most in city)	39	50	11	64
About the same (as other neighborhoods in city)	11	0	22	7

Housing Activities of CDCs

Table 9.3 presents findings on the housing activity of the CDCs surveyed. The first question concerned housing's share of total nonprofit activity at

Table 9.3
Housing Activity of CDCs in Three Cities

1. Housing activity as a percent of total CDC activity, by year				
Year	COMBINED	CIN	CLE	PIT
First year of operations	59%	59%	83%	13%
1985	64	63	86	30
1990	74	91	84	44
2. Percent of CDCs with housing activity, by type, since origin				
In support of homeownership	COMBINED	CIN	CLE	PIT
New construction	75%	86%	50%	100%
Substantial rehabilitation	83	86	100	57
Conversion to residential use	13	14	0	29
Home improvements and repairs	79	71	90	71
Energy cost reduction	71	86	90	29
Home maintenance	42	43	60	14
Property management	45	43	70	14
Home owner counseling	75	43	90	86
Equity participation	29	29	30	29
Reverse mortgages for elderly	8	14	10	0
Lease purchase	63	29	90	57
Condominium ownership	17	0	10	43
Cooperative ownership	13	29	0	14
Loan underwriting and/or administration	25	0	50	14
Other	17	17	20	14
Average number of homeownership activities per CDC	7	6	7	6
In support of rental housing	COMBINED	CIN	CLE	PIT
New construction	25%	42%	0%	43%
Substantial rehabilitation	79	71	80	86
Conversion to residential use	21	0	30	29
Improvements and repairs	63	86	60	43
Energy cost reduction	58	86	70	14
Rental maintenance	21	0	40	14
Property management	79	71	80	71
Renter counseling	54	43	30	29
Equity participation	33	43	0	29
Loan underwriting and/or administration	4	0	30	14
Other	17	14	20	14
Average number of rental housing activities per CDC	4	5	5	4

Table 9.3 (continued)

3. Level of housing activity, in units, in 1990 (for CDCs reporting the type of housing activity				
In support of homeownership	**COMBINED**	**CIN**	**CLE**	**PIT**
New construction	12%	5%	24%	12%
Substantial rehabilitation	11	3	24	8
Repaired or improved	34	16	63	17
Weatherized	63	6	121	4
Managed as rentals (e.g., lease purchase)	28	12	52	2
In support of rental housing	**COMBINED**	**CIN**	**CLE**	**PIT**
New construction	15%	30%	5%	13%
Substantial rehabilitation	14	14	7	18
Repaired or improved	7	10	6	2
Weatherized	78	78	0	0
Managed as rentals	50	82	25	20
4. Percent expressing opinion about the degree of innovation in CDC housing activity	**COMBINED**	**CIN**	**CLE**	**PIT**
Percent of housing activity identified as "innovative"	58%	57%	51%	67%

three times: the first year of operation, 1985, and 1990. In Cincinnati and Pittsburgh, this share increased dramatically over time—in Pittsburgh, from 13 to 44 percent, and in Cincinnati, from 59 to 91 percent. In comparison, Cleveland CDCs reported housing's share as consistently high, ranging from 83 to 86 percent overall.

The second question concerned the extent of support for homeownership and rental housing since the nonprofit's origin. Over two-thirds of the nonprofits identified involvement in six homeownership categories: new construction (75 percent), substantial rehabilitation (83 percent), home improvement and/or home repairs (79 percent), energy cost reductions (71 percent), lease-purchase (63 percent), and pre- or postpurchase counseling (75 percent). Forty-two percent operated home maintenance programs (e.g., tool loan or paint programs). On the rental side, 79 percent had done substantial rehabilitation, and the same percentage had property management experience.

Program involvement in certain categories varied substantially among cities. For example, all CDC respondents from Pittsburgh identified new homeownership construction programs. In contrast, only half of the Cleveland nonprofits surveyed indicated new home construction. Instead, all of Cleveland's CDCs reported involvement in the substantial rehabilitation of homes, while only 57 percent of Pittsburgh's CDCs were involved. In the area of energy cost reduction (e.g., home energy audits or weatherization programs), nonprofits in both Cleveland and Cincinnati identified substantial involvement (86 to 90 percent), while less than one-third (29 percent) of the Pittsburgh nonprofits operated such programs. Here, the difference may be explained by active state and private utility support of energy conservation in Ohio.

The third question regarded the level of housing activity in 1990 in terms of units produced, repaired, managed, and so forth. For nonprofits active in single-family construction in 1990, an average of twelve new homes were built. For CDCs doing substantial rehabilitation, an average of eleven single-family homes were completed during the year. Higher unit counts were experienced by nonprofits involved in home repair and improvement (thirty-four) and weatherization (sixty-three). In all homeownership categories, Cleveland CDCs reporting activity were dominant. In contrast, on the rental side, Cleveland nonprofits were least active in producing new or substantially rehabilitated units. CDCs in Cincinnati were much more active, especially in new construction.

The survey results from the three cities suggest that CDC support of homeownership and rental housing in the three cities is substantial. While average production in any one activity may be small, aggregate involvement in housing is large. CDCs in the three cities reported an average of eleven different housing programs since origin—seven supporting homeownership and four supporting rental housing. Based on interviews with CDC executive directors, it is likely that 1990 activity levels were the highest since nonprofit sponsorship of Great Society programs in the early 1970s.[30]

Life Cycle Support

CDCs provide housing supports to residents at three stages in the home-ownership life cycle: first, in the transition from rentership to ownership; second, in maintaining and sustaining ownership; and third, in the transition out of ownership to alternative housing. The outline below identifies, by example, the kinds of program supports provided by housing nonprofits at each stage.

Stage 1. Transition to homeownership

  Prepurchase counseling

  Enhanced affordability, e.g., lease-purchase

Stage 2. Maintaining/sustaining ownership over time

  Early years

    –Postpurchase and default counseling

    –Emergency repair programs

    –Energy audits and weatherization

–Tool loan programs

Later years

  –Emergency home repairs

  –Scheduled maintenance/monitoring programs

  –Home improvement programs (age-related or health-related needs)

  –Reverse mortgages

  –In-home services (e.g., Meals-on-Wheels)

  –Transportation services

Stage 3. Transition out of homeownership

Information sharing on alternative housing

Development and management of alternative housing (e.g., independent living, house sharing, level of care housing, congregate care facilities, etc.)

Respondents were asked the extent to which they viewed their housing activities as innovative. On average, the nonprofits identified nearly 60 percent of their activity as involving "some degree of innovation on the part of the nonprofit or other organizations working with the nonprofit." The innovations described included the following, by stage of homeownership:

Transition to Homeownership from Rentership

Obtaining mortgages that cover "appraisal gaps" for low- and moderate-income purchasers.

Building new homes on 25-foot-wide lots.

Designing and implementing a lease-purchase program for families on public assistance.

Enabling home purchase while retaining the deed to the land (through a resident-owned cooperative) for the common good of the community.

Assisting in a tenant cooperative buy-out and management of 330 units of scattered-site Section 8 housing.

Renovating a condominium project resulting in lower prices to buyers.

Assisting purchasers in the design of their housing.

Maintaining/Sustaining Ownership over Time

Operating a "labor-free" home repair program.

Converting single-family homes owned by the elderly into two units to provide rental income to supplement relatively fixed incomes.

Hiring a safety coordinator who works with city police to protect residences.

Transition out of Homeownership

> Developing, along with three other nonprofits, an independent living complex for the elderly with incomes below 60 percent of median.

> Conversion of an elementary school to housing for the elderly and handicapped.

Comprehensive life cycle perspectives on housing ownership and renter-ship are important to effective program delivery in declining neighborhoods. For example, many prospective buyers in the central city come from renter families with limited knowledge of ownership responsibilities. Further, in emergencies, younger home owners may not be able to turn to their parents for financial assistance or to private banks because of poor credit.

The housing problems of older homeowners are also complicated. Unlike their suburban counterparts, most older homeowners in center city neigh-borhoods have not experienced much appreciation in the value of their homes, and some properties have actually lost value. Thus, the opportunity to convert home equity in order to remain in the home (meet rising main-tenance and repair costs, make improvements) or to pay for alternative housing is limited.

Finally, when ownership is not affordable, CDCs may acquire, fix up, and rent apartment units to lower-income households. As property managers, they control long-term use and occupancy, unless the management or own-ership is transferred to the tenants. In either case, the goal is to ensure continued occupancy by households in need.

Incomes Targeting by CDCs

Table 9.4 presents data on the income distribution of owners and renters in CDC-sponsored housing in the three cities. On the ownership side, one-third of all units are targeted to families with incomes below 50 percent of the area median income. The rate is doubled on the rental side, where two-thirds of all tenants have such income. Targeting on both sides is greatest in Cincinnati, where almost half of the owners and over three-quarters of all renters have incomes below 50 percent of area median.

CONCLUSION

The failure of nonprofit organizations to become major providers of housing for low- and moderate-income households during most of America's history has been attributed to the ethos of individualism and a preference for private sector entrepreneurship (Howenstine, 1983: 106). Only since the last 1960s have nonprofits been major providers.

The first wave of modern nonprofits emerged in the 1960s, as sponsors of federally assisted housing. It was not until the 1980s, however, that non-

Table 9.4
Distribution of Household Incomes in CDC Housing Programs in Three Cities,
1990

In support of homeownership	COMBINED	CIN	CLE	PIT
-- Below 50% of Median	33%	48%	33%	21%
-- 50% to 80% of Median	46	35	53	48
-- Above 80% of Median	21	17	14	31
In support of rental housing	**COMBINED**	**CIN**	**CLE**	**PIT**
-- Below 50% of Median	67%	78%	67%	55%
-- 50% to 80% of Median	26	18	31	37
-- Above 80% of Median	4	4	1	8

profits became the predominant private sector participants in the development, management, and improvement of low- and moderate-income housing. Without them, little if any housing activity would have occurred in central cities (Roberts and Portnoy, 1990: 306–307).

Beginning in the 1970s, policymakers have had to address four major housing problems: availability, affordability (the ratio of housing expenses to income), adequacy (including both quality and overcrowding), and neighborhood conditions (Bratt, 1989: 6). CDCs have been much better suited to address these problems than for-profit housing developers.

To increase the supply of affordable housing, CDCs commonly have had to attract multiple funding sources. They have offered programs ranging from basic maintenance to long-term preservation and ownership. To improve neighborhoods, CDCs have developed housing strategies consistent with neighborhood preservation and revitalization goals. This is, in part, because of the high level of community representation on CDC boards.

For the foreseeable future, the nonprofits' role as the primary provider of housing for inner-city residents seems assured. First, unlike the early 1970s, when nonprofits were criticized for their failure to perform, CDCs today are almost universally well regarded. There is also increased recognition that sole reliance on the for-profit sector in the provision of low- and moderate-income housing and economic development is unworkable. Second, CDCs have broadened their base of financial support, including revenue from operations. Third, through leveraging (e.g., converting grants into revolving loan funds), they have expanded available resources. Fourth, CDCs are supported by a growing network of local, state, regional, and national organizations.

Given the size and resources of the federal government, one must also ask the question: Why nonprofits? One view is that housing nonprofits are well suited to a complementary relationship with government (Rasey et al., 1989: 37). The federal government's strengths are centered primarily in its taxing powers and in its ability to establish national priorities. Local government is often unresponsive to neighborhoods, especially the poorest, whose needs (welfare, health, education, and job training) require substantial public expenditures. As potential competitors to CDCs, for-profit participants have short-term objectives that are generally inconsistent with the long-term needs of poor neighborhoods. One reason nonprofits are so responsive to changing local needs is that their charters are usually explicit regarding their long-term commitment to the communities they serve.

Keys to the future of CDCs as housing providers include the availability of deep subsidies from government in order to assist lower-income households, increased access to private equity and long-term financing, and administrative flexibility to respond to neighborhood and community needs (Roberts and Portnoy, 1990). At the same time, keys to the success of the target neighborhoods CDCs appear to require much more. High on most neighborhood lists are welfare reform, educational reform, and increased job training and employment programs.

Aside from central concerns such as capacity and resource availability, other issues will influence the future of nonprofits. Will CDCs retain their unique characteristics—among them, high degree of innovation, long-term frame of reference, community orientation—or become nonprofit versions of for-profit corporations with business principles as their primary motivation, or alternatively, become bureaucratic agents for government (akin to local public housing authorities) (Eisenberg, 1990)?

Current pressures for change include calls for the professionalization of nonprofit staff and a "production" focus favoring housing development over other housing activities. Advocates of these changes, often found within the intermediaries, are well intentioned. Their goals of efficiency, economies of scale, and short-term impact are worthy. However, fears about such changes expressed by Eisenberg and others include the potential for separation from grass-roots organizers and support networks, a possible retreat from advocacy (leaving it to other organizations not involved in development), and a failure to retain a comprehensive neighborhood strategy (instead relying on expertise in one or two areas).

The nonprofits' preferred status as housing provider for center city neighborhoods should be based not solely on their capacity to produce or on organizational efficiency but on their ongoing willingness to address unmet housing needs. In an era of severe budget constraints, organizations that seek comprehensive solutions, involving the effective integration and targeting of available resources, should be nurtured and sustained.

NOTES

1. While funding for homeownership counseling was authorized by Section 106(a)(iii) of the Housing and Urban Development Act of 1968, funds were not made available for counseling during the Nixon-Ford administrations (HUD, *Housing Production with Non Profit Sponsors*, 1975).

2. Edith Elmer Wood, an early housing scholar and reformer, found that only two housing projects that were purely nonprofit in character were built before 1919 (Friedman, 1968: 76–77).

3. Some early sponsors viewed this outcome as favorable in the long run to the extent the housing improvements would filter down to the very poor (Adams, 1990: 5).

4. State governments, constitutionally responsible for the welfare of their residents, were judged unable to finance the massive relief effort required.

5. Fewer than ten projects received funding.

6. The general view in the late 1930s was that other institutions were already in place to provide housing: public housing authorities would house the lower third of the income spectrum, limited-dividend corporations and cooperatives the middle third, and federal and private credit programs the upper third (Adams, 1990: 5).

7. NAREB's sponsorship of nonprofit housing legislation may have reflected, at least in part, its strong opposition to the public housing program enacted in 1937.

8. The United Housing Foundation was credited with having provided housing for over thirty thousand families in New York City during the 1950s and 1960s (Milgram, 1977: 175–176).

9. Saul Alinsky was one of its leading proponents and activists.

10. The use of the term *community development corporation* instead of *community action agency* may have been preferred for political reasons by a Congress anxious to respond to a growing urban crisis.

11. A year earlier Senator Robert F. Kennedy (D, New York) had testified to the need for "community development corporations," which would carry out the work of construction, the hiring and training of workers, the provision of services, and the encouragement of associated enterprises in urban neighborhoods. In the same hearings, Mayor Sorenson of Omaha, Nebraska, described how he, out of frustration with "the federal obstacle course," personally obtained a commitment of $250,000 from a local foundation in order to form the Omaha Development Corporation to engage in housing rehabilitation (Hearings on the Federal Role in Urban Affairs before the Subcommittee on Executive Reorganization of the Committee of Government Operations, U.S. Senate, 89th Cong., 2d sess., August 15, 16, 1966).

12. Garn described the CDCs funded by OEO as "hybrid organizations, quasi-private and quasi-public," linked in some way to a particular community, and involved in "operating some commercial and business enterprises, providing assistance to other entrepreneurs; providing manpower training; building, rehabilitating, and managing housing; providing access to welfare and related services; and dealing with

publicly-funded agencies (such as the police, fire department, and schools) on behalf of community residents" (Garn, 1975: 564).

13. The estimates are based primarily on various HUD and General Accounting Office reports on assisted housing. Bratt (1989: 279–281) provides a useful summary of published sources.

14. In reporting on a comparative evaluation of limited-dividend and nonprofit sponsors of Section 236 projects, HUD research staff found that "non profit groups rent their units to the poorest possible tenants, given the structure of the program" (HUD, *Housing Production with Non Profit Sponsors*, Staff Study, November 1975).

15. A small Neighborhood Development Demonstration program was created by Congress in 1983, but early funding was limited to only about $2 million a year (Bratt, 1989: 170–171).

16. The National Equity Fund (NEF) and the Local Initiatives Managed Assets Corporation (LIMAC) were set up in 1987.

17. In comparison with CDC service areas, NRC affiliates tend to operate in neighborhoods with higher median incomes and higher homeownership rates. In part, this is because of the substantial reliance on voluntary resident participation in the programs.

18. In 1943, Richard King Mellon convened the Allegheny Conference on Community Development (ACCD) to plan Pittsburgh's future. Mellon, a Republican, obtained the close cooperation of Democratic mayor David Lawrence and the Democratic political machine that ran the city and Allegheny County. Several other key public and private planning organizations were to follow, including ACTION-Housing.

19. The state law was passed in 1945; Pittsburgh's URA was created in 1946.

20. The NHS model was soon adopted by housing activist Gale Cincotta, who helped to set up an NHS in Chicago. Obtaining bank agreements in the two cities to lend in older, redlined center city neighborhoods contributed to the passage of the Home Mortgage Disclosure Act in 1975 and the Community Reinvestment Act in 1977 which supported the creation of NHS programs across the country (Metzger, 1992: 4).

21. Among the first in the country, the PPND model was later applied in several other U.S. cities, including Washington, D.C., Philadelphia, Cleveland, and Denver.

22. A political minority had to garner one-ninth of the vote, plus one, to secure a council seat.

23. The first public housing project, Laurel Homes, was built on a slum clearance site and contained over a thousand units. The second project, Greenhills, planned as a 1,200- to 1,500-unit new town, was located on vacant land outside the city (Fairbanks, 1988: 104–109).

24. This was changed by a successful constitutional referendum in 1990 making rental housing a public purpose under state law.

25. The black share of Hough's population increased from less than 2 percent in 1950 to 91 percent in 1960 (U.S. Census).

26. Prior to the Hough riot, there was street talk in Hough about arson and rioting as "instant urban renewal" (Swanstrom, 1975: 100).

27. NOAH, Inc. was one of the early nonprofit sponsors of federally assisted housing development in Cleveland. The nonprofit survived the 1970s and 1980s by expanding its geographical base and becoming both developer and manager of housing

units for low- and moderate-income families and special-needs housing for the elderly and disabled.

28. It is likely that the percentage of CDCs with service areas larger than one neighborhood increased in the 1980s. A sample survey of nonprofit recipients of CDBG funds in the state of Ohio in 1988 found over half had increased the size of their service areas, in part, to increase revenue from CDBG awards and other sources (Rasey et al., 1989: 39).

29. The low response rates for government, especially given the level federal program funding over the years, may reflect the broadened revenue mix of most neighborhood-based nonprofits engaged in housing and economic development in the late 1980s and early 1990s.

30. It is very likely that 1991 and 1992 activity will exceed 1990 levels based on expanded revenue sources, including income from operations.

REFERENCES

Adams, Carolyn T. 1990. "Nonprofit Housing Producers in the U.S.: Why So Rare?" Paper presented at the Annual Conference of the Urban Affairs Association, Charlotte, North Carolina.

Ahlbrandt, Roger S., Jr., and Paul C. Brophy. 1975. *Neighborhoods, People and Community*. New York: Plenum.

Atlas, John, and Peter Dreier. 1986. "The Tenants' Movement and American Politics." In *Critical Perspectives on Housing*, 378–397. Edited by Rachel G. Bratt, Chester Hartman, and Ann Meyerson. Philadelphia: Temple University Press.

Austin, David M. 1968. "Influence of Community Setting on Neighborhood Change." In *Neighborhood Organization for Community Action*, 76–96. Edited by John B. Turner. New York: National Association of Social Workers.

Birch, Eugene L., and Deborah S. Gardner. 1981. "The Seven-Percent Solution: A Review of Philanthropic Housing, 1870–1910." *Journal of Urban History* 7: 403–438.

Blaustein, Arthur I., and Geoffrey Faux. 1972. *The Star-Spangled Hustle*. Garden City, N.Y.: Doubleday.

Bowly, Devereux, Jr. 1978. *The Poorhouse: Subsidized Housing in Chicago, 1895–1976*. Carbondale: Southern Illinois University Press.

Bratt, Rachel G. 1989. *Rebuilding a Low-Income Housing Policy*. Philadelphia: Temple University Press.

Cleveland State University. Center for Neighborhood Development. June 1991. *Directory of Neighborhood-Based Organizations in Cleveland*. Cleveland: Author.

Eisenberg, Pablo. 1990. Keynote address to the Seventh Annual Conference of the Ohio CDC Association. Washington, D.C.

Enterprise Foundation. 1990. *Annual Report*. Columbia, Md.

Fairbanks, Robert B. 1988. *Making Better Citizens: Housing Reform and the Community Development Strategy in Cincinnati, 1890–1960*. Urbana: University of Illinois Press.

Famicos Foundation. 1990. *Mission Statement*. Cleveland, Ohio.

222 Alternative Forms of Housing Control

Friedman, Lawrence M. 1968. *The Government and Slum Housing: A Century of Frustration.* Chicago: Rand McNally.

Futterman, Robert A. 1961. *The Future of Our Cities.* Garden City, N.Y.: Doubleday.

Garn, Harvey A. 1975. "Program Evaluation and Policy Analysis of Community Development Corporations." In *The Social Economy of Cities*, 561–588. Edited by Gary Gappert and H. M. Rose. Beverly Hills, Calif.: Sage.

Gillette, Howard, Jr. 1983. "The Evolution of Neighborhood Planning: From the Progressive Era to the 1949 Housing Act." *Journal of Urban History* 9 (4): 421–444.

Glaab, Charles N., and A. T. Brown. 1967. *A History of Urban America.* New York: Macmillan.

Goetz, Edward G. 1992. "Local Government Support for Nonprofit Housing: A Survey of U.S. Cities." *Urban Affairs Quarterly* 27 (3): 420–435.

Grier, Eunice, and George Grier. 1960. *Privately Developed Interracial Housing: An Analysis of Experience.* Berkeley: University of California Press.

Hampden-Turner, Charles. 1975. *From Poverty to Dignity.* Garden City, N.Y.: Anchor Books Edition.

Hays, R. Allen. 1985. *The Federal Government and Urban Housing: Ideology and Change in Public Policy.* Albany: State University of New York Press.

Howenstine, E. Jay. 1983. *Attacking Housing Costs: Foreign Policies and Strategies.* New Brunswick, N.J.: Rutgers University.

Keating, Dennis. 1990. "Community-Based Housing Development in Cleveland." In *Mainstreaming the Community Builders: Case Studies of the Development Process in Six Cities.* Edited by Phillip L. Clay. Cambridge, Mass.: MIT Press.

Lenz, Donald. 1991. Interview. Cincinnati, Ohio. May 2.

Local Initiatives Support Corporation. 1990. *Annual Report.* New York, N.Y.

Lubove, Roy. 1962. *The Progressives and the Slums: Tenement House Reform in New York City: 1890–1917.* Reprinted in 1974. Westport, Conn.: Greenwood Press.

Marris, Peter, and Martin Rein. 1967. *Dilemmas of Social Reform.* New York: Atherton.

Mayer, Neil S. 1990. "The Role of Nonprofits in Renewed Federal Housing Efforts." In *Building Foundations: Housing and Federal Policy*, 365–388. Edited by Denise DiPasquale and Langley C. Keyes. Philadelphia: University of Pennsylvania Press.

Metzger, John T. 1992. "The Community Reinvestment Act and Neighborhood Revitalization." In *From Redlining to Reinvestment: Community Responses to Urban Disinvestment.* Edited by Gregory D. Squires. Philadelphia: Temple University Press.

Milgram, Morris. 1977. *Good Neighborhood: The Challenge of Open Housing.* New York: W. W. Norton.

Miller, Zane, and Bruce Tucker. 1990. "The New Urban Politics: Planning and Development in Cincinnati, 1954–1988." In *Snowbelt Cities: Midwestern Politics in the Northeast and Midwest since World War II*, 91–108. Edited by Richard M. Bernard. Bloomington: Indiana University Press.

Milon, Barbara. 1992. Conversation. March 31.

National Congress for Community Economic Development. 1991. *Changing the Odds: The Achievements of Community-based Development Organizations.* Washington, D.C.: Author.

NOAH, Inc. 1989. *Annual Report.* Cleveland, Ohio.

Peirce, Neal R., and Carol F. Steinbach. 1987. *Corrective Capitalism: The Rise of America's Community Development Corporations.* New York: Ford Foundation.

Perry, Stewart E. 1971. "A Note on the Genesis of the Community Development Corporation." In *The Case for Participatory Democracy: Some Prospects for a Radical Society,* 55–63. Edited by George C. Benello and Dimitrious Roussopoulos. New York: Grossman.

———. 1987. *Communities on the Way: Rebuilding Local Economies in the United States and Canada.* Albany: State University of New York Press.

Pittsburgh Partnership for Neighborhood Development. 1990. *Progress Report.* Pittsburgh: Author.

Rasey, Keith P., et al. 1989. *Community Development in Ohio: Issues and Policy Opportunities.* Research report. Cleveland: Cleveland State University.

Rasey, Keith P., W. Dennis Keating, Norman Krumholz, and Philip D. Star. 1991. "Management of Neighborhood Development: Community Development Corporations." In *Managing Local Government: Public Administration in Practice,* 214–236. Edited by Richard D. Bingham et al. Newbury Park, Calif.: Sage.

Roberts, Benson F., and Fern C. Portnoy. 1990. "Building a New Low-Income Housing Industry: A Growing Role for the Nonprofit Sector." In *The Future of National Urban Policy.* 305–318. Edited by Marshall Kaplan and Franklin Jones. Durham, N.C.: Duke University Press.

Shafer, Robert, and Charles G. Field. 1973. "Section 235 of the National Housing Act: Homeownership for Low-Income Families?" in *Housing Urban America,* 460–471. Edited by Jon Pynoos, Robert Shafer and Chester Hartman. Chicago: Aldine Publishing Company.

Shafer, Robert, and Helen F. Ladd. 1981. *Discrimination in Mortgage Lending.* Cambridge, Mass.: MIT Press.

Sullivan, Donald G. 1969. *Cooperative Housing and Community Development: A Comparative Evaluation of Three Housing Projects in East Harlem.* New York: Praeger.

Swanstrom, Todd. 1985. *The Crisis of Growth Politics: Cleveland, Kucinich, and the Challenge of Urban Populism.* Philadelphia: Temple University Press.

Taggart, Robert III. 1970. *Low-Income Housing: A Critique of Federal Aid.* Baltimore: Johns Hopkins Press.

U.S. Congress. Senate. Committee on Government Operations. Subcommittee on Executive Reorganization. 1969. *Hearings on the Federal Role in Urban Affairs.* 89th Cong., 2d sess., August 15, 16.

U.S. Department of Housing and Urban Development. 1969. *HUD Statistical Yearbook.* Washington, D.C.: U.S. Government Printing Office.

———. 1975. *Housing Production with Non Profit Sponsors.* A Staff Study. Washington, D.C.: U.S. Government Printing Office.

U.S. General Accounting Office. 1978. *Section 236 Rental Housing—An Evaluation with Lessons for the Future.* PAD–78–13. Washington, D.C.: U.S. Government Printing Office.

Vidal, Avis et al. 1989. *Community Economic Development Assessment: A National Study of Urban Community Development Corporations (Preliminary Findings).* New York: New School for Social Research.

10

Nonprofit Housing Cooperatives in Canada: Changing Features and Impacts of an Alternative Housing Form

FRANCINE DANSEREAU

The provision of nontraditional housing services to households considered marginal on a variety of grounds has been a mission vested in governments since the beginning of this century. Long confined within the realm of service to the poor marginalized on account of their inability to meet the financial conditions required for access to normal or majority housing services, this mission has been enlarged since the 1970s to serve a variety of new needs and life situations. New housing solutions have emerged, enlarging the range of choice and giving residents more control over their immediate environment. We have seen, for example, a mushrooming of housing cooperatives and other alternative housing solutions, usually taking the form of self-help by various social groups.

The state has been called upon to provide an institutional framework and, in certain cases, financial support. This has been done with a vacillation indicative of great ambivalence as to the proper responsibility of the state in monitoring the overall functioning of the housing market. Housing cooperatives are here treated as an illustration of these hesitant developments: they are situated at the nexus of choices in social housing policies, especially within the context of inner-city revitalization and housing stock management in general.

SOCIAL MIX VERSUS CORE NEED: A RECURRING AMBIVALENCE

Nonprofit housing cooperatives, along with nonprofit housing corporations, have become the favored vehicle for delivery of social housing in Canada since the mid–1970s. In 1973, amendments to the National Housing

Act shifted the emphasis from public provision of low-rent housing to reliance on these so-called third-sector initiatives. This was a response to the financial burden represented by the rapidly growing public housing portfolio as well as a solution to the alleged ghettoization and bureaucratization of public housing projects, repeatedly pointed to by social critics and groups active on the urban scene of the late 1960s.

Third-sector initiatives encompass both housing cooperatives and housing corporations. The main difference is that the first are self-managed by member tenants, whereas the latter are run by directorships appointed by municipal, charitable, or other non-profit organizations. Also, target groups tend to differ: nonprofit housing corporations are mainly used to serve special-needs client groups (handicapped, seniors, battered women, etc.) in contrast with cooperatives, which were originally designed to produce socially mixed projects and communities. Since their inception in 1973, cooperatives have been aimed at modest to moderate-income households whose incomes fell between that of clients eligible for public housing and that of households able to afford homeownership with little or no direct governmental help.

These distinguishing features have evolved over time, especially through changes in financial arrangements, but, in essence, the cooperative formula has remained a tenure choice—in contrast to a second-best or last-resort housing solution—that has appealed to many segments of the population. For this reason what follows will focus primarily on cooperatives.[1]

Between 1973 and 1978, both housing cooperatives and housing corporations were (under Article 61 of the National Housing Act) heavily subsidized by the federal government. Their financing included a direct subsidy covering 10 percent of capital costs and a mortgage loan (with a fixed interest rate of 8 percent over a fifty-year amortization period) for the remaining 90 percent of capital costs. In addition, grants up to $10,000 were available to cooperative groups willing to develop a project; other grants were aimed at organizations providing technical and advisory help to would-be cooperative groups. Finally, rent supplements were planned for households unable to meet the rents determined on the basis of net operating costs: the proportion of such households was not to exceed 25 percent of a project's units in order to preserve the income mix objective. The main difference from public housing was that no deficit in operating costs was to be allowed and absorbed, as had previously been the case under the system of federal-provincial subsidies. The absorption of such operating losses had, in fact, proved to be the most costly aspect of the public housing program.

In 1979, the federal financing mechanism of cooperatives was changed in order to serve a larger number of low-income families. Henceforth, mortgage loans were to be obtained from private lenders at market rates, with a federal guarantee (NHA, Art. 95). The loan maximum remained at 100 percent of capital costs, but the maximum amortization period was reduced to thirty-five years. Federal subsidies to cooperatives consisted chiefly of a grant, which reduced the interest rate to as low as 2 percent for three years, after which net mortgage costs were to increase 5 percent annually until the mortgage was paid off. Rents were determined by Canada Mortgage and Housing Corporation (CMHC), the federal housing agency, on the basis of the low end of market rents in the project's neighborhood. The unused portion of the subsidy was available to low-income households in order to bring their rent-to-income ratio down to 25 percent. At least 15 percent of a project's units were reserved for such households.

The cooperative program became increasingly popular in this period, especially since some provincial and municipal governments added their own incentives, such as land or rehabilitation grants, start-up grants, or operating grants, to technical resource groups. However, as interest rates jumped to a peak of over 20 percent during the early 1980s, the financial burden carried by the federal government again appeared excessive, and a new program was devised. This program, enacted in 1986, was part of a major revision of the federal role in housing, limiting state expenditures and channeling aid exclusively to the "core needy."[2] The social mix ideal was thus abandoned. Other levels of government soon followed this neoconservative lead, given the general spirit of the times and their limited financial capabilities to follow an independent course.

The new program, termed the *index-linked mortgage* (ILM), was the result of a long bargaining process between the Cooperative Housing Foundation— an influential lobby speaking on behalf of the cooperative movement—and the federal government. Its rationale was to sever links between the cooperative concept and social housing and link it rather with homeownership and private rental market stabilization objectives. In fact, cooperative housing units built under the ILM program are not treated as social housing at all by CMHC but as market housing. The ILM is a loan in which the interest rate is stated in terms of a fixed real rate of return that is combined with a variable rate adjusted periodically for inflation. It is obtained in the private mortgage market. Under the ILM program, the initial occupancy charge corresponds to the full market rent, whereas in the previous federal cooperative program, the initial occupancy charge corresponded to the low end of market rent.

This shift made the cooperative formula much less attractive and, together with a net reduction in funds available, resulted in a marked decrease in the number of units built annually. The number of units had reached 26,334 across Canada during the 1980–1984 period; it fell to 10,255 between 1985 and 1990 with the new ILM program.[3] The number of units built under the federal housing cooperative programs totaled 56,745 in 1990; of these, 46 percent had been built between 1980 and 1984 and 18 percent between 1985 and 1990. Currently, cooperative units represent only 9 percent of the nearly 600,000 social housing units built with CMHC assistance.[4]

While decreasing in numbers, the groups reached by cooperatives since

the late 1980s have, in comparison with previous programs' clienteles, become somewhat more segregated in socioeconomic terms both within and
between projects. The majority tend to be low-income households eligible
for rent supplements or income-based rent. At the other end of the scale,
a small fraction are able to afford full market rents. Indeed, according to
many technical resource group workers, it is often difficult to attract the
latter to cooperative housing, in contrast to previous programs, where sim-
ilar-income households were getting a bargain. Table 10.1 shows various
indicators of differences between programs in terms of income levels of
groups reached and the internal diversity of each project.

Since its inception, the federal program has left room for wide variation
in application between provinces. For instance, earlier versions of the program (Art. 61, Art. 95) have tended to serve much lower-income groups in
Quebec than in Ontario. The trend since 1973 has run in opposite directions:
in Quebec, the proportion of residents living under the Statistics Canada's
low-income cutoff has gone down, with each successive version, from 55
percent to 43 percent to 35 percent, while it has risen from 22 percent to
27 percent to 33 percent in Ontario. The proportion of residents paying an
income-based rent has decreased markedly between Article 95 projects and
more recent ILM projects, especially in Quebec. An important reason for
this is that beneficiaries of income-based rents under the ILM program tend
to have much lower incomes than was the case under previous program's
provisions.

Nationally the proportion of residents paying an income-based rent whose
income levels are at or above the median income of all Canadian renters in
1989 ($20,000) has been reduced dramatically (from 36 percent for house-
holds living in units built under Art. 95 or 39 percent for units built under
Art. 61 to a mere 10 percent for those built under the more recent ILM).
In fact, the government's appeal for closer targeting of low-income populations has met with considerable success. The result is a reduction in income
diversity, although the various indexes of income mix or segregation are
contradictory. The income mix index in table 10.1 shows a decrease in
diversity, but this is in fact due to a concentration around modal categories:
under the ILM program, cases where 60 percent or more of a project's
residents pay an income-based rent have disappeared, whereas such a situation prevails in four of ten cooperatives built under Article 95.

To sum up, there are definite signs of a trend toward greater homogeneity
of clientele over time, but one can still point to considerable diversity between projects and localities; this testifies to the basic malleability of the
cooperative housing program. More important, these changes show that the
separation of the cooperative program from social housing does not have
much significance in concrete terms since the proportions of rent supplement
recipients have never been so high. The conditions for bringing a cooperative

Table 10.1
Indicators of Socioeconomic Status and Income Mix of Residents in Nonprofit
Housing Cooperatives

	ILM (1986-1992)	ARTICLE 61 (1973-1978)	ARTICLE 95 (1979-1985)
Part A Percentage of residents with incomes under Statistics Canada low income cut-offs, 1989.			
Canada	32.1	32.3	35.5
Quebec	34.8	54.9	43.0
Ontario	32.5	22.1	26.6
Part B Percentage of residents paying an income-based rent.			
Canada	33.8*	42.8	55.8
Quebec	27.1	22.0	44.9
Ontario	36.0	40.6	42.4
Part C Percentage of residents paying an income-based rent for various income strata.			
Under $10,000	39.9	21.8	24.4
$10,000-$19,000	49.7	38.9	39.9
$20,000 or more	10.4	39.3	35.7
Part D Percentage of residents in cooperatives characterized by "income mix"**			
Canada	44.8	67.2	48.3

*   Only 38 percent of these households quote employment as a major
        source of income (in contrast with 61 percent for same group under
        Article 61 and 53 percent under Article 95 programs.)

**   "Income mix" is defined as at least 20 % of a cooperative's residents
        fall into each of the following categories; (1) under core
        need;(2)between core need and 150% over core need; (3) more than
        150 % over core need.

SOURCE: Evaluation of Federal Cooperative Housing Programs. CMHC,
           Program Evaluation Division, 1990.

into existence have simply been made much more difficult with rent supplements restricted to core needy households.

DIVERSITY IN PHYSICAL DESIGN

There has been a great diversity in physical options—project size, building
type, and choice of new construction, rehabilitation of residential buildings,
or recycling or nonresidential buildings (schools, abandoned warehouses, or
factories) into residential use. Across Canada (table 10.2), the distribution
of building types increasingly favors apartment buildings (60 percent of ILM
projects totaling 48 percent of dwelling units compared with 38 percent of
projects totaling 33 percent of dwelling units built under Art. 95) as opposed
to low-rise multifamily buildings or, much less common, single-family units.
Building size tends to remain small. Although very small projects (under
ten units) have become a thing of the past with the disappearance of rehabilitation as the main tool for delivering cooperative units, the majority of
projects still contain fewer than thirty units. Large projects (one hundred
units or more) have also become a thing of the past.

Regional variation in the delivery of physical products must be stressed.
In Quebec, for example, cooperatives have tended to be small and have
favored rehabilitation over new construction, especially those developed
before 1986. Since then, physical characteristics have tended to converge
with those found in Ontario. This partly explains the difference between
Quebec and Ontario in income levels of members and proportions of rent
supplement recipients.

COOPERATIVES AS A DISTINCT SOCIORESIDENTIAL
PACKAGE

Over and above such spatial variation and changes through time, cooperatives represent a unique residential package with specific characteristics
consistently reported by members in various surveys:

1. Good-quality housing at affordable rents. Although the financial advantage over
   private market rents has decreased, housing cooperatives still offer better-quality
   housing at reasonable prices, and the fact that an important fraction of households
   can benefit from rent supplements is a definite advantage.

2. Security of tenure. This is absolute as long as a member fulfills his or her obligations
   and is transmissible to the member's descendants. It is a stronger right than that
   enjoyed in public housing and is, in fact, equivalent to that enjoyed by homeowners. The difference between cooperatives and ownership or condominium
   titles is that no profit may be realized from holding a share in a cooperative. This
   is considered a major drawback by middle-class households who can afford homeownership. It should not be a surprise, in this respect, to find that the most
   common motive mentioned in the 1990 survey of members by those who intended

Table 10.2
Physical Characteristics of Nonprofit Housing Cooperatives

	ILM (1986-1992)		ARTICLE 61 (1973-1978)		ARTICLE 95 (1979-1985)	
	Projects	Units	Projects	Units	Projects	Units
Part A Percentage of projects and dwelling units by type of dwelling (Canada)						
Single-family	4.0	2.6	13.0	5.8	8.3	3.8
Low-Rise	26.7	35.5	29.6	31.0	32.9	40.0
Apartment	60.2	47.9	41.7	36.4	37.7	32.6
Other	0.3	0.4	1.8	1.0	1.8	1.1
Mixed	8.7	13.7	13.9	25.7	19.3	22.5
Part B Percentage of projects and dwelling units by size of project (Canada)						
< 10 units	9.0	2.4	47.5	6.8	16.0	2.9
10-29	48.8	28.8	18.4	11.2	42.9	22.0
30-49	22.7	26.5	12.1	14.5	18.9	20.2
50-99	17.7	35.0	16.1	37.2	16.7	32.8
100 +	1.6	7.3	5.8	30.4	5.5	22.2
Part C Percentage of cooperatives and dwelling units by mode of realization (Canada)						
New construction	63.6	75.6	32.2	50.7	51.7	65.6
Existing building	11.1	7.5	27.6	25.3	18.0	12.9
Mixed	25.3	17.0	38.2	24.0	30.3	21.4
SOURCE: Evaluation of Federal Cooperative Housing Programs. CMHC, Program Evaluation Division, 1990.						

to leave their cooperatives was the wish to buy a home or an apartment (mentioned by over 20 percent of members paying a full rent, twice the rate of those on income-based rents).

3. Self-management. For most households, this is an advantage over the management structures of both public housing and private market rental housing. For some, however, it may represent a burden or a source of conflict with neighbors. Members of cooperatives have to participate actively in their cooperative's activities as executive board members or on various committees (finance, social activities, maintenance, etc.). At least 80 percent of members do participate in such activities, spending an average of around eight hours per month, according to a 1990 survey. Of course, the number of hours is much higher during the first year or two of operation, and a considerable fraction of members take on a much heavier burden; for instance, 15 percent of members in recent ILM-type cooperatives devote at least fifteen hours per month to their cooperative's activities. Earlier surveys have raised the question as to whether some types of households—female-led single-parent families (Klodawsky, Spector, and Rose, 1985), for example—would find such obligations excessive. Also, the pressure to participate has been mentioned as a potential source of conflict and the major reason cited by leavers in the past (Myra Schiff Consultants, 1983).

4. Control over one's individual and collective living environment. This can be seen as the reverse side of the pressure to participate in management and maintenance. Cooperatives provide ample opportunities for involvement in the design and maintenance of one's living environment. Collective decision making concerning the overall design of buildings and the detailed layout and allocation of apartments as well as of outdoor space can be time-consuming and frustrating but also a gratifying learning process. Personalization of apartments occurs gradually and contributes to the sense of belonging to the cooperative (Deslauriers and Brassard, 1989).

5. Stepping-stone toward a more general process of empowerment in the community and the work environment. Participation in one's cooperative enhances self-image and management skills; this can spill over into other areas of life, increasing personal control over the neighborhood or work environment. The 1990 survey indicates that residents tend to emphasize the acquisition of general psychosocial skills (self-confidence, communication skills, better ability to participate in group discussions or decisions, to work with others on a particular project) as opposed to specific management skills, such as budgeting or management, bookkeeping, or secretarial work.

The 1990 survey found that, depending on the program, the proportion of residents asserting that they acquired no new competence through participation in their cooperative varied between 30 percent and 41 percent. This may appear somewhat surprising, given the usual discourse on cooperative living's benefits. As to more tangible effects, such as going back to school or getting a degree (mentioned respectively by 16 percent to 20 percent and 9 percent to 14 percent, depending on the program, of residents paying an income-based rent), reentering the labor market (10 percent to

21 percent of same), or starting one's own business (1 percent to 6 percent), these are mentioned by approximately one-third of respondents. This is no modest achievement. Acquiring new skills or general social competence may be seen as corresponding to a somewhat restricted, if not purely egocentric, view of a housing cooperative's social benefits. Other aspects related to community building, including the formation of a sense of identity, strong informal networks that develop mutual help and social support, as well as new services and activities, are all important benefits, which have been pointed to by various case studies or surveys.

COOPERATIVES AS AGENTS OF CHANGE IN THE COMMUNITY

Most housing cooperatives have acted as active agents in the development of services such as day care, food banks, or leisure activities for various age groups at the community level, either through direct provision or self-help or through pressure on municipal or school organizations. In other words, housing cooperatives supply a pool of militants who are likely to become involved in a variety of causes. Members are described as "involved" or "very involved" in the community by housing cooperatives' managers or coordinators in 37 percent to 57 percent of cases, depending on the program version.

From the community's viewpoint, many benefits linked with the emergence of housing cooperatives can be noted. The most obvious is the supply of well-maintained, good-quality rental housing at modest cost. This is especially important in inner-city neighborhoods in need of rehabilitation or experiencing speculative pressure. The action of community investment or development corporations deserves special mention here. Such corporations (which emanate directly from the cooperative movement, through regional or local federations) try to buy available properties at low prices in order to rehabilitate them and turn them into cooperatives. The liquid assets gained from resale to the cooperative allow the corporation to buy more property, thus enabling the conversion process to continue.

Such specialized community corporations have met with some success in Montreal, especially in neighborhoods where private market activity has tended to be slow. But they can become quickly neutralized in high-pressure neighborhoods and, for this reason, have recently requested special treatment from municipal authorities: right of first refusal on municipal land put up for development, short-term loans at preferential rates, and so forth. However, the existence of such corporations is not a requirement for cooperatives to have tangible effects on a neighborhood's livability and residential quality. They simply allow for more local concentration of cooperatives, which, in turn, are likely to influence neighborhood rents and physical housing quality. This is analogous, albeit with potentially reverse price effects, to developments brought about by the spread of condominium conversion in a neighborhood.

Also similar is the increased demand for local services sensitive to the needs of the new settlers. In the case of cooperatives, this usually means services directed at young families (e.g., playgrounds and other facilities, day care, after-school supervision) or teenagers (sports and recreation facilities) that are not commonly provided in inner-city neighborhoods with aging and primarily single-person households. The scope and variety of amenities is thus enlarged, along with increased claims for neighborhood improvement in areas such as traffic safety, street lighting and cleanliness, tree planting, and park maintenance. Cooperatives provide a pool of militants and community watchdogs who are able to mobilize or revitalize many community organizations and therefore produce a more lively and better served neighborhood.

This activity inevitably increases the neighborhood's desirability, with gentrification accompanied by higher rents and conversion of rental buildings into condominium or undivided co-ownership (*cooperatives* in U.S. terminology) as a highly possible outcome.[5] One cannot draw causal links between these developments—for example, conceptualize the creation of housing cooperatives as the prime cause of a more general gentrification process— but synergistic effects are discernable, as if alternative tenure forms were feeding into each other. In a study conducted in 1986 (Choko and Dansereau, 1987) in areas immediately bordering Montreal's central business district (CBD), we found that neighborhoods with high rehabilitation activity tended to be affected by both high rates of conversion to condominium or co-ownership and high rates of cooperative formation.

Yet this general statement must be qualified. The profile of tenure changes depends heavily on locational advantages, surrounding urban activities, architectural and environmental form, and the incumbent population's socioeconomic characteristics. For instance, as observed elsewhere (Ley, 1985), areas located close to the CBD and favored by natural amenities or visual perspectives, as well as highly valued Victorian architecture, experienced the most drastic changes. The Milton Park neighborhood in Montreal is a clear example in this respect. It is located close to Mount Royal Park, Montreal's most dominant landmark. On the north and west, it is encircled by major hospitals, research institutions, and the McGill University campus. Major commercial and business concentrations form its southern boundary. The neighborhood's transformation started in the early 1970s as a battleground between private bulldozer-type redevelopment with high-rise office and residential structures and heritage conservationist groups, which succeeded in having a major portion of the territory turned into housing cooperatives largely for existing neighborhood residents.

In subsequent years, remaining properties were quickly seized by real estate professionals to be rehabilitated, reconverted to larger units, or subdivided and resold as condominium units. Transitional housing forms—student rooming houses and low-rent dilapidated apartments, which had been a distinct feature of the area since the 1930s—virtually disappeared. The only remaining exceptions consist of a few buildings that have recently been renovated, with the help of the city and provincial-federal grants and are now run as "social" rooming houses for low-income singles by nonprofit corporations or cooperatives.

The social mix in the neighborhood now tends to be weighted toward highly educated households but with varied financial means. High-rise apartments are occupied mainly by low-level professional or semiprofessional (nurses, lab technicians, etc.) and clerical workers, the majority of whom are young and single. In comparison, residents in cooperatives and, much more so, in condominiums show higher professional qualifications. Our 1986 survey revealed that 69 percent of them had university degrees compared to 12 percent among the men and 7 percent among the women aged 15 and over in the inner city (with an exceptional peak at 22 percent and 15 percent, respectively, for the CBD). High-level managerial and traditional professional occupations (lawyers, doctors) represented 16 percent of the total, with the bulk of residents, 35 percent, belonging to the "new professional" categories (artistic and intellectual occupations: journalists, theater directors, media and advertising copy writers, university professors, etc.); the rest was distributed between middle management (office supervisors, sales managers: 18 percent), technicians and clerical workers (19 percent), "inactive" (students, pensioners: 11 percent), and blue-collar workers (1 percent).

An important line must be drawn between owners of condominiums and those of co-ownership apartments. The former have less formal education: 56 percent have university degrees, in contrast to 77 percent of co-owners. However, condominium owners occupy better-paid professional positions, 84 percent of them have incomes over $40,000, while only 28 percent of co-owners have incomes this high. The lower income of educated co-owners reflects their concentration in new professional occupations, while condominium owners are more concentrated in high management or traditional professional occupations. In addition, inactive (mostly students) and blue-collar occupants are found exclusively in co-ownership units.

The major reason for such discrepancies lies in the process by which these two groups have had access to homeownership. On the one hand, the market for rehabilitated undivided co-ownership units, which appeared earlier in Montreal and reached its peak in 1983, has drawn on a relatively limited, homogeneous client pool, linked into personal and professional networks, which tended to take an active part in the processes of rehabilitation and tenure conversion. On the other hand, the market in rehabilitated condominiums has been dominated by real estate professionals and addressed to a much larger and more anonymous client group that is less prone to do-it-yourself rehabilitation work.

As a result, residents in undivided co-ownership apartments fall somewhere between condominium owners and tenants in nonprofit cooperatives in socioeconomic and family profile. The major exception is that cooperatives in the inner city recruit more elderly and female-headed single-parent families with very limited financial means.

It must also be noted that the picture drawn using Milton Park as an illustration does not prevail in all areas. The district lying east of the CBD, known as Centre-sud, can serve as a counterexample. This traditional working-class district, which suffered dramatic population losses over the past three decades due to major demolition, the erosion of its manufacturing base, and a general flight of families, has been the principal recipient of public housing construction and cooperative rehabilitation of dilapidated housing.[6] The best-known and most active neighborhood development corporation in Montreal—the Corporation de développement communautaire du Centre-sud—has played a leading role in this mushrooming of cooperatives. Conversion of rental to ownership has almost exclusively taken the form of undivided co-ownership, with much self-rehabilitation of buildings bought at low prices. Such operations have nonetheless been conducted by groups that differ markedly from their immediate environment, especially in terms of age and educational level.

The three groups—residents in condominium or undivided co-ownership and those in nonprofit cooperatives—express strikingly similar motives for their residential choice. All point to "the only financially affordable option to live near the downtown" as a major consideration. The "good investment" criterion also ranks high for owners of condominium or undivided co-ownership units. Reasons related to social relations ("better neighbors," "influence of friends") play an important though generally secondary part, especially for residents in undivided co-ownership or cooperative apartments. The choice for a central location and for older housing seems particularly firm in the light of both the other possibilities considered during the respondents' prepurchase "shopping" process and those contemplated for the future. The ideal of the centrally located upper-middle class "better neighborhoods" that offer older single-family homes is, however, contemplated as a next step by one-third of the owner sample, made up essentially of the younger (less than age 40) segment.

These various features, which emphasize the strong sociocultural component of the rise of alternative tenure forms, have important implications for inner-city evolution. The emergence of alternative tenure forms is propelled by young households committed to making the inner city a good place to live, as well as an instrument in class constitution (Jager, 1986), that is, in defining and consolidating their own position in the marketplace or on the job. Because many of these actors are in the design and media professions, symbolic attributes play a crucial part in this process. But this activity also creates new models that are assimilated by more conservative elements

elements of the population—the risk averse of the stage model of the gentrification process (Clay, 1979). Clearly, in Montreal, as in many other cities, alternative tenure forms are regarded as regular options by diverse parts of the middle classes and by various players on the real estate and building scene.

The impact of the rise of alternative tenure forms, in conjunction with major rehabilitation initiatives, is obviously an entrenching of new client groups, which reduces the fluidity of the housing market in central areas. The reverse side of the picture, which has drawn most attention in the literature, is displacement of older, established residents. In half of the dwellings renovated with municipal subsidies before 1976, the tenant left (Vachon, 1976). Ten years later, such moves were observed in nineteen out of twenty cases of major renovation work (LARSI, 1985; Dansereau, 1988).[7]

The major explanation for this escalating proportion is that by 1986, owners, and especially new owners of rehabilitated buildings, had systematically become owner residents (co-owners or owners of a condominium unit). The result is increasing control over their living conditions for that fraction of ex-tenants who have gained access to homeownership or security of tenure in a cooperative. But for the vast majority, the transformation of the inner city has meant an erosion of both tenure security and housing affordability. Also, tighter access to the CBD and surrounding areas has meant a blocking out of newly arriving groups—international immigrants, students and young workers from peripheral regions or even suburbs—from that hotbed for socialization to urbanity that the city center had traditionally represented.

EFFECTS ON RENTAL MARKET CONDITIONS

What are some of the possible consequences of these alternative tenure forms for the overall evolution of the rental market in the city of Montreal? Montreal has traditionally been a city of renters, representing over 80 percent of its households from the turn of the century until the early 1980s. This proportion has dropped more recently, from 81 percent in 1971 to 74 percent in 1986. The parallel change has been a growing proportion of renters whose rent-to-income ratio ranked above 25 percent (rising from 38 percent to 48 percent between 1981 and 1986) (Ville de Montréal, 1989: 15). This is due not mainly to rising rents but to the relative impoverishment of renters, especially in the case of nonfamily households.[8]

In a survey conducted in 1990 on a representative sample of rental buildings, we observed wide variation in these figures between household types and building types (Dansereau et al., 1991). For instance, single-parent families and persons living alone show a rent-to-income ratio above 30 percent in 53.1 percent and 44.3 percent of cases, respectively.[9] Couples, on the other hand, are better off, with rent-to-income ratios above 30 percent in 38.5 percent of cases for couples with children at home and 21.0 percent for couples without children. Differences across building types are also striking: renters in small "plex" structures (buildings containing two or three units, each with a separate entry, and usually run by a resident landlord) have a rent-to-income ratio under 30 percent in 63 percent of cases, whereas those living in high-rise or large (twelve or more units) walk-up apartment buildings show rent-to-income ratios reaching 50 percent or more in 29 percent and 25 percent of cases, respectively. Moreover, small "plex" structures offer a much better residential quality than any other type of building in Montreal. They also are much more affordable financially.

The problem is that this particular segment of the rental market, which still accounts for approximately 35 percent of Montreal's residential rental stock, is eroding in relative terms. It has been the major target for step-by-step conversion from rental to undivided co-ownership and now to condominium tenure over the past decade. The reasons lie partly in low maintenance costs and intrinsic as well as locational desirability. They also lie in the institutional rules governing its transition from rental to ownership. There has been a ban on conversion from rental to condominium property in Montreal since December 1975, which was tightened in 1980 in order to rule out repossession by an owner of a unit (usually held in undivided co-ownership based on purely person-to-person agreements) located in a building containing more than four units. This ban on repossession was extended to smaller buildings only in December 1988. These rules have channeled pressures toward homeownership and rehabilitated housing into smaller buildings, held in undivided co-ownership, and have prompted the use of heavy rehabilitation to gain vacant possession of buildings and effect otherwise prohibited condominium conversions. The risks and the complexities involved in operations concerning larger buildings have kept most would-be developers or speculators at bay.

The effects of the relative decrease in the general ability to pay of renters and the ensuing poor profitability prospects (or, at least, the pessimistic views of investors in the rental housing market) offer rather bleak prospects as to the level of maintenance and quality in the rental stock. Walk-up apartment buildings, in particular, are often found wanting in fire safety and general maintenance (e.g., poorly fitting windows were mentioned by almost 50 percent of respondents in our 1990 survey, pests by 28 percent, insufficient heat or the need for additional heating sources by 20 percent). The owners are not prone to correct these deficiencies; faced with high turnover rates and difficult tenants who do not pay their rent regularly, they are eager to resort to evictions. High-rise buildings, most of them built during the 1960s, are also entering a phase of major and costly repair needs regarding underground parking structures, balconies, and so forth. Half of the owners of such buildings are simply waiting for an opportunity to resell their property within the next five years.

TIME TO DRAW UP A BALANCE SHEET?

If drawing up a balance sheet of the benefits and costs involved in the growth of alternative tenure forms were a sensible exercise after a period of only fifteen years marked by major economic swings and U-turns in policy, one would certainly recognize that new opportunities have been created for households previously limited to an excessively narrow range of housing choices. Pure rental market tenancy was formerly the rule for nonfamily households since access to homeownership meant purchasing a single-family home or a large "plex" with apartments to maintain and tenants to manage. Social housing was restricted to highly stigmatized public housing, perceived either as a last resort or as a final achievement after a lengthy and exhausting detour through the bureaucracy of municipal waiting lists. In contrast, nonprofit housing cooperatives have opened new opportunities in diverse locations for a variety of household types, ages, and income strata. Through time, however, the choices available under cooperative tenure have narrowed. Similarly, the spread of condominium or undivided co-ownership has opened new possibilities for homeownership, especially in central districts, but also with a tendency to narrow choices around the higher end of the price spectrum as this market became standardized.

It is nonetheless a fact that many households that previously had very little control over their housing conditions made clear gains in terms of security of tenure and control over the design and arrangement of their living quarters, as well as over their housing costs. Access to a new housing status has also meant greater control over their local environment and life situation, including the acquisition of new skills. This has been clearly demonstrated in the case of women living in cooperatives as well as women (mainly divorced) for whom the purchase of a condominium or an undivided co-ownership unit has represented a new start in life.

On the other hand, there are now fewer apartments for rent in central districts. In Montreal's city center, for instance, no private rental building has been built since 1976 except for two or three complexes heavily subsidized by government and run by nonprofit housing corporations (Dansereau, 1988). There also remain fewer tenants with the ability to afford good-quality market rents. The fact that a city is inhabited by fewer tenants than a decade ago is not an ill in itself. The problem is the doubts that this situation raises as to the future collective capacity to manage and maintain the rental stock. These doubts are especially acute in these times of fiscal restraint when governments seem reluctant to influence the course of events with refashioned and much needed housing improvement or rehabilitation programs.

NOTES

1. Most of the information contained in the following paragraphs has been extracted from the report, "Evaluation of the Federal Co-operative Housing Programs," conducted by CMHC's Program Evaluation Division (CMHC, 1990).

2. This expression applies to households faced with either an affordability (rent-to-income ratio above 25 percent, raised, since 1986, to 30 percent) or a physical adequacy (substandard conditions) problem or overcrowding. If a household living in substandard or overcrowded conditions can afford the rent required to improve its condition, it is not counted as being in core need.

3. During the 1985–1990 interval author 12,267 units, which had been approved under the previous (Art. 95) program's provisions, were built.

4. If, as CMHC currently does, one removes units built under the ILM program from social housing figures, this percentage falls just below 8 percent.

5. Undivided co-ownership here refers to equity cooperatives, distinct from the nonprofit tenant cooperatives normally found in Canada, but synonymous with the term *cooperative* used in the United States. The distinguishing feature is that all of the property of the building is shared between partners who are jointly responsible for all financial and legal aspects. This tenure form is found mainly in Quebec.

6. Through highway construction, major fires, and construction of the Canadian Broadcasting Corporation and the Université du Québec complexes, among others.

7. After 1987, with rehabilitation the coming into power of a "progressive" municipal party and later, in 1989, with the withdrawal of the federal landlord rental residential rehabilitation program, municipal rehabilitation subsidies have been reserved exclusively for operations conducted by nonprofit housing corporations or cooperatives.

8. According to the 1986 census, the proportion of households living under the poverty threshold in Montreal had reached 50 percent for "unattached individuals" (or single-person household) and 26 percent for "economic families."

9. Rent calculations presented here include rent as well as heating, hot water, and (exceptionally) parking payments.

REFERENCES

Canada Mortgage and Housing Corporation (CMHC). 1990. *Evaluation of the Federal Co-operatives Housing Programs*.

Choko, M. H., and F. Dansereau. 1987. *Restauration résidentielle et copropriété au centre-ville de Montréal*. Montreal: INRS-Urbanisation.

Clay, P. L. 1979. *Neighborhood Renewal: Middle-Class Resettlement and Incumbent Upgrading in American Neighborhoods*. Lexington, Mass.: Lexington Books.

Dansereau, F. 1988. *Habiter au centre: tendances et perspectives socio-économiques de l'habitation dans l'arrondissement Centre*. Montréal: Ville de Montréal et INRS-Urbanisation.

Dansereau, F., C. Beaudoin, F. Charbonneau, M. H. Choko, and A.-M. Séguin. 1991. *L'Etat du parc résidentiel locatif de Montréal*. Montréal: INRS-Urbanisation.

Deslauriers, J.-P., and M.-J. Brassard. 1989. *Pouvoir habiter*. Chicoutimi: UQAC, Groupe de recherche et intervention régionales.

Jager, M. 1986. "Class definition and the esthetics of gentrification: Victoriana in Melbourne." In N. Smith and P. Williams, eds., *Gentrification of the City*, 78–91. Boston: Allen and Unwin.

Klodawsky, F., A. Spector, and D. Rose. 1985. *Single Parent Families and Canadian Housing Policies: How Mothers Lose*. Ottawa: Canada Mortgage and Housing Corporation.

Laboratoire de recherche en sciences immobilières. 1985. *Impacts de la restauration dans les quartiers centraux de Montréal*. Montréal: UQAM.

Ley, D. 1985. *Gentrification in Canadian Inner Cities: Patterns, Analysis, Impacts and Policy*. Vancouver: University of British Columbia, Department of Geography.

Myra Schiff Consultants. 1983. "Housing Cooperatives in Montréal: A Survey of Members, a Report." CHF Research Bulletin 6. Ottawa: Co-operative Housing Foundation of Canada.

Vachon, B. 1976. *Analyse des programmes de restauration résidentielle à Montréal*. Annexe 7 du Rapport du Groupe de travail sur l'habitation. Québec: Editeur officiel.

Ville de Montréal. 1989. *Habiter Montréal*.

Selected, Annotated Bibliography

Amin, Ruhul, and A. G. Mariam. 1987. "Racial Differences in Housing: An Analysis of Trends and Differentials, 1960–1978." *Urban Affairs Quarterly*. 22(3): 363–376.
This article provides a good background paper on housing and race.

Andrusz, Gregory. 1984. *Housing and Urban Development in the USSR*. London: Macmillan/SUNY.
This book examines the evolution of the major types of housing tenure which dominated until the dawning of perestroika and which still influence policy.

———. 1992. "Housing Cooperatives in the Soviet Union." *Housing Studies*, 7(2).
This article traces the fortunes of this tenure and suggests that it seems to be favored in perods of liberalization and crisis in the political/economic cycle.

Ball, M. 1983. *Housing Policy and Economic Power*. Methuen: Andover, Hants.
This book offers a critical discussion of housing policy in Britain, focusing on the production process.

Birchall, J. 1988. *Building Communities the Cooperative Way*. London: Routledge and Kegan Paul.
This book presents arguments for the cooperative form of housing ownership, a history of cooperative housing in Britain, and six case histories of operating cooperatives.

Blaustein, Arthur I., and Geoffrey Faux. 1972. *The Star-Spangled Hustle*. Garden City, N.Y.: Doubleday.
This book provides a historical account of federal legislative initiatives in the 1960s supporting the creation of community development corporations.

Bratt, Rachel G. 1989. *Rebuilding a Low-Income Housing Policy*. Philadelphia: Temple University Press.

244   Selected, Annotated Bibliography

This book offers a comprehensive critique of housing policy options, including consideration of the past and future role of community development corporations in the United States.

——. 1991. "Mutual Housing: Community-based Empowerment." *Journal of Housing* 48: 173–180.
This article provides a good introduction to the concept of mutual housing as it is evolving in the United States, including discussion of its strengths and weaknesses.

Canada Mortgage and Housing Corporation. 1990. *Evaluation of the Federal Co-operatives Housing Programs.*
The most complete and up-to-date research report on federally supported housing cooperatives in Canada, it contains useful data drawn from administrative records and an extensive survey of projects' members.

Choko, Marc H., and Francine Dansereau. 1987. *Restauration résidentielle et co-propriété au centre-ville de Montréal.* Montréal: INRS-Urbanisation.
This report is based on a survey of owners of rehabilitated apartments in core areas of Montreal. It contrasts purchasers of condominium units and those of units held in undivided co-ownership (equity cooperatives).

Dansereau, Francine. 1988. *Habiter au centre: Tendances et perspectives socioé-conomiques de l'habitation dans l'arrondissement Centre.* Montréal: Ville de Montréal et IRNS—Urbanisation.
This report summarizes the evolution of housing over the 1951–1986 period in downtown Montreal and discusses policy options for the fostering of socially balanced neighborhoods in downtown districts.

Dansereau, Francine, C. Beaudoin, F. Charbonneau, M. H. Choko, and A. M. Séguin. 1991. *L'etat du parc résidentiel locatif de Montréal.* Montréal: IRNS—Urbanisation.
This book reports a three-component survey of four hundred rental buildings in Montreal, including detailed physical inspections, landlord questionnaires, and tenant interviews.

Forrest, Ray, and Alan Murie. 1988. *Selling the Welfare State: The Privatisation of Public Housing.* London: Routledge.
This book presents the most complete description and analysis of the privatization of public housing in Britain, and is the definitive work in this area.

——. 1990. *Moving the Housing Market.* Aldershot: Avebury.
This book reports the results of a research on the role in the housing market of public sector dwellings which have been bought by tenants and resold.

——. 1988. *Selling the Welfare State.* London: Routledge and Kegan Paul.
This book offers a full account of developments and debates surrounding privatization of housing and the sale of council houses in particular.

Forrest, R., A. Murie, and Williams, P. 1990. *Homeownership: Fragmentation and Differentiation.* London: Unwin Hyman.
This book provides the most recent discussion of homeownership in Britain, referring to the contemporary debates about the nature and meaning of tenure.

Frey, William H. 1978. "Black Movement to the Suburbs: Potentials and Prospects for Metropolitan-Wide Integration." In Frank D. Bean and W. Parker Frisbie,

The Demography of Racial and Ethnic Groups. New York: Academic Press.
This article reports on black suburbanization, emphasizing residential mobility and suburban movement.

Galster, George. 1990. "Racial Discrimination in Housing Markets during the 1980s: A Review of the Audit Evidence." *Journal of Planning Education and Research* 9(3): 165–176.
This article provides evidence of continuing discrimination in housing markets.

Glendinning, Richard, Patrick Allen, and Helen Young. 1989. *The Sale of Local Authority Housing to the Private Sector*. London: HMSO.
This describes a government-sponsored survey of the sale of public sector housing estates to private developers, rather than to sitting tenants.

Hampden-Turner, Charles. 1975. *From Poverty to Dignity*. Garden City, NY: Anchor Books.
This book provides an interesting theoretical interpretation of the rise of community-based development corporations in the United States.

Heisler, B. S., and L. M. Hoffman. 1987. "Keeping a Home: Changing Mortgage Markets and Regional Economic Distress." *Sociological Focus* 20: 227–247.
This article examines the loss of an owner occupied home and its effect on the household.

Holmans, A. E. 1987. *Housing Policy in Britain*. London: Croom Helm.
This book offers a full and detailed account of the history of housing policy in Britain up to 1980.

Kemeny, Jim. 1981. *The Myth of Home-Ownership*. London: Routledge and Kegan Paul.
This book offers a treatment of the basic philosophical and economic issues surrounding homeownership.

Kerr, Marian. 1988. *The Right to Buy: A National Survey of Tenants and Buyers of Council Housing*. London: HMSO.
This reports on a government-sponsored survey of the socioeconomic characteristics of buying and nonbuying tenants of public sector dwellings.

Kunze, C. 1981. "Public Housing Cooperatives Reduce Dependence on Operating Subsidies, Modernization Funding." *Journal of Housing* 38(9): 489–493.
This article presents an analysis of the potential advantages and limitations of converting public housing into cooperatives.

Ley, D. 1985. *Gentrification in Canadian Inner Cities: Patterns, Analysis, Impacts and Policy*. Vancouver: University of British Columbia, Department of Geography.
This is a theoretically grounded and well-documented discussion of gentrification processes based on 1971–1981 comparative census data and on case studies of various inner-city districts in major Canadian cities.

Manpower Demonstration Research Corporation. 1981. *Tenant Management: Findings from a Three Year Experiment in Public Housing*. Cambridge, Mass.: Ballinger.
This report provides the first comparative study of resident-managed public

housing in the United States, it chronicled some of the successes and failures of these groups during their early years of operation.

Mayer, Neil S. 1990. "The Role of Nonprofits in Renewed Federal Housing Efforts." In *Building Foundations: Housing and Federal Policy*, edited by Denise DiPasquale and Langley Keyes. Philadelphia: University of Pennsylvania Press, 365–388.
This is a practical evaluative review of the role and performance of community development corporations in the United States.

Meehan, Eugene. 1979. *The Quality of Federal Policymaking: Programmed Failure in Public Housing.* Columbia: University of Missouri Press.
This is a systematic treatment of the origins of U.S. public housing. It shows the basic contradictions built into the program and how these contradictions resulted in many of its current problems.

Merrett, S. 1982. *Owner Occupation in Britain.* Andover: Routledge and Kegan Paul.
This book offers a full and critical account of the history of homeownership in Britain.

Monti, Daniel J. 1989. "Economic Development in Low Income Neighborhoods: The Case of Tenant-Managed Public Housing Sites in the U.S." *Built Environment* 14(5): 201–208.
This analyzes the ability of resident management firms to create jobs for persons living at the site and to develop business ventures that complement the firm's community organizing and management functions.

———. 1989. "The Organizatonal Strengths and Weaknesses of Resident Managed Public Housing Sites in the United States." *Journal of Urban Affairs* 11: 39–52.
This is an organizational analysis of ten more recent and better established resident management sites in the United States. It describes and assesses the ability of RMCs to carry out community organizing and management functions at the same time.

National Center for Neighborhood Enterprise. 1984. *The Grass Is Greener in Public Housing: From Tenant to Resident to Homeowner.* Report on Resident Management of Public Housing, submitted to U.S. Department of Housing and Urban Development, Washington, D.C.
Published by an organization that actively supports resident management and ownership (and that has been influential in shaping Reagan administration policy), this report summarizes the arguments on behalf of these reforms. It views resident management as a transitional phase leading to ownership.

National Congress for Community Economic Development. 1991. *Changing the Odds: The Achievements of Community-based Development Organizations.* Washington, D.C.
This report presents the results of a 1991 survey of community development corporations in the United States, including their activities and housing production record in the late 1980s.

Ong, Paul M., and J. Eugene Grigsby, III. 1988. "Race and Life-Cycle Effects on Homeownership in Los Angeles: 1970 to 1980." *Urban Affairs Quarterly* 23

(4): 601–615.
This article examines the combined impact of race and life cycle on homeownership.

Peterman, W., and M. Young. 1991. "Alternatives to Conventional Public Housing Management." Technical Note No. 1–91. Chicago: Voorhees Center for Neighborhood and Community Improvement, University of Illinois.
This report describes five alternatives to conventional public housing management: resident management, community-based management, private management, cooperative ownership, and community-based ownership.

Rohe, W., and M. Stegman. 1990. *Public Housing Homeownership Assessment.* Vols. 1 and 2. Washington, D.C.: U.S. Department of Housing and Urban Development.
Volume 1 of this report presents findings of an evaluation of HUD's Public Housing Homeownership Demonstration, involving the sale of units to public housing tenants in seventeen communities. Volume 2 presents detailed case studies of the seventeen programs.

Sewel, John, Fred Twine, and Nicholas J. Williams. 1984. "The Sale of Council Houses—Some Empirical Evidence." *Urban Studies* 21: 439–450.
This article describes the pattern of sales of council houses in Aberdeen.

Sillince, John, ed. 1990. *Housing Policies in Eastern Europe and the Soviet Union.* New York: Routledge.
This book examines trends in housing conditions and construction since 1945 and discusses the importance of factors external to the housing market.

Silver, H., J. McDonald, and R. J. Oritz. 1985. "Selling Public Housing: The Methods and Motivations." *Journal of Housing* 42: 213–228.
This article offers a good discussion of the policy implications of the sale of public housing to tenants.

Turner, Bengt, et al. 1990. *The Reform of Housing in Eastern Europe and the Soviet Union.* New York: Routledge.
This book highlights various aspects of housing reform: rehabilitation, private initiatives, housing quality, and homeownership. It explores the wide divergence between countries in the region in the relative size of the private and public sectors.

Williams, Nicholas J., John Sewel, and Fred Twine. 1986. "Council House Sales and Residualisation." *Journal of Social Policy.* 15: 273–292.
This article discusses the residualization thesis and offers conclusions drawn from an Aberdeen case study.

Index

About the Editor and Contributors

R. ALLEN HAYS is Associate Professor of Political Science at the University of Northern Iowa. He is the author of a 1985 State University of New York Press book on federal housing policy, which he is currently revising for a second edition. He has also published articles on various aspects of housing policy at the local level in the United States and housing policy under the Reagan administration.

GREGORY D. ANDRUSZ is Principal Lecturer in the Department of Sociology, Middlesex University, England; the Director of the Kazakhstan-UK Centre; and Research Fellow at the Centre for Russian and East European Studies, University of Birmingham, England. He has carried out post-graduate research in Poland and in the Ukraine. His current research, funded by the Economic and Social Research Council, is on homelessness in Moscow and Sofia.

MARC H. CHOKO is a Professor at the Université du Québec à Montréal and an invited professor at the Institut National de la Recherche Scientifique—Urbanisation. He is the author of numerous books and articles on various housing issues. He is currently involved in comparative and historical research on homeownership in Montréal, Paris, Brussels, and Geneva, supported by a grant from the Social Sciences and Human Research Council of Canada.

FRANCINE DANSEREAU is a sociologist who has been active in urban- and housing-related research since 1971, when she joined the Institut National de la Recherche Scientifique—Urbanisation in Montreal. She has published a number of research reports and scientific articles on topics such as urban renewal and local improvement policies, residential quality in relation to user satisfaction and aspirations, "alternative" tenure forms (cooperatives, condominiums), as well as neighborhood socioeconomic and ethnic change. Her current research is focused on social mix in public and semi-public residential space and on family residential strategies.

DANIEL J. MONTI is Associate Professor of Sociology and Urban Studies at Boston University. He has written extensively on race and ethnic relations, school desegregation, inner-city redevelopment, and gangs. His most recent book is entitled *Gangs: The Origins and Impact of Contemporary Youth Gangs in the United States* (1993), edited with Scott Cummings.

HAZEL A. MORROW-JONES is an Associate Professor in the Department of City and Regional Planning at Ohio State University. Her research interests are in residential mobility over the life course, homeownership, housing, finance, and housing policy. She has had grants from the National Science Foundation, the Department of Housing and Urban Development, and the Ohio Board of Regents. Her work has been published in such journals as *Environment and Planning A, Urban Geography,* and *Urban Studies.*

ALAN MURIE is Professor of Planning and Housing in the School of Planning and Housing at Heriot Watt University in Edinburgh, Scotland. He is the editor of *Housing Studies* and has published widely on housing issues in Britain. He has also served in an advisory role for a number of housing organizations in Britain.

WILLIAM PETERMAN is Associate Professor of urban planning and policy at the University of Illinois at Chicago. As the founding director of the Voorhees Center for Neighborhood and Community Improvement, he has worked with community-based development groups and low-income housing providers. He has assisted several public housing resident management corporations and was a prime consultant associated with the development of LeClaire Courts, Chicago's first resident-managed public housing.

KEITH P. RASEY is a Ph.D. candidate in Urban Studies at Cleveland State University. His dissertation research, supported by the Aspen Foundation, focuses on the role of nonprofit organizations in the provision of housing for low-income and special-needs populations. Previously, he served as policy and program development director for the National Council of State Housing Agencies and as director of program evaluation in the Office of Housing at the Department of Housing and Urban Development.

WILLIAM M. ROHE is a Professor in the Department of City and Regional Planning at the University of North Carolina, Chapel Hill. He is co-author of *Planning with Neighborhoods* (1985) and *Public Housing Homeownership Assessment* (U.S. Department of Housing and Urban Development). He is also author of numerous articles on federal housing policy, community crime prevention, and community development planning. He has served as the Director of the American Planning Association's Neighborhood Planning Division and is on the editorial board of the *Journal of Planning Education and Research*. His current research includes a longitudinal study of the social impacts of homeownership on low-income persons and an evaluation of an innovative public housing self-sufficiency program.

MICHAEL A. STEGMAN is Cary B. Boshamer Professor and Chair of both the Department of City and Regional Planning and the Ph.D. curriculum in Public Policy at the University of North Carolina, Chapel Hill. He has written extensively on national housing policy. His most recent books include: *More Housing More Fairly: The Limits of Privatization, The Public Housing Homeownership Demonstration Assessment* (with William Rohe), and *Non-Federal Housing Programs: How States and Localities are Responding to Federal Cutbacks*. His current research includes an analysis of alternative mortgage instruments to finance affordable housing and two five-year panel studies—one examining the social and economic impacts of homeownership on lower-income families and the other an evaluation of a demonstration program in Charlotte, North Carolina, designed to promote economic self-sufficiency among single-parent families in public housing.

NICHOLAS J. WILLIAMS is Senior Lecturer in Geography at Aberdeen University in Scotland. He was formerly the Research Officer for the Local Government Boundary Commission in Wales. He is Vice-Chair of the Castlehill Housing Association, which provides affordable housing for low-income households in Northeast Scotland.